RAPE AND SEXUAL ASSAULT III

A Research Handbook

Garland Reference Library of the Social Sciences
(Volume 672)

1991

RAPE AND SEXUAL ASSAULT III

A Research Handbook

■

Ann Wolbert Burgess, Editor

Garland Publishing, Inc.
New York & London
1991

Rape and sexual assault III : a research handbook /
Ann Wolbert Burgess, editor.
    p.   cm. — (Garland reference library of the social
sciences ; v. 672.)
    Includes index.
    ISBN 0-8240-7181-6 (alk. paper)
    1. Rape—United States. 2. Rape—United States—
Psychological aspects. 3. Rape victims—United States—
Psychology. 4. Rape victims—Services for—United States.
5. Rapists—United States—Psychology. I. Burgess, Ann
Wolbert. II. Series: Garland reference library of social
science : v. 672.
HV6561.R369 1991
362.88'3'0973—dc20   91-14696
                     CIP

Design by Julie Threlkeld

Printed on acid-free, 250-year-life paper
Manufactured in the United States of America

Table of Contents

■

Contributors

∎

Barbara Anderson, M.S.
Western Psychiatric Institute
and Clinic
Pittsburgh, PA

Jeanne L. Azarovitz, B.A.
University of Lowell
Lowell, MA

Timothy Baker, Ph.D.
Director, Penn Relays
University of Pennsylvania
Philadelphia, PA

Ellen Brickman, Ph.D.
Victim Services Agency
New York, NY

John Briere, Ph.D.
Department of Psychiatry
and the Behavioral Sciences
University of Southern California
School of Medicine
Los Angeles, CA

Ann Wolbert Burgess,
R.N., D.N.Sc.
van Ameringen Professor of
Psychiatric Mental Health
Nursing
University of Pennsylvania
School of Nursing
Philadelphia, PA

Rob Davis, M.A.
Victim Services Agency
New York, NY

Lisa A. Eddy, B.A.
University of Lowell
Lowell, MA

Diana M. Elliott, Ph.D.
Rosemead School of Psychology
Biola University
La Mirada, CA

Ellen Frank, Ph.D.
Western Psychiatric Institute
and Clinic
University of Pittsburgh School
of Medicine
Pittsburgh, PA

Evelina Giobbe
Program Director, WHISPER
Minneapolis, MN

Christine Grant, R.N., Ph.D.
Assistant Professor of
Psychiatric Nursing
Widenor University
Philadelphia, PA

Carol R. Hartman, R.N., D.N.Sc.
Chair and Professor of Psychiatric
Mental Health Nursing
Boston College School of Nursing
Chestnut Hill, MA

Robert R. Hazelwood, M.S.
Supervisory Special Agent
National Center for the Analysis
of Violent Crime
FBI Academy
Quantico, VA

Paul J. Isley, M.A., M.Ed.
Riverside Community Mental
Health and Retardation
Center, Inc.
West Newton, MA

ix

Ron Langevin, Ph.D.
The Clarke Institute of Psychiatry
Toronto, Canada

Mary Ann Largen
Executive Director
National Network for Victims of
Sexual Assault
Arlington, VA

Anna T. Laszlo, M.A.
Research Associate
The Circle
McLean, VA

Linda E. Ledray, R.N., Ph.D.
Director, Sexual Assault Resource
Service
Hennepin County Medical Center
Minneapolis, MN

Laurinda A. Michaud, B.A.
University of Lowell
Lowell, MA

Pamela Brede Minden, R.N., M.S.
Coordinator for Special Nursing
Projects
Charles River Hospital
Wellesley, MA

Arlene McCormack, Ph.D.
Professor of Sociology
University of Lowell
Lowell, MA

Michael Newcomb, Ph.D.
University of Southern California
Los Angeles, CA

Cindy M. Notgrass, Ph.D.
University of California
 Los Angeles
Los Angeles, CA

Kathryn J. Pailes, B.A.
University of Lowell
Lowell, MA

Robert Alan Prentky, Ph.D.
Director of Research
Massachusetts Treatment Center
Bridgewater, MA

Roland Reboussin, Ph.D.
National Center for the Analysis
of Violent Crime
FBI Academy
Quantico, VA

Louise Skolnik, D.S.W.
School of Social Work
Adelphi University
Garden City, New York

Carole-Rae Reed, R.N., M.S.N.
Doctoral Candidate
University of Pennsylvania School
of Nursing
Philadelphia, PA

Janet I. Warren, Ph.D.
Assistant Professor, General
Medical Faculty
Department of Behavioral
Medicine and Psychiatry
University of Virginia
Charlottesville, VA

Gail Elizabeth Wyatt, Ph.D.
Associate Professor of Medical
Psychology
University of California Los
Angeles
Los Angeles, CA

Preface

∎

Rape and abuse affect the lives of thousands of people each year. Contrary to popular belief, they are not uncommon events. Since 1977, the rate of forcible rape has increased by 21 percent. That is the largest increase in all violent crimes. The 1989 FBI Uniform Crime Report cites 94,504 cases of forcible rape to females of consenting age reported in 1988. And while an estimated 250,000 cases of child sexual abuse are reported annually, many sexually abusive acts are never reported.

There are also statistics on the subject of "hidden rape." Social science researcher Mary Koss, studying the incidence and prevalence of sexual aggression and victimization on college campuses, argues that because of the inadequacies in the methods used to measure sexual assault, national crime statistics, criminal victimization studies, and conviction or incarceration rates fail to reflect the true scope of rape.

What is the scope of violence? Both men and women are approximately equally likely to be the victims of criminal violence but intimate violence impacts disproportionately on women and girls. Criminal violence includes acts of larceny, burglary, aggravated assault, forcible rape, and homicide. Intimate violence includes acts labeled child abuse, child sexual abuse and incest, courtship violence, date rape, wife beating or battering, marital rape, and elder abuse.

At current crime rates, almost everyone will be a victim of crime during his or her lifetime. According to 1988 statistics compiled by the Bureau of Justice Statistics (BJS) in *The Report to the Nation on Crime and Justice*, an estimated five-sixths of Americans will be victims of attempted or completed violent crime. Many will be victimized more than once. Most will be victims of personal larceny three or more times. The rates of some violent crimes are higher than those of serious life events. For example, the risk of being the victim of a violent crime is higher than the risk of death from cancer or injury or death from a fire. Still, continues the Report, a person is much more likely to die from natural causes than as the result of a criminal victimization.

The strong forces that operate to keep intimate violence secret have been inadequately countered in the collection of official statistics where underreporting is a serious methodological problem. Although comprehensive national prevalence data do not exist, it is speculated by Koss's research that the cumulative risk of all forms of violence on women is of epidemic proportions.

In fact, in a November 15, 1990 *USA Today* report by Sam Meddis, rape reports to police are soaring toward record levels, with the heaviest increases in middle-sized cities. A *USA Today* computer analysis of FBI data for the first six months of 1990 (see Table I-1), finds:

■ Rape reports overall surged 10 percent—the sharpest six-month rise in a decade.

■ Mid-sized cities—populations of 100,000 to 500,000— reported a 14 percent increase.

■ Almost a third of the 171 cities surveyed reported at least a 25 percent increase.

■ About one in six cities reported a 50 percent jump.

And that's only for the first half of the year, which historically accounts for fewer than half the rapes reported annually. In Table I-1, cities are listed in order of percentage increase in rapes. The "rate" figures are based on incidents reported per 10,000 population—a more accurate reflection of an individual's chances of being assaulted in those cities.

Key reasons cited in *USA Today* for the increase: more violence and greater willingness by women to report sex crimes; growing fear of AIDS; increased sensitivity of law enforcement's sex crimes units and more community support for rape crisis centers; and heightened media attention to the issue of sexual assault, following highly publicized cases earlier in the year.

Historically, the realization of rape as a violent act committed in a sexual context signaled the beginning of national efforts to address the problems inherent in this traumatic life event. Prior to the resurgence of the women's movement, avoidance and silence dominated the professional reactions to victims of rape. Given this pattern, the first efforts of feminist women's groups and professionals were to raise the awareness of others that rape was a criminal act not desired by the victim. Furthermore, the victim was not responsible for the behavior

Table I-1

RAPE PER 10,000 POPULATION

(IN ORDER OF PERCENTAGE OF CHANGE)

City	State	Pop.	No. of '89 Rapes	No. of '90 Rapes	'89 Rape per 10,000 Pop.	'90 Rape per 10,000 Pop.	Rape Rate Pct. Chng.
Cedar Rapids	IA	110,526	2	9	.18	.81	350.00
Sunnyvale	CA	119,255	7	18	.59	1.51	157.14
Fort Lauderdale	FL	149,575	27	58	1.81	3.88	157.14
Lexington	KY	225,918	32	67	1.42	2.97	109.38
Des Moines	IA	193,305	24	49	1.24	2.53	104.17
Honolulu	HI	848,959	131	267	1.54	3.15	103.82
Yonkers	NY	183,417	9	18	.49	.98	100.00
Bakersfield	CA	161,823	19	36	1.17	2.29	94.74
Gary	IN	133,318	36	70	2.70	5.25	94.44
Pueblo	CO	101,560	25	47	2.46	4.64	88.00
Oceanside	CA	115,611	26	48	2.25	4.15	84.62
Irving	TX	134,207	26	47	1.94	3.50	80.77
Arlington	VA	156,115	15	27	.96	1.73	80.00
Warren	MI	145,932	20	34	1.37	2.33	70.00
Jersey City	NJ	218,020	40	68	1.83	3.12	70.00
Abilene	TX	110,100	26	44	2.36	4.00	69.23
Chula Vista	CA	129,581	12	20	.93	1.54	66.67
Lakewood	CO	119,918	15	25	1.25	2.08	66.67
Laredo	TX	125,862	3	5	.24	.40	66.67
Washington	DC	604,000	90	149	1.49	2.47	65.56
Waco	TX	104,358	38	62	3.64	5.94	63.16
Plano	TX	119,868	8	13	.67	1.08	62.50
Inglewood	CA	106,671	34	53	3.19	4.97	55.88
Hampton	VA	132,596	15	23	1.13	1.73	53.33
Pasadena	TX	117,941	21	32	1.78	2.71	52.38
Corpus Christi	TX	263,298	85	129	3.23	4.90	51.76
Hialeah	FL	166,494	22	33	1.32	1.98	50.00
Denver	CO	494,589	122	182	2.47	3.68	49.18
Newport News	VA	162,298	31	46	1.91	2.83	48.39
Eugene	OR	110,119	21	31	1.91	2.82	47.62
Santa Rosa	CA	111,084	19	28	1.71	2.52	47.37
Wichita	KS	297,391	98	144	3.30	4.84	46.94
Mesa	AZ	285,883	31	45	1.08	1.57	45.16
Pasadena	CA	135,504	20	29	1.48	2.14	45.00
Buffalo	NY	314,284	117	166	3.72	5.28	41.88
Erie	PA	113,155	29	41	2.56	3.62	41.38
Norfolk	VA	290,434	78	109	2.69	3.75	39.74
Glendale	AZ	142,931	36	50	2.52	3.50	38.89
Portsmouth	VA	108,976	31	43	2.84	3.95	38.71
Arlington	TX	259,797	50	69	1.92	2.66	38.00
Ontario	CA	126,646	24	33	1.90	2.61	37.50
Huntington Beach	CA	191,826	19	26	.99	1.26	36.84
Akron	OH	222,588	83	113	3.73	5.08	36.14
Jackson	MS	201,350	69	93	3.43	4.62	34.78
Bridgeport	CT	140,029	30	40	2.14	2.86	33.33
Aurora	CO	219,780	65	86	2.96	3.91	32.31
Montgomery	AL	194,146	35	46	1.80	2.37	31.43
Salinas	CA	103,766	23	30	2.22	2.89	30.43
Syracuse	NY	154,960	41	53	2.65	3.42	29.27
Waterbury	CT	104,714	14	18	1.34	1.72	28.57

Table I-1 (continued)
RAPE PER 10,000 POPULATION
(IN ORDER OF PERCENTAGE OF CHANGE)

City	State	Pop.	No. of '89 Rapes	No. of '90 Rapes	'89 Rape per 10,000 Pop.	'90 Rape per 10,000 Pop.	Rape Rate Pct. Chng.
Ann Arbor	MI	108,830	23	29	2.11	2.66	26.09
Columbus	OH	572,341	223	281	3.90	4.91	26.02
Pomona	CA	123,659	31	39	2.51	3.15	25.81
Las Vegas	NV	536,148	147	184	2.74	3.43	25.17
Tulsa	OK	336,297	132	165	3.60	3.50	25.00
Orange	CA	108,508	8	10	.74	.92	25.00
Vallejo	CA	103,396	25	31	2.42	3.00	24.00
Grand Rapids	MI	186,036	145	179	7.79	9.62	23.45
Livonia	MI	101,463	9	11	.98	1.08	22.22
Modesto	CA	152,605	32	39	2.10	2.56	21.88
San Diego	CA	1,098,639	176	213	1.60	1.94	21.02
Kansas City	KS	161,756	63	76	3.89	4.70	20.63
Toledo	OH	342,418	170	205	4.96	5.99	20.59
Fremont	CA	170,999	15	18	.88	1.05	20.00
Baltimore	MD	763,138	254	303	3.33	3.97	19.29
Houston	TX	1,713,499	510	608	2.98	3.55	19.22
Oxnard	CA	133,523	27	32	2.02	2.40	18.52
Virginia Beach	VA	370,316	66	78	1.78	2.11	18.18
Cleveland	OH	523,906	375	442	7.16	8.44	17.87
Phoenix	AZ	941,948	196	231	2.08	2.45	17.86
Portland	OR	425,788	185	218	4.34	5.12	17.84
Chattanooga	TN	164,155	87	102	5.30	6.21	17.24
Charlotte	NC	372,612	149	174	4.00	4.67	16.78
Salt Lake City	UT	154,304	60	70	3.89	4.54	16.67
Long Beach	CA	426,025	117	136	2.75	3.19	16.24
Oklahoma City	OK	431,982	150	173	3.46	4.00	15.33
Elizabeth	NJ	105,324	20	23	1.90	2.18	15.00
Amarillo	TX	167,516	35	40	2.09	2.39	14.29
Fresno	CA	315,218	116	132	3.68	4.19	13.79

and choices of the predator. The rapist was acting out of his own intentions and patterns of belief. Previously, the act of rape and victim response was strongly linked to social discrimination and oppression surrounding the sex role attributes ascribed to women.

Compiled in this third volume of the *Rape and Sexual Assault* series is a collection of reports on a wide range of topical issues. The purpose of the book is twofold: First, we hope to provide research conducted since the 1988 volume on the scientific literature on rape and sexual assault. Second, by this effort, we hope to advance the knowledge base in this area through the contributions of historical analysis, theoretical conceptualizations, research findings, and treatment and policy innovations.

This volume is organized into four sections.

Table I-1 (continued)

Rape Per 10,000 Population
(in Order of Percentage of Change)

City	State	Pop.	No. of '89 Rapes	No. of '90 Rapes	'89 Rape per 10,000 Pop.	'90 Rape per 10,000 Pop.	Rape Rate Pct. Chng.
Greensboro	NC	184,321	44	50	2.39	2.71	13.64
Shreveport	LA	217,734	52	59	2.40	2.72	13.46
Glendale	CA	165,477	15	17	.91	1.03	13.33
Indianapolis	IN	484,056	220	249	4.54	5.14	13.18
Milwaukee	WI	600,898	226	255	3.76	4.24	12.83
Albuquerque	NM	384,801	104	117	2.70	3.04	12.50
Colorado Springs	CO	284,482	89	100	3.13	3.52	12.36
Lubbock	TX	189,797	66	74	3.48	3.90	12.12
Detroit	MI	1,039,599	717	800	6.90	7.70	11.58
Memphis	TN	651,081	364	404	5.59	6.21	10.99
Fullerton	CA	112,645	20	22	1.78	1.95	10.00
Winston-Salem	NC	1,560,111	72	79	4.78	5.25	9.72
San Francisco	CA	750,964	199	218	2.65	2.90	9.55
Lansing	MI	125,419	78	85	6.22	6.78	8.65
Dallas	TX	996,320	601	653	6.03	6.55	8.65
New Orleans	LA	528,589	160	173	3.03	3.27	8.12
Hayward	CA	106,342	13	14	1.22	1.32	7.69
Little Rock	AR	180,932	119	128	6.58	7.07	7.56
Mobile	AL	209,507	67	72	3.20	3.44	7.46
El Paso	TX	515,607	131	140	2.54	2.72	6.87
Kansas City	MO	440,435	235	251	5.34	5.70	6.81
Lincoln	NE	188,922	45	48	2.38	2.54	6.67
Cincinnati	OH	372,282	169	180	4.54	4.84	6.51
Beaumont	TX	115,246	67	71	5.81	6.16	5.97
Stockton	CA	195,727	88	93	4.50	4.75	5.68
Garland	TX	182088	59	62	3.24	3.40	5.08
Fort Worth	TX	430,481	207	217	4.81	5.04	4.83
Garden Grove	CA	138,891	21	22	1.51	1.58	4.76

Section 1: The Aftermath of Rape and Sexual Assault

The consequences of sexual assault are serious and long lasting. Criminal victimization is a public health problem of major importance. For many victims, responses during and after the assault correspond to the critical symptoms of post-traumatic stress disorder. Chapter 1, "Neurobiology in Rape Trauma," by Carol R. Hartman and Ann W. Burgess, reviews the emerging evidence that traumatic life events are responsible for basic disrupted adaptive patterns of brain biology. This, in turn, affects cognition and patterns of interpersonal reactions by influencing memory on sensory, perceptual, cognitive, and interpersonal levels. A particular focus is on the impact of rape and sexual assault as a traumatic experience capable of biological

Table I-1 (continued)

RAPE PER 10,000 POPULATION
(IN ORDER OF PERCENTAGE OF CHANGE)

City	State	Pop.	No. of '89 Rapes	No. of '90 Rapes	'89 Rape per 10,000 Pop.	'90 Rape per 10,000 Pop.	Rape Rate Pct. Chng.
Concord	CA	110,900	23	24	2.07	2.16	4.35
Topeka	KS	123,218	34	35	2.76	2.84	2.94
Columbus	GA	180,328	37	38	2.05	2.11	2.70
New York	NY	7,369,454	1600	1633	2.17	2.22	2.06
St. Petersburg	FL	241,862	86	87	3.56	3.60	1.16
Allentown	PA	105,531	14	14	1.33	1.33	0.00
Amherst	NY	112,285	2	2	.18	.18	0.00
Baton Rouge	LA	233,894	53	53	2.27	2.27	0.00
Chicago	IL	2,988,260	0.00	0.00	0.00		
Peoria	IL	109,955	0.00	0.00	0.00		
Roanoke	VA	99,042	17	17	1.72	1.72	0.00
Scottsdale	AZ	124,138	8	8	.64	.64	0.00
Spokane	WA	175,051	51	51	2.91	2.91	0.00
Springfield	IL	99,860	0.00	0.00	0.00		
Tallahassee	FL	129,061	47	0.00	3.63	0.00	
Springfield	MA	150,920	63	62	4.17	4.11	-1.59
Savannah	GA	148,155	54	53	3.64	3.58	-1.85
San Jose	CA	757,964	207	203	2.73	2.68	-1.93
Hartford	CT	131,544	77	75	5.85	5.70	-2.60
Los Angeles	CA	3,441,449	995	967	2.89	2.81	-2.81
Sacramento	CA	347,172	100	97	2.88	2.79	-3.00
Tempe	AZ	143,207	31	30	2.16	2.09	-3.23
Madison	WI	178,642	30	29	1.68	1.62	-3.33
Atlanta	GA	426,482	339	324	7.95	7.60	-4.42
Seattle	WA	514,398	219	209	4.26	4.06	-4.57
Richmond	VA	216,229	85	81	3.93	3.75	-4.71
Boston	MA	580,095	223	212	3.84	3.65	-4.93
Santa Ana	CA	245,880	39	37	1.59	1.50	-5.13
Brownsville	TX	105,458	18	17	1.71	1.61	-5.56
Tacoma	WA	167,943	121	113	7.20	6.73	-6.61
Torrance	CA	141,599	15	14	1.06	.99	-6.67

changes in brain functioning and that these changes drive some of the dysfunctional cognitive, behavioral, and interpersonal reactions documented in survivors.

Chapter 2, "Victim Assessment: The Dimensions of Rape Interview Schedule (DORIS)," by Carole-Rae Reed, Ann W. Burgess, and Carol R. Hartman, provides a systematic method of collecting data regarding rape and sexual assault. The theoretical model for this semistructured interview schedule is information processing of trauma. This model assumes sexual assault to be a major trauma to a victim and that the biological as well as psychological strategies used to survive

Table I-1 (continued)
RAPE PER 10,000 POPULATION
(IN ORDER OF PERCENTAGE OF CHANGE)

City	State	Pop.	No. of '89 Rapes	No. of '90 Rapes	'89 Rape per 10,000 Pop.	'90 Rape per 10,000 Pop.	Rape Rate Pct. Chng.
Berkeley	CA	106,404	29	27	2.73	2.54	−6.90
Riverside	CA	216,205	69	62	3.19	2.87	−10.14
Boise	ID	112,270	29	26	2.58	2.32	−10.34
Fort Wayne	IN	180,975	46	41	2.54	2.27	−10.87
Orlando	FL	160,197	92	82	5.74	5.12	−10.94
Jacksonville	FL	654,737	376	353	5.74	5.09	−11.44
Tampa	FL	289,463	204	180	7.05	6.22	−11.76
Philadelphia	PA	1,652,188	311	269	1.88	1.63	−13.50
Rochester	NY	230,303	81	70	3.52	3.04	−13.58
Newark	NJ	313,839	209	180	6.66	5.74	13.88
Youngstown	OH	101,642	28	24	2.75	2.36	−14.29
Durham	NC	116,921	34	29	2.91	2.48	−14.71
Macon	GA	119,698	34	29	2.84	2.42	−14.71
Alexandria	VA	109,888	31	26	2.82	2.37	−16.13
West Covina	CA	97,120	11	9	1.13	.93	−18.18
El Monte	CA	97,640	34	27	3.48	2.77	−20.59
San Antonio	TX	949,691	268	212	2.82	2.23	−20.90
Providence	RI	157,030	56	44	3.57	2.80	−21.43
Flint	MI	142,129	100	78	7.04	5.49	−22.00
Anaheim	CA	251,146	50	39	1.99	1.55	−22.00
Irvine	CA	102,780	9	7	.88	.68	−22.22
Paterson	NJ	138,846	53	40	3.82	2.88	−24.53
Miami	FL	381,206	165	124	4.33	3.25	−24.85
Stamford	CT	100,446	11	8	1.10	.80	−27.27
Chesapeake	VA	149,830	22	16	1.47	1.07	−27.27
Manchester	NH	100,295	10	7	1.00	.70	−30.00
Independence	MO	115,479	12	8	1.04	.69	−33.33
Clearwater	FL	97,650	40	26	4.10	2.66	−35.00
Sterling Hts.	MI	115,132	16	10	1.39	.87	−37.50
Hollywood	FL	123,412	35	19	2.84	1.54	−45.71
Overland Park	KS	107,609	12	6	1.15	.56	−50.00

the experience play a key role in symptom manifestation and adaptation over time.

Rape trauma seriously taxes a victim's personal coping resources. The need for identifying variables and factors that influence recovery from rape is imperative. In Chapter 3, Gail Elizabeth Wyatt, Michael Newcomb, and Cindy M. Notgrass report on data collected from a multiethnic community sample of fifty-five women who had been victims of rape or attempted rape. Internal and external factors were examined as mediational processes and/or coping strategies that link four aspects of women's rape experiences to the initial and lasting effects on their postrape adjustment, attitude toward sex and intimacy, and lifestyle changes to prevent future assaults. A measured or observed variable simultaneous path analysis model was used to test the relationships among the traumatic circumstances, mediators, and outcome variables. More self-blame, high involvement of police or other agencies, a greater number of repeated rapes per incident, and severity of abuse predicted women's negative initial and lasting attitudes toward sex and intimacy.

Although it has been shown that most types of crime have a psychological impact on victims, sexual assault has been shown to be particularly deleterious. Long-term problems in the areas of psychological functioning, social adjustment, and sexual behavior have been identified. Chapter 4, by Diana M. Elliott and John Briere, "Studying the Long-Term Effects of Sexual Abuse: The Trauma Symptom Checklist (TSC) Scales," reports on the psychometric characteristics of the TSC-33 in a clinical sample of adult women and the TSC-40 in a large, nonclinical sample of professional women. Also, data are presented from six other studies that used the TSC scales in discriminating a history of sexual abuse or to correlate specific characteristics of sexual abuse to adult symptomatology.

Treatment of rape and sexual assault victims continues to be a critical but neglected area of study. In Chapter 5, Barbara Anderson and Ellen Frank report on the efficacy of psychological interventions with recent rape victims. They studied two treatment interventions, Psychoeducational Intervention and Psychological Support, and found that both treatment interventions were associated with comparable levels of symptom reduction. The researchers then studied the efficacy of short-term therapy versus brief intervention therapy by comparing their two group treatment findings with Cognitive Behavior Therapy and Systematic Desensitization-treated groups. Again, findings note that both treatment protocols were associated with comparable levels of symptom reduction.

One of the areas that has been identified as important to the recovery of the rape survivor has been the support she or he receives from others. In Chapter 6, "The Social Support of Survivors of Rape," Timothy Baker, Louise Skolnick, Rob Davis, and Ellen Brickman report on the differences between rape survivors and survivors of other violent crimes and between husbands, boyfriends, and women friends. No significant differences were found on the positive support measure between the rape survivors and the survivors of other violent crimes.

However, the two groups were significantly different with regard to negative support. Rape survivors were found to receive considerably more negative support from their significant others than do nonrape survivors.

Section 2: Victim Populations

This section contains reports on three victim populations that are not well understood and that are often the recipients of strong emotional reaction and bias. In Chapter 7, Arlene McCormack, with Jeanne L. Azarovitz, Lisa A. Eddy, Laurinda A. Michaud, and Kathryn J. Pailes, report on peer-to-peer harassment in "Sexual Assaults on College Campuses." This study of 176 undergraduate women who entered a northeastern university in the fall of 1986 indicates that one in every four women (25 percent) have experienced an incident of sexual harassment involving a member of the university community. Although harassment by faculty members accounted for a third of the reports, and personnel in seven other areas of the university were named, most of the students reported other students as the source of harassment (68 percent). Further, a disturbing number (25 percent) of written descriptions of sexual harassment by students mentioned sexual assaults and rapes.

Since its inception in 1985, WHISPER (Women Hurt In Systems of Prostitution Engaged in Revolt) has grown from a small grass-roots movement to a respected Minnesota based organization. WHISPER has provided educational forums around the country about prostitution as a system of exploitation and abuse, and it advocates for the expansion of services to women and girls attempting to escape the sex industry. In Chapter 8, "Prostitution: Buying the Right to Rape," Evelina Giobbe, director and founder of WHISPER, documents the violence and manipulation used to recruit and trap women in the sex industry. Prostitution, writes Giobbe, is not a "career choice" or a "victimless crime," but rather, prostitution creates an environment in which crimes against women and children are defined as a commercial enterprise.

Chapter 9, "Adult Male Sexual Assault in the Community," by Paul J. Isely, reviews the literature on the male victim and presents a group treatment model. This chapter seeks to inspire therapists to conduct similar groups for male victims as well as to encourage more research on the issues, concerns, and aftermath of rape trauma for males.

Section 3: Care Providers

This section contains four chapters that focus on the care provider and/or victim counselor and outlines protocols used in several agencies. Victims have many worries and fears following a sexual assault. Chapter 10, "Sexual Assault and Sexually Transmitted Disease: The Issues and Concerns," by Linda E. Ledray, describes the medical concerns of victims and the Sexual Assault Resource Service (SARS) in Minneapolis. The review of 1,007 records of victims seen within seventy-two hours of a sexual assault provides data for the STD protocol options and considerations used at SARS.

In Chapter 11, Pamela Brede Minden writes on perspectives for victims and care providers in "Coping with Interpersonal Violence and Sexual Victimization." The first section of the chapter describes the author's personal account of her thoughts and reactions to leaving her tenure at Boston City Hospital and the Victim Counseling Program and the implications for care providers of sexual assault victims. The second part of the chapter describes the five-phase Victim Counseling Program that is organized around six fundamental assumptions.

Chapter 12, "Confidentiality in the Sexual Assault Victim/Counselor Relationship," by Mary Ann Largen, describes the nature of the sexual assault victim and counselor relationships, the need to protect confidential communications between victims and counselors from criminal proceedings, and the results of a nationwide survey of states' laws concerning sexual assault victim/counselor confidentiality. Although the majority of states have yet to assign privilege to sexual assault victim/counselor communications, the findings in this survey should be of interest to policy makers, victim advocates, and others interested in the general question of confidential communications privileges for the newer mental health service providers and their clients.

Increasing concern is being expressed by victims about possible HIV exposure. Chapter 13, "HIV Counseling Issues and Victims of Sexual Assault," by Anna T. Laszlo, Ann W. Burgess, and Christine A. Grant, reviews the scant literature on counseling rape victims on HIV testing and presents the issues and a sample protocol based on guidelines from the Center for Disease Control.

Section 4: Aggressors

Three chapters focus on research findings in the aggressor population. Chapter 14, "Hypothetical Biological Substrates of a Fantasy-Based Drive Mechanism for Repetitive Sexual Aggression," by Robert Alan Prentky and Ann W. Burgess, presents the hypothesis that the fantasy life of a sex offender may be importantly related to repeated acts of sexual violence. The second half of the chapter addresses the putative biological factors that may help to explain the repetitive component of repetitive sexual violence.

Chapter 15, "The Sex Killer," by Ron Langevin, reports on a sample of thirteen sex killers and thirteen nonsex killers. The study describes method of killing, motive for the crime, substance abuse, mental illness, sexual behavior, elements of the sex killing, phallometric test results, sexual dysfunction, family background and childhood of the sex killer, and biological factors.

In Chapter 16, Janet I. Warren, Robert R. Hazelwood and Roland Reboussin report on their study forty-one serial rapists who were responsible for 837 rapes and more than 400 attempted rapes. Data collection consisted of lengthy, in-depth interviews through which an attempt was made to "step into" the mind of the rapist and, from this vantage point, decipher the motivation and behavior that characterized the development and execution of his rape behavior. The results of the study are summarized in terms of methodology, case vignettes, developmental history, sexual history, crime scene characteristics, and classification analyses.

Part 1

The Aftermath of
Rape and Sexual Assault

■

Chapter 1

Neurobiology of Rape Trauma

Carol R. Hartman
Boston College

Ann W. Burgess
University of Pennsylvania

■

What has been done in the basic sciences on the topic of violence and psychological trauma? What are the etiological factors to symptoms encountered in the trauma response? This chapter reviews some of the basic research indicating that sexual violence creates changes in the nervous system that have lasting consequences to victims. These consequences become a challenge to our clinical efforts and to the development of intervention services.

Basic Research

From the beginning of our work with victims who had been raped and/ or sexually assaulted, we have believed that a certain type of learning occurred during the assault. This learning had to be understood on a sensory, perceptual, cognitive, and interpersonal level. We have pursued our thoughts about the presentation and level of symptoms. This has led to an assumption that this special type of learning is a manifestation of disregulation of primary processes related to fundamental operations in the management of information; that is, information generated internally as well as in the environment. This assumption that something structurally and functionally changed because of the trauma and that this change was basic to the array of symptoms that we witnessed is now more clearly documented in basic research regarding brain, behavior and post-traumatic stress disorder.

The brain may be understood to be an array of neurons organized into circuits. Different circuits process different kinds of information, and they do so in different ways. Researchers are giving much more attention to the question of just how and where experience-dependent circuit changes take place, because that is how and where memory is stored.

As background for the presentation of neuroscience findings related to response patterns to rape trauma, it is important to organize the symptoms into two broad categories, positive symptoms and negative symptoms. Positive symptoms refer to those manifestations of hyperarousal. This arousal can be of a consistent tonic nature; for example, someone is consistently tense, or it can be phasic with episodic periods of being startled, frightened, or terrorized by external and internal cues.

This is in contrast to the group of symptoms that are classified as negative symptoms. These symptoms range from a sense of numbness, apathy, or depression to various states of dissociation. The assumption is that this presentation of positive and negative symptoms occurs after traumatic events and represents compensatory patterns of organization of a damaged alarm system. This disregulatory process is responsible for the biphasic characteristics of one outcome of the trauma response, which is post-traumatic stress disorder. The mounting scientific evidence indicates that the disruption of the alarm system is central to the basic processes and operations for coding, sorting, sequencing, and developing information systems, be they visual, auditory, kinesthetic, olfactory, motor, or gustatory (Aysto, 1987; Horowitz, 1976; van der Kolk, 1987).

To begin to understand why there is disruption in arousal and numbing processes we have to remember that the natural response set of the human being is to protect and promote survival. All incoming information is processed on the most fundamental level of awareness of threat. The major neuro-arrangement for the intake of stimulation, its categorization, and its organization of action begins in the systems that relate to the flight/fight/freezing aspect of the alarm system. These primary points for directing and regulating response are located in the pons and limbic system and the cerebral cortex. Research on the impact of trauma on neurological systems and ultimately on higher cortical functioning will elaborate on this major premise.

Pitman (1989) evaluates research on the arousal and alarm system and its relationship to post-traumatic stress disorder by organizing the key symptoms as follows: First are the tonic symptoms—these are the symptoms a patient manifests almost all of the time, especially when evoked by salient environmental stimuli that reminds the person of the traumatic event. Next are phasic symptoms—these are frequently intermittently experienced symptoms. They are the dramatic symptoms of flashbacks, reliving experiences, nightmares, and intrusive recollection of the traumatic events. The third are a mix of tonic and phasic symptoms that are not necessarily tied directly to salient cues in the environment but are presented when there is mild or sometimes no stimuli. These symptoms are the hypervigilance, insomnia, and exaggerated startle response as well as the generalized physiological reactivity (phasic). There are also the avoidant symptoms such as a diminished interest, numbing, estrangement, and avoidance of reminders.

Giller (1990) arranges the symptoms in terms of their specificity to the traumatic event itself: Intrusive symptoms, such as flashbacks, are those symptoms most closely allied with the event itself. The next are avoidant symptoms, including the numbing, detachment and restricted affect. These symptoms are most often a direct response to the psychic representation of the traumatic events, that is, a memory. Last are the least specific symptoms, in that they can be associated with situations and stimuli that have minimal connection with the actual event. These are irritability, hypervigilance, increased startle reaction, and difficulty concentrating.

John Krystal (1990) explains this constellation of symptoms by a variety of models derived from animal and human research, thus laying down the foundation for the biology of trauma. First is the Noradrenergic-Alarm Model or LC Model (Locus Coerulus). Research basic to this model suggests that the LC activation affects the limbic system during stress. This activation is aimed at not only the alerting and preparing of the organism, but through elaborate feedback systems, modulating the surge of noradrenergic hormones. In trauma, research suggests that this basic regulation of the LC process is altered resulting in a flooding of noradrenergic and adrenergic hormones that lead to overlearning and stimulation of key areas of the limbic system as well as the activation of the opioid, diazapine systems that lead now to the numbing, amnesias, and dissociative experiences.

A second model, supported by animal and clinical research, is the Fear-Enhanced Startle Model (Krystal, 1990). This model suggests that during a traumatic experience there is a sensitization of pathways that involve the startle response during a fear-provoking situation. Subsequently there is an enhancement of the fear response without direct association to the traumatic stimuli. Neuroscience theories considered in this model are those that focus on the suspected phenomena of "kindling." The area of sensitization assumed is the amygdala in the limbic system. This nonassociative fear enhancement is felt to be central to the long-lasting fear response found in many survivors of trauma.

A third model is the Traumatic Alterations in Neural Activity and Memory (Krystal, 1990). This model attempts to explain three major characteristics of memory disturbance associated with trauma. One is the long-lasting effects, if not lifelong disturbances of memory. Second is the impairment and fragmentation of memory experienced as intrusive thoughts, nightmares, and flashbacks. All of these are characterized as if the event, upon recall, is being relieved. And third is the hyperarousal and defensive posture (lack of trust) found in unrelated stressful situations. The assumptions here, gathered from research on the Aplysia snail, is that micro structural changes appear to play a role in the long-lasting traumatic enhancement of alarm, avoidance, and memory. Transient avoidance learning operates through a spectrum of intracellular processes that increase or decrease the activity of simple sensorimotor systems. The activation of this system is via the brain stem and limbic system. Severe or repeated exposure to aversive stimuli produces long-lasting enhanced reactivity in the snail. This activation has an impact on the long- and short-term memory of the snail. Evidence for molecular change was obtained when products were injected that blocked gene transmission material (RNA) and gene translation material (DNA). When these products were given (during traumatic exposure), long-term avoidant learning disappeared. When they were not given, long-term avoidant learning occurred. Further, if the gene products had appeared, the blocking agents did not work after the trauma; thus, there was a chronic state of avoidance. There was a proliferation of certain receptor sites and a reduction in others under conditions of trauma and trauma with injections.

A fourth model explaining the manifestations of PTSD is that of Inescapable Shock (IS). Van der Kolk (1987) has summarized the findings from primate studies and human subjects. The research on monkeys, dogs, and humans under different stressful situations in which escape was limited or prevented provides evidence for massive multisystem brain activation. This activation results in the depletion of noradrenergic, dopaninergic, and serotonergic neurons, in the alterations in receptor function systems as well as benzodiasepin and endogenous opiate systems.

These animal studies, combined with the poignant studies on maternal deprivation and its impact on affective regulations, social behavior, and vulnerability to stress have led to a fifth model on the biology of trauma. This model combines the IS, maternal deprivation findings and the concepts of hormonal disregulation. This combined model suggests that the PTSD symptoms may arise purely from activation-induced disturbances in homeostatic neuronal systems and not as goal-directed learned responses. Rather, stress-induced disregulation may produce learned behavioral syndromes that adaptively dampen arousal through mechanisms such as cognitive patterns that decrease level of arousal or phobic avoidance.

Implications of Models for Human Response to Trauma

The implication of these models and the latter in particular, for clinical practice, resides in a movement away from mentalistic explanations regarding the symptoms of victims. We suggest that social, behavioral patterns are more profitably understood as adaptive responses to biologically driven phenomena than as psychologically derived conclusions. For example, the woman who remains in a battering situation may be more directly assisted in moving to protect herself when the overwhelming numbing state is addressed as an adaptive response to the disorganizing experience of a noradrenergic flooding. Her self-appraisal is altered if not impaired by biological alterations that have an impact on differentiation and discrimination of internal and external cues. Rather, repetitive nonfunctional behaviors dominate. To interpret her behavior in terms of psychological motivations, that is, feeling deserving or to blame, is better understood as psychological reasons given by the woman to explain her confusion in taking more functional actions. That is, she blames her response selection on personal will, motivations, rather than on a biological response to overwhelming threat.

Pitman (1989) reviews the major positions put forth in the animal models with existing studies of traumatized human populations and cautions against extrapolating from animal models to human models.

Nevertheless, human clinical studies deriving many of their hypotheses from animal models does suggest a strong argument for the biological underpinnings for much of the behavior we witness in people who have been traumatized.

The pattern of response to trauma, abstracted from the models and research data, can be summarized as follows. Basically, three key circuits are activated when a person is confronted with a traumatic stressor. First, the *preparatory circuit* mobilizes the body for an emergency and is influenced by the locus coeruleus and Raphe nucleus, which secrete two known catecholamines that are associated with different states of stress. There is the noradrenergic hormone associated with arousal and serotonin that has a major function in modulating the noradrenergic system initiated by the locus coeruleus. This is the seat for arousal and when in a dysregulated state is a source of unresolved stress and positive symptoms.

Second, the *stress response circuit* is known for increasing the secretion of the corticotropin releasing factor (CRF) and in some cases cortisol. This is one of the main hormones mobilizing the body to fight/flight (handling the emergency). This hormone is regulated by key structures in the limbic system. The pituitary gland responsible for CRF interacts with the hypothalmus (limbic structure). This circuitry is innervated by the adrenergic system. In Post-Traumatic Stress Disorder (PTSD), there is an increase in norepinephrine and a decrease in cortisol. The ratio of norepinephrine/cortisol is a biological benchmark for PTSD. This circuit interacts with the third circuit and accounts not only for fight and avoidance responses but accounts for negative symptoms such as detachment, dissociation, and apathy.

Third, the *blunting circuit* is regulated by hormones secreted from the opiod-benzodiazopin system. This response blunts the feeling of pain. This circuit includes the locus coeruleus, hypothalmus, and amygdala, which registers strong emotion.

Stress and/or trauma have been shown to alter all three key circuits. These circuits interconnect via feedback loops that aim at achieving homeostasis. Rather than these adaptive systems being depleted, they accommodate the imbalance to preserve a protective response as well as homeostasis. These accommodations err in priming the alarm system to react with less provocation and less capacity to discriminate error.

Disorder behaviors are assumed to arise out of stress/trauma overwhelming these adaptive systems, throwing them into states of disregulation via processes of hyposecretion and/or hypersecretion. Dysregulation occurs in the primary center for the regulation of major life-engaging functions, for example, sleep, memory, attachment, sexual behavior, aggression, and self-defense (limbic system). Stress/ trauma is seen to have a significant effect on personal and interpersonal behavior patterns. This includes actions and thinking.

After Circuit 1 has been activated and a person has moved into Circuit 2, the release of CRF can lead to an increase in plasma cortisol, which leads to an increased tryptophan hydroxylase (which is a neuro activator, activating seratonin circuits), which because of sustained stress/trauma results in decreased serotonin, which results in a decrease in its modulating effects. The result is an unchecked excretion of norandrenalin from the locus coeruleus. This is just one example of disregulation. There can be disregulation in the HPA axis or between the opiod system and the noradrenergic system.

All three circuits influence memory. Experience is remembered at a basic level that some refer to as taxonomic or primarily categorical memory. The key aspect of this memory is that it is sensory-motor and not related to time and space. Therefore, it is immediate, as if it is happening.

The primary memory system is basic to higher order memory structures. When there is disregulation of sensory input, alterations in primary memory influence the elaboration of secondary memory. When there is inference with basic categorization (discrimination, sorting, etc.), there is disruption in the processing and storing of information on a secondary level. For example, the interpretation cues that clarify the intentions and motivations of others can be disturbed because basic patterns of response are limited by a restricted repertoire of response that is also biased to produce avoidant responses.

Trauma and Its Impact on Cognition

The pursuit of the biological underpinnings of trauma suggests that trauma response may be understood as an adaptive consequence of change in the alarm system of living organisms. The call to arousal and preparation for fight/flight and the analgesic inducement to manage and control physical pain and injury and maintain psychic integrity, are basic operations in the survival of the species. When there is an accumulation of stress due to factors that restrict the resetting of the various innervated hormonal systems, adjustments occur that influence the basic structures and operations of the brain. Alterations in the behavior of victims can be seen in victim assumptions regarding cause and effect; in attention, cue selection, and interpretation; in the presentation of self; in attributional patterns; in memory and sequencing of intra- and interpersonal experiences; in levels of consciousness; in self-appraisal capacities; in the modulation of emotion; in repetitive behaviors; in disturbed sleep patterns; and in the integration and expression of moral judgment. Although psychological explanations have been useful to some extent in the treatment of victims, the maintenance of severe symptoms over time suggests a need for a broader frame of reference for understanding and treatment.

For years, there has been an emphasis on higher order cognitive function, direction, behavior, and motivation. MacLean (1990) stated that it came to him as a wondrous insight, that thought emanates from the "animal brains" in man. In his famous discussion of the "triune brain," he posits that the initial response to introceptive and proprioceptive stimuli is addressed first in the primitive brain areas and elaborated in the more advanced area of the brain, such as the cortex and the frontal lobe.

Recognition that symptom formation may reflect learning has been basic to the behaviorist position. Pitman (1989), adopting a behavioral perspective, suggests that the symptoms of PTSD might be explained by two types of learning, classical conditioning and operant conditioning or instrumental learning. He suggests that there is nonassociative learning and associative learning, thus explaining the generalization of fear/anxiety responses.

Foa and Kozak (1986) challenge this traditional two-factor learning paradigm and suggest that symptoms of PTSD are best explained by fear structures in memory that take into account information about the feared stimulus situation; information about verbal, physiological, and other behavioral responses; and interpretive information about the meaning of the stimulus-and-response elements of the structure.

Edelman's model (1989) of memory and learning suggests more complex alterations in basic perceptual categorization processes that are highly dependent on basic survival. In turn, these alterations at the primary level of consciousness influence higher order consciousness.

While this does not rule out the appraisal schema proposed by Foa and Kozak, it suggests that at a primary level of consciousness, categorical discriminations and categories are reorganized. This reorganization influences the higher order consciousness, in particular, conceptualizations of the present state of events. Thus, the response on the primary consciousness level shapes and influences reorganization of the higher order consciousness. This hypothesis then makes some of the judgment errors in victims who are subject to revictimization as understandable as victims who manifest exaggerated fear to innocuous situations.

The important point is that the fear schema arises out of a primary consciousness that consists of basic memory processes that for all intents and purposes are out of awareness and are only suggested in the higher order consciousness. The survival adaptive orientation of the primary consciousness is such that trauma alters saliency and discriminatory mappings. This leaves to clinical efforts the task to search out and identify these alterations and devise interventions that reestablish more flexibility at the level of primary consciousness as well as at the level of higher consciousness. The model of learning assumed by Pitman appears simplistic as to what is known regarding brain functioning, and the fear schema suggested by Foa and Kozak can gain strength by the theoretical proposition of Edelman.

Dissociation, Trauma, and Memory

In trauma, there is biological evidence that the alarm systems functioning is severely altered. Of particular importance is the alterations in arousal and analgesic systems. The result is discontinuity in the basic operations of selecting and categorizing new and ongoing experiential stimuli and developing new memory constructs.

The influence of dissociation and hyperarousal on memory and learning at this basic level alters thinking (solving problems) and is at the heart of understanding the impact of trauma on cognition.

Altered states of consciousness was pivotal in Janet's conceptualization of causes of repetitive behaviors, be they reenactments of a basic upsetting experience or fragmented stereotypes. He believed that altered states of consciousness brought about these patterns because of severe trauma that with its contextual basis had been dissociated from conscious awareness. He believed that trauma overwhelmed and impaired the capacity of the individual to feel, think, and act in a unified, purposeful way. The key lay in how memory is stored, retrieved, and integrated in the face of "vehement emotional" experiences (van der Hart & Horst, 1989).

Freud (1920) struggled with the concept of fixation and the concept of repetition compulsion throughout his intellectual career.

Whereas Freud viewed psychological trauma rooted in infantile sexuality, Janet noted how a variety of traumatic experiences result in the disruption of personality and behavior and are marked by disturbances in memory (van der Kolk & van der Hart, 1989). Van der Kolk and van der Hart (1989) concluded their presentation of Janet's work on trauma and psychological adaptation by noting that after more than 100 years much remains to be learned about how memories operate, are stored, and interact with emotions and behavior in order to diminish their hold over current experience.

Clinical Implications

These current neurobiological findings have direct implications for clinical practice. First, the long-term symptom sequelae of rape and sexual abuse victims has to be understood not only from a psycho-social-political perspective, but from a biological basis. Trauma learning is realized in alterations in primary and secondary memory processes. The search for appropriate biological interventions that can reestablish dysregulation is an optimum outcome. However, the associative damage done via the prolongation of symptoms and the interpersonal violations require a variety of approaches from self-help support groups to focused psychotherapeutic approaches.

References

Aysto, S. 1987. Neuropsychological aspects of simultaneous and successive cognitive process. In J.M. Williams and C.J. Long (eds.), *Cognitive Approaches to Neuropsychology*. New York: Plenum, 229–72.

Edelman, G. 1989. *The Remembered Present: A Biological Theory of Consciousness*. New York: Basic Books.

Foa, E.B., and M.J. Kozak. 1986. Emotional processing of fear: Exposure to corrective information. *Psychological Bulletin* 99:20–35.

Freud, S. 1920. *Beyond the pleasure principle*. Trans. and ed. by J. Strachey (1961). Liveright ed. (1970), New York.

Giller, E. (ed). 1990. *Biological Assessment and Treatment of Posttraumatic Stress Disorder*. Washington: American Psychiatric Press.

Horowitz, M. 1976. Intrusive and repetitive thoughts after experimental stress. *Archives of General Psychiatry* 32:1457–63.

Krystal, J. 1990. Animal models for posttraumatic stress disorder. In E. Giller (ed.), *Biological Assessment and Treatment of Posttraumatic Stress*. Washington, DC: American Psychiatric Press, 1–26.

MacLean, P. 1990. *The Triune Brain in Evolution*. New York: Plenum.

Pitman, R. 1989. Biological findings in PTS: Implications for DSM-IV Classification. Unpublished position paper. NH Veterans Administration Medical Center/Dept. of Psychiatry, Harvard Medical School Research Services, 151.

van der Hart, O. and R. Horst. 1989. The dissociation theory of Pierre Janet, *Journal of Traumatic Stress* 2:399–411.

van der Kolk, B.A. 1987. *Psychological Trauma*. Washington DC: American Psychiatric Press.

van der Kolk, B.A., and O. van der Hart. 1989. Pierre Janet and the breakdown of adaptation in psychological trauma. *American Journal of Psychiatry* 146 (12):1530–40.

Chapter 2

Victim Assessment: The Dimensions of Rape Interview Schedule (DORIS)

Carole-Rae Reed, Ann W. Burgess
University of Pennsylvania

Carol R. Hartman
Boston College

■

Introduction

To date, the majority of research concerning rape victims has concentrated on the aftermath and symptom response. Little research has been done concerning the relationship of various aspects of the rape experience and specific symptoms. The lack of a systematic, standardized method of assessing various features of the rape event has hampered research in this area, although such instruments have been recently introduced for use with child abuse victims (Burgess, Hartman, & Kelley, 1990) and adult survivors of incest (Edwards & Donaldson, 1989). Furthermore, clinicians have traditionally had to base assessments on the victim's description and recall of the actual rape event, which may be influenced by emotional state, cognition, and trauma response. Amnesia for aspects of the event in rape victims is well documented. If clinicians do not ask about significant aspects of the rape event, the fact that victims have gaps in their recall may not be recognized.

In order to facilitate assessment of victims' experience of the rape event for use in both clinical and research settings, a semi-structured interview schedule was developed by the authors. The interview is meant to supplement commonly used clinical assessment techniques, such as the mental status examination and other diagnostic procedures. The interview is based on the theoretical constructs of information processing of trauma. Individual items included are based on extensive review of the literature combined with clinical experience in the assessment of rape victims.

Theoretical Basis and Rationale

Theoretical basis

Information-processing theories of trauma account for the psychological, behavioral, and somatic symptoms seen in victims following traumatic experience, an advantage over other theories that account for only limited aspects of the trauma response (Burgess & Hartman, 1988; Burgess et al., 1990).

Rape is conceptualized as a traumatic experience. Burgess & Hartman (1988; Hartman & Burgess, 1986; 1988) have developed a model of information processing of trauma that is specific to sexual trauma in childhood. Because rape is a form of sexual trauma, and no other model of trauma takes into account effects which may be specific to a sexual type of traumatic experience, this model was adapted to serve as the theoretical framework for developing the DORIS. The following description briefly illustrates how this model can be used to explain adult victims' response to rape.

Experiences are processed on sensory, perceptual, cognitive, and interpersonal levels (Burgess & Hartman, 1988; Hartman & Burgess, 1986; 1988; Horowitz, 1976; 1986; Kolb, 1987). In the case of rape, the information to be processed is the rape experience. The individual registers the experience on a sensory level, which includes all sights, sounds, tactile and spatial sensations, smells, and tastes. On the perceptual level, information is subjectively interpreted and classification begins. At the cognitive and interpersonal level, the person attaches meaning to the experience and organizes or processes experience into systems of meaning (Hartman & Burgess, 1986). The constructive representation of the rape experience, and current needs and drives, are matched or compared with enduring schemata of the individual self and the world (Horowitz, 1976).

Dimensions of Rape

The dimensions of rape assessed in the interview include: type of abuse, assailant characteristics and relationship to victim, event characteristics; victim characteristics at the time of rape and now,

Table 2-1

DIMENSIONS OF RAPE INTERVIEW SCHEDULE

Type of Abuse

A. Physical Acts
   1. Hit, punched, or beaten
   2. Cut, stabbed, or bitten
   3. Tied up or restrained, gagged, or blindfolded
   4. Forced to walk or crawl long distance
   5. Burned
   6. Given drugs or alcohol
   7. Other (describe)

B. Sexual Acts
   1. Oral penetration by assailant/object (oral sex)
   2. Vaginal penetration by assailant/object (sexual intercourse)
   3. Anal penetration by assailant/object (anal sex)
   4. Assault witnessed by other people
   5. Victim witnessed sexual acts of others
   6. Pornographic materials used or produced
   7. Other (describe)

C. Use of Weapon
   1. Gun
   2. Knife
   3. Other (describe)

D. Threats
   1. Threatened with death
   2. Threatened with disfigurement or physical injury
   3. Threatened with loss of job or income
   4. Threatened with harm to loved ones
   5. Threatened with repeat rape
   6. Other

---

victim response, and aftermath. Rape is commonly defined as having three basic elements; penetration, nonconsent, and threat or force. (See Table 2-1.)

Type of abuse

Rape may include aspects of three types of abuse: physical, sexual, and psychological. The most distressing features of the rape may or may not be the sexual elements. For example, if the victim's life is threatened, or if physical torture or abuse is used, the victim's initial symptom response may often be related to physical survival. One pattern of abuse may dominate over others (Burgess et al., 1990). The

Table 2-1 (continued)

DIMENSIONS OF RAPE INTERVIEW SCHEDULE

Assailant Characteristics and Relationship to Victim

A. Verbal Strategies
1. Threats (see above)
2. Orders
3. Ploy used to gain access to victim (confidence line)
4. Personal inquiries of victim
5. Personal revelations by rapist
6. Obscene names/racial epithets
7. Exploitation of victim's forced sexual response ("you like it")
8. Soft-sell departure (apologies, safe return, socializing)
9. Sexual put-downs
10. Possession of victim ("you're mine now")
11. Taking property from another male (partner statements)

B. Relationship of Rapist to Victim
1. Stranger
2 Acquaintance or friend
3. Current or former spouse or cohabitant
5. Date
6. Authority figure (describe)
7. Relative or in-law
8. Other (describe)

C. Assailant(s) Characteristics
1. Gender
2. Approximate age
3. Race/ethnicity
4. Use of alcohol or drugs (describe)

Event Characteristics

A. Characteristics of Rape
1. Multiple rapists
2. Multiple victims
3. Time of day/night, approximate date (month and year)

---

various methods of force and or threats used against the victim throughout the rape experience are assessed in this section, as well as objects and/or weapons used in conducting the assault.

Physical acts include: being hit, punched, or beaten; being cut, stabbed, or bitten; being tied up, restrained, gagged, or blindfolded; being forced to walk or crawl a long distance; being burned; and/or

Table 2-1 (continued)
DIMENSIONS OF RAPE INTERVIEW SCHEDULE

    4. Location/setting
    5. Robbery or other crime committed
    6. Duration of attack
    7. Awakened from sleep
    8. Ritualism (describe)

Victim Characteristics

A. Characteristics of Victim
    1. Race
    2. Age at time of attack/now
    3. Education at time of attack/now
    4. Occupation at time of attack/now
    5. Marital/relationship status at time of attack/now

Response/aftermath

A. Lifestyle Change in Response to Rape
    1. Change in residence
    2. Change in significant interpersonal relationships
    3. Change in job, shift, or hours worked
    4. Change in telephone number
    5. Change in sleep habits, times
    6. Use of rituals such as checking locks, etc.
    7. Use of drugs/alcohol increased/decreased/same
    8. Change in life/career goals
    9. Change in eating habits/weight (loss, gain)

B. Other Consequences of Rape
    1. Development of physical illness/somatic complaints, permanent disability
    2. Development of emotional/mental disorder
    3. Development of sexual difficulties
    4. Development of sexually transmitted disease
    5. Pregnancy (abortion, miscarriage, birth)
    6. Victim or rapist tested for HIV (results)
    7. Other (describe).

other physical acts the victim may describe. Sexual acts assessed include: oral penetration by assailant(s)/object (oral sex); vaginal penetration by assailant(s)/object (sexual intercourse); anal penetration by assailant/object (anal sex); assault witnessed by other people; victim witnessed sexual acts of others; pornographic materials used or produced; other sexual acts.

Determining whether or not the assault was witnessed by others has several purposes. If the assault was witnessed by others who were unwilling or unable to assist the victim, feelings of anger, abandonment, and mistrust may result. If friends or family members witnessed the assault, the clinician is alerted that there are several victims, and that family counseling may be necessary. The production of pornographic materials may indicate the assailant(s) involvement with a group or other such organized operation, and the probability that others have been victimized. The fear that others may view an assault may give rise to feelings of embarrassment and shame in the victim. Viewing pornographic materials and/or witnessing the sexual acts of others constitutes additional traumatic information that must be processed by the victim.

The presence of a weapon and specific threats used to access and control the victim constitutes psychological abuse. Clinical symptoms, especially specific fears, and intrusive imagery are theorized to be directly related to methods of control and access (Hartman & Burgess, 1988). Gun use, knife use, or use of any other object as a weapon is assessed in the interview. Threats assessed include: death, disfigurement or physical injury, loss of job or income, harm to loved ones, repeat rape, and other threats described by the victim.

Characteristics of assailant and relationship to victim

Assessed in this section are the verbal strategies used by the assailant during the rape, the relationship of the assailant to the victim, and other characteristics of the assailant.

Verbal strategies used by the assailant are similar to threats in that they represent information to be processed by the victim, and are a form of psychological abuse. However, they are classified here as assailant characteristics as they give important clues to the assailant's style of attack and motivation (Holmstrom & Burgess, 1978). The following eleven verbal strategies and their descriptions were adapted from a study of 115 rape victims interviewed in a hospital emergency ward (Holmstrom & Burgess, 1980).

Orders: Victims are frequently commanded to do things by the rapist. This establishes the rapist's control. Examples are orders to perform specific sexual activities, to keep quiet, to get money or valuables, or not to tell anyone. Orders are often combined with threats: "Keep smiling or I'll kill you."

Confidence line: A ploy is used to gain access to the victim or to get the victim to a location where the rape can take place undiscovered. Common ploys are: requests or offers of assistance; promises of social activities, material items, drugs, or alcohol; promises of information; references to someone whom the victim knows; promises of potential employment; trading on social niceties. The latter ploy is often seen in date or acquaintance rape.

Personal inquiries of the victim: Victims may be asked details of their lives, their addresses, their phones numbers, and sexual details. Younger victims may be asked if they are virgins. Victims may disclose information out of fear that causes them distress later or may be used against them.

Personal revelations by rapist: These may be used to gain sympathy from the victim, "I was abused as a child," or to gain further control, "I just got out of jail for killing a woman," or both: "Since you left me I've been so lonely; I'll kill you if you don't let me in." Rapists may reveal information that ultimately leads to their apprehension, such as a name, workplace, or even a phone number.

Obscene names/racial epithets: Victims may be called "whore" or "slut" and/or other obscene names, which further adds to their humiliation. Derogatory references may be made to the victim's racial or ethnic background or social class. One victim was told that "this is all your fault because you're white."

Exploitation of victim's forced sexual response: Victims are frequently told: "You know you like it." Victims may be coerced into saying they "enjoyed" one of the most traumatic experiences in their lives.

Soft-sell departure: Some rapists, in an attempt to normalize what has occurred, or to make a safe departure, will apologize, socialize, or even arrange or assist in the victim's safe return. A rapist who terrorized a seaside resort town for several weeks was known as "the polite rapist" because he would apologize, help his victims locate their belongings and get dressed, and generally treat them nicely following the rape.

Sexual put-downs: Rapists may tell victims they didn't get any satisfaction, that the victim was "cold," or otherwise comment on the victim's sexual performance. Victims may be told that no one will want them anymore, or that they weren't really worth raping. It is possible these put-downs may contribute to the low self-esteem and sexual difficulties often experienced by victims in the aftermath of rape, although the relationship has not been empirically investigated.

Possession of victim: The emphasis in this strategy is to gain the victim for the rapist's own personal use: "You're mine now, I own you," either as a sexual partner or as a prostitute. This is often seen in cases of interracial rape.

Partner statements: The theme in these verbal statements is that of taking property from another male, or exploiting the powerlessness of the victim's partner to prevent the rape. Partner statements are often made in rapes where the partner is present and forced to watch.

Relationship of rapist to victim

According to Koss, Dinero, Seibel, and Cox (1988),

> the relationship context has been postulated to affect both the victim's and offender's behavior before, during, and after the crime. It may take the woman who is acquainted with her offender longer to perceive that an interaction is progressing to rape (Koss et al., p. 2)

Furthermore,

> . . . the victim offender relationship may predict some of the important choices that rape victims must make, including: whom to tell, from whom to seek help, what changes in life circumstances to make, how to protect oneself in the future, what other actions to take in political and social terms, and how to reorganize oneself. (Koss et al., 1988, p. 3)

However, it is well established that victims who are acquainted with their rapist do not necessarily differ from victims of stranger rape in terms of psychological symptoms present at various times following the rape (Ellis, Atkeson, & Calhoun, 1981; Frank, Turner, & Stewart, 1980; Kilpatrick, Best, Saunders, & Veronen, 1988; Kilpatrick, Veronen, & Best, 1985; Koss et al., 1988; Parrot & Bechhofer, 1991; Ruch, & Chandler, 1983).

There is limited empirical evidence that victims of acquaintance rape are significantly less likely than victims of stranger or marital rape to view their experience as rape (Koss et al., 1988; Kilpatrick et al.,

1988). This suggests that the rapist's relationship to the victim may affect the victim's perception and the meaning the victim attaches to the incident. Acquaintance rapes are more likely to involve an individual offender over a period of time and involve more than one assault (Alzenon & Kelley, 1988; Koss et al., 1988). An associated finding of the study was that a percentage of victims of date rape continue the relationship (Alzenon & Kelley, 1988).

Rapist characteristics: Other rapist characteristics assessed include gender, approximate age, race/ethnicity. and use of drugs and/or alcohol. Use of drugs and /or alcohol on the part of the rapist has implications for the victim. First of all, if intravenous drug use is involved, the victim may be at risk for exposure to the human immunodeficiency virus (HIV) and subsequent autoimmune deficiency disease (AIDS). Clinicians working with such victims should be aware of these concerns, and issues regarding testing of both the offender and victim (Burgess et al., 1990). In our clinical work, we have noted that rape victims often offer the fact that the offender had been using drugs or alcohol as a reason for the assault: "He was high; he didn't know what he was doing," or for their inability to stop the attack: "He had been drinking, I told him no, but he just wouldn't stop."

Characteristics of rape

Among the items assessed in this section are: whether or not there were multiple rapists or more than one victim; the time of day and approximate date (month and year); the location and setting; whether or not a robbery or crime other than rape was committed, the duration of the attack; whether or not the victim was awakened from sleep; and the presence or absence of ritualism.

It is important to determine the characteristics of the rape event, since in terms of information to be processed this is some of the most disturbing. Amnesia for the event for or aspects of the event will become evident. Aspects of the event may be the source of ensuing phobic avoidance, or intrusive imagery such as nightmares or flashbacks (Burgess & Hartman, 1988; Hartman & Burgess, 1986; 1988; Horowitz, 1976; 1986). The existence of other victims is important in case finding and may be an important source of verification of victim recall. The location, setting, and general context of the rape are important in terms of establishing the victim's present level of safety and need for other services and may affect symptom response (Burgess & Hartman, 1988; Hartman & Burgess, 1986; 1988; Horowitz, 1976; 1986). There is growing concern on the part of clinicians regarding ritualistic abuse (Hill & Goodwin, 1988; Kelley, 1988; 1989). Unless specifically asked about possible ritualistic aspects of the abuse, many victims will not offer the information or believe it too bizarre to be an actual memory (Hill & Goodwin, 1988; Kelley, 1988; 1989).

Characteristics of victim

The following demographic characteristics are assessed in the DORIS: race, age at time of attack and now, education at time of attack and now, occupation at time of attack and now; and marital status at time of attack and now. It is important to establish the victim's status at the time of the attack and at present to determine change, if any, post assault, and duration of time since assault. this information is useful to clinicians and researchers alike in determining immediate and long-term response to the rape.

Aftermath and consequences of rape

Lifestyle change in response to rape: It is well established that rape victims alter various aspects of their lives in response to rape (Burgess & Holmstrom, 1986; Becker, Skinner, Abel, & Treacy, 1982; Divasto, 1985; Ellis, et al., 1981; Gilmartin-Zena, 1985; Frank & Stewart, 1984; Ipema, 1979; Mezey & Taylor, 1988; Nadelson, Notman, Zackson, & Gornick, 1982). These alterations may reflect attempts at self-protection, and/or avoidance of upsetting reminders of the assault. Sleep disturbances or sleep problems (including nightmares) have been associated with the aftermath of rape (Binder, 1981; Divasto, 1985; Forman, 1980; Becker et al., 1984; Libow & Doty, 1979; Frank, Turner, & Duffy, 1979; Frank & Stewart, 1984; Mezey & Taylor, 1988; Nadelson et al., 1982; Norris & Feldman-Summers, 1981). Alcohol and/or substance abuse following rape has been reported in several studies (Divasto, 1985; Mezey & Taylor, 1988, Meyer & Taylor, 1986) as has resumption of previous substance abuse (Ellis et. al., 1981; Kasniak, Nussbaum, Berren, & Santiago, 1988). Appetite and weight disturbance following rape have been documented by several researchers (Becker et al., 1984; Divasto, 1985; Frank & Stewart, 1984; Frank et al., 1979; Norris & Feldman-Summers, 1981).

Other consequences of rape: Other consequences of rape assessed are development of the following: physical illness/somatic complaints, sexually transmitted disease; emotional or mental disorder; HIV concerns; pregnancy; scarring or permanent physical disability; or other not previously mentioned consequences attributed to the rape experience.

Physical illness/somatic complaints: The existence of physical illness and somatic complains among rape victims, both immediately postassault and as long-term consequences, is frequently described in the research literature (Binder, 1981; Burgess & Holmstrom, 1974; Burt & Katz, 1988; Divasto, 1985; Domino & Haber, 1987; Gill & Stein, 1982; Norris & Feldman-Summers, 1981). This category includes fatigue or loss of energy (Ellis, Atkeson, & Calhoun, 1981; Frank, Turner, & Duffy, 1989; Frank & Stewart, 1984).

Emotional/mental disorder: The development of emotional or mental disorders subsequent to rape is well documented (Becker et al., 1984; Burgess & Holmstrom, 1974; Burnam, Stein, Golding, Siegal, Sorenson, Forsythe, & Telles, 1988; Forman, 1980; Frank & Stewart, 1984; Kasniak et al., 1988; Kilpatrick et. al., 1988; Meyers, 1989; Mezey & King, 1989; Mullen, Romans-Clarkson, Walton, & Herbison, 1988; Nadelson et al., 1982; Resnick, Jordan, Girelli, & Hutter, 1988; Santiago et al., 1985; Winfield, George, Swartz, & Blazer, 1990). The most common disorders seen in clinical practice are post-traumatic stress disorder and depression.

Sexual difficulties: Sexual difficulties and dysfunctions, including sexual fears, identity confusion and difficulties in intimate relationships are frequently reported consequences of rape (Becker et al., 1982; 1984; 1986; Burgess & Holmstrom, 1974; Ellis, Atkeson, & Calhoun, 1981; Feldman-Summers, Gordon, & Meaghet, 1979; Kilpatrick, et al., 1988; Mezey & King, 1989; Mezey & Taylor, 1988; Myers, 1989; Norris & Feldman-Summers, 1981; Resnick et al., 1988).

Sexually transmitted disease: An infrequently discussed consequence of rape is the development of sexually transmitted disease (Osterholm, MacDonald, & Danita, 1987). The item is included to provide an opening for the interviewer to discuss the topic with the victim. If testing has not been done and is desired by the victim, appropriate referral is indicated.

Pregnancy: Another infrequently discussed consequence of rape is pregnancy. It is important that the interviewer determine the outcome of the pregnancy, that is, abortion, miscarriage, birth, or adoption. This provides an opportunity to discuss the victims feelings and fears surrounding pregnancy and her decisions regarding pregnancy. If she suspects she may be pregnant and has not been examined or tested, a referral for pelvic examination and pregnancy testing and options counseling is recommended.

Victim or assailant tested for HIV (results): There is increasing concern over HIV testing and disease among sexual assault victims (Baker, Burgess, Davis, & Brickman, 1990) and professionals working with them (Burgess, et al., 1990). A victim of spousal rape, when asked if she or her husband had been tested for HIV, replied, "No, but I've thought of it. He's a real womanizer and I think he's been to prostitutes. Who knows who he's been with?" Furthermore, she stated that this was the first time anyone ever asked her about the issue or was willing to discuss it. She did not know where or when to get tested, and was unaware of anonymous testing sites. This is alarming, since she had been in therapy for several months and was involved in a rape related legal proceeding. There is evidence of HIV transmission following rape (Forster, Pritchard, Munday, & Goldmeir, 1987; Murphy, Kitchen, Harris, & Forster, 1989). If the assailant is known to belong to an at-risk population for HIV, the testing issue is extremely important. Referral for testing is necessary should the victim express concern or desire. Most cities have anonymous testing centers if the victim prefers to keep the results confidential.

Clinical Use

The DORIS is designed for use as an adjunct to the standard clinical interview. We have found that it is best to allow the victim to describe his or her experience, with the clinician writing in *yes* or *no* for presence or absence of specific items and filling in brief descriptions on the DORIS form. When the victim has finished relating the event, the interviewer then asks about specific items on the DORIS that the victim either did not mention or that need further clarification. When it is known by the clinician that the victim will be seen on two or more occasions, we have found it useful to conduct the standard clinical interview during the first session, and use the DORIS during the second session. The use of the DORIS during the second session is a good technique to introduce talking about the traumatic experience for information processing of the trauma.

References

Alzenon, M., and G. Kelley. 1988. The incidence of violence and acquaintance rape in dating relationships among college men and women. *Journal of College Student Development* 29:305–19.

Baker, T., A. Burgess, R. Davis, and E. Brickman. 1990. Rape victims' concern about possible exposure to AIDS. *Journal of Interpersonal Violence* 5:49–60.

Becker, J., L. Skinner, G. Abel, and E. Treacy. 1982. Incidence and types of sexual dysfunctions in rape and incest victims. *Archives of Sexual Behavior* 8(1):65–74.

———, L. Skinner, G. Abel, G. Axilrod, and E. Treacy. 1984. Depressive symptoms associated with sexual assault. *Archives of Sexual Behavior* 10(3):185–92.

———, L. Skinner, G. Abel, and J. Cichon. 1986. Level of postassault sexual functioning in rape and incest victims. *Archives of Sexual Behavior* 15(1):37–49.

Binder, R. 1981. Difficulties in follow-up of rape victims. *American Journal of Psychotherapy* 35(4): 534–41.

Burgess, A., and C. Hartman. 1988. Response patterns of traumatized children. In A. Burgess and C. Grant (eds.) *Children Traumatized in Sex Rings*, pp. 21–25. Washington, DC: National Center for Missing and Exploited Children.

———, C. Hartman, and S. Kelley. 1990. Assessing child abuse: The TRIADS checklist. *Journal of Psychosocial Nursing and Mental Health Services* 28(4):6–14.

———, and L. Holmstrom. 1974. Rape trauma syndrome. *American Journal of Psychiatry* 131(9): 981–86.

———, and L. Holmstrom. 1986. *Rape: Crisis and Recovery*. West Newton, MA: Awab, Inc.

———, B. Jacobsen, J. Thompson, T. Baker, and C. Grant. 1990. HIV testing of sexual assault populations: Ethical and legal issues. *Journal of Emergency Nursing* 16(5): 331–38.

Burnam, M., J. Stein, J. Golding, J. Siegal, S. Sorenson, A. Forsythe, and C. Telles. Sexual assault and mental disorders in a community population. *Journal of Consulting and Clinical Psychology* 56(6): 843–50.

Burt, M., and B. Katz. 1988. Coping strategies and recovery from rape. *Annals of the New York Academy of Sciences* 528: 345–58.

Divasto, P. 1985. Measuring the aftermath of rape. *Journal of Psychosocial Nursing and Mental Health Services* 28(2):33–35.

Domino, J., and J. Haber. 1987. Prior physical and sexual abuse in women with chronic headache; Clinical correlates. *Headache* 27: 310–14.

Edwards, P. and M. Donaldson. 1989. Assessment of symptoms in adult survivors of incest: A factor analytic study of the responses to childhood incest questionnaire. *Child Abuse and Neglect* 13:101–10.

Ellis E., B. Atkeson, and K. Calhoun. 1981. An assessment of long-term reaction to rape. *Journal of Abnormal Psychology* 90(3):263–66.

Feldman-Summers, S., P. Gordon, and J. Meagher. 1979. The impact of rape on sexual satisfaction. *Journal of Abnormal Psychology* 88(1):101–5.

Forman, B. 1980. Cognitive modification of obsessive thinking in a rape victim: A preliminary study. *Psychological Reports* 47(3 pt. 1):819–22.

Forster, G, S. Pritchard, P. Munday, and D. Goldmeir 1987. Risk of AIDS after rape. *Genitourinary Medicine* 63: 217.

Frank, E., and B. Stewart. 1984. Depressive symptoms in rape victims: A revisit. *Journal of Affective Disorders* 7(1): 77–95.

———, S. Turner, and B. Duffy. 1979. Depressive symptoms in rape victims. *Journal of Affective Disorders* 1(4): 269–77.

———, S. Turner, and B. Stewart. 1980. Initial response to rape: The impact of factors within the rape situation. *Journal of Behavioral Assessment* 2:39–53.

Gill, J., and H. Stein. 1982) Occult emotional trauma: A trigger factor to certain headaches. Paper presented at the Twenty-fourth Annual A.A.S.H. Meeting, New Orleans, LA.

Gilmartin-Zena, P. 1985. Rape impact; Immediately and two months later. *Deviant Behavior* 6:347–61.

Hartman, C., and A. Burgess. 1986. Child sexual abuse: Generic roots of the victim experience. *Journal of Psychotherapy and the Family* 2:83–92.

———. 1988. Information processing of trauma: A case application of a model. *Journal of Interpersonal Violence* 3(4): 443–57.

Hill, S., and J. Goodwin. 1988. Satanism: Similarities between patient accounts and pre-Inquisition historical sources. Paper presented at the International Society for the Study of Multiple Personality Disorders, Chicago, IL.

Holmstrom, L., and A. Burgess. 1980. Rapists' talk: Linguistic strategies to control the victim. *Deviant Behavior* 1:101–25.

Horowitz, M. 1976. *Stress Response Syndromes*. Northvale, NJ: Jason Aronson.

———. 1986. *Stress Response Syndromes*, 2nd ed.) Northvale, NJ: Jason Aronson.

Ipema, D. 1979. Rape: The process of recovery. *Nursing Research* 28(5):272–75.

Kasniak, A., P. Nussbaum, N. Berren, and J. Santiago. 1988. Amnesia as a consequence of male rape; a case report. *Journal of Abnormal Psychiatry* 97(1):100–04.

Kelley, S. 1988. Ritualistic abuse of children: Dynamics and impact. *Cultic Studies Journal* 5(2): 228–36.

———. 1989. Stress responses of children to sexual abuse and ritualistic abuse in day care centers. *Journal of Interpersonal Violence* 4(4): 501–12.

Kilpatrick, D., C. Best, B. Saunders, and L. Veronen. 1988. Rape in marriage and in dating relationships: How bad is it for mental health? *Annals of the New York Academy of Sciences* 528:335–44.

———, L. Veronen, and C. Best. 1985. Factors predicting psychological distress among rape victims. In C. Figley (ed.), *Trauma and Its Wake: The Study and Treatment of Post-Traumatic Stress Disorder*, pp. 113–41. New York: Brunner/Mazel.

Kolb., L. 1987. A neuropsychological hypothesis explaining posttraumatic stress disorders. *American Journal of Psychiatry* 144(8): 989–95.

Koss, M., T. Dinero, C. Seibel, and S. Cox. 1988. Stranger and acquaintance rape: Are there differences in the victim's experience? *Psychology of Women Quarterly* 12:1–24.

Libow, J., and D. Doty. 1979. An exploratory approach to self-blame and self-derogation by rape victims. *American Journal of Orthopsychiatry* 49(4):670–79.

Meyer, C., and S. Taylor. 1986. Adjustment to rape. *Journal of Personality and Social Psychology* 50(6):1226–34.

Meyers, M. 1989. Men sexually assaulted as adults and sexually abused as boys. *Archives of Sexual Behavior* 18(3): 203–15.

Mezey, G., and M. King. 1989. The effects of sexual assault on men: A survey of 22 victims. *Psychological Medicine* 19(1): 205–09.

————, and P. Taylor. 1988. Psychological reactions of women who have been raped. *British Journal of Psychiatry* 152:330–39.

Mullen, P., S. Romans-Clarkson, V. Walton, and G. Herbison. 1988. Impact of sexual and physical abuse on women's mental health. *The Lancet* 1(8950): 841–45.

Murphy, S., V. Kitchen, J. Harris, and S. Forster. 1989. Rape and seroconversion to HIV. *British Medical Journal* 299: 718.

Nadelson, C., M. Notman, H. Zackson, and J. Gornick. 1982. A follow-up study of rape victims. *Journal of Abnormal Psychiatry* 146(10):203–15.

Norris, J., and S. Feldman-Summers. 1981. Factors related to the psychological impacts of rape on the victim. *Journal of Abnormal Psychiatry* 90(6):562–67.

Osterholm, M., K. MacDonald., and R. Danita. 1987. Sexually transmitted diseases in victims of sexual assault. *New England Journal of Medicine* 316:1024.

Parrot, A., and L. Bechhofer. 1991. *Acquaintance Rape*. New York: Wiley Interscience.

Ruch, L., and S. Chandler. 1983. Sexual assault trauma during the acute phase: An exploratory model and multivariate analysis. *Journal of Health and Social Behavior* 24:174–85.

Resick, P., C. Jordan, S. Girelli, and C. Hutter. 1988. A comparative outcome study of behavioral group therapy for sexual assault victims. *Behavior Therapy* 19(1): 385–401.

Santiago, J., F. McCall-Perez, M. Gorcy, and A. Beigel. 1985. Long-term psychological effects of rape in 35 rape victims. *American Journal of Psychiatry* 142(11): 1338–40.

Winfield, I., L. George, M. Swartz, and D. Blazer. 1990. Sexual assault and psychiatric disorders among a community sample of women. *American Journal of Psychiatry* 147(3):333–41.

Chapter 3

Internal and External Mediators of Women's Rape Experiences

Gail Elizabeth Wyatt
University of California, Los Angeles

Michael Newcomb
University of Southern California

Cindy M. Notgrass
University of California, Los Angeles

∎

This research is funded by the National Institute of Mental Health, Grant R01 MH33603, a Research Scientist Career Development Award K01 MH00269 to the first author and Grant DA01070 from the National Institute on Drug Abuse to the second author. The authors wish to thank the Women's Project Staff for data collection, Stefanie Peters, Ph.D., for her invaluable assistance with data preparation, and Vicki Mays, Ph.D., and Ivan Mensh, Ph.D., for their editorial input.

Reprinted, with changes, from Psychology of Women Quarterly *14:153–76, 1990, by permission.*

∎

Incidents of attempted and completed rape are known to be some of the more serious forms of sexual assault (Russell, 1983). In the past ten years, the initial and lasting effects of rape on women's psychological adjustment (Cohen & Roth, 1987; Holmes & St. Lawrence, 1983; Kilpatrick, Veronen, & Resick, 1982; Marhoefer-Dvorak, Resick, Hutter, & Girelli, 1988; Meyer & Taylor, 1986; Ruch & Chandler, 1983; Sales, Baum, & Shore, 1984), sexual functioning (Becker, Skinner, Abel, & Cichon, 1986; Cohen & Roth, 1987; Feldman-

Summers, Gordon, & Meagher, 1979) and subsequent intimate relationships (Cohen, 1988; Cohen & Roth, 1987; Meyer & Taylor, 1986; Resick, 1983) have been well documented (also see Koss & Burkhart, 1989). There is, however, still no universal consensus that rape is as stressful an experience as many report it to be. For example, until recently (Wright, 1985), rape was not conceived of as a major life event or as a daily stressor in studies of psychological problems (Hammen, Marks, Mays, & DeMayo, 1985; Kanner, Koyne, Schaefer, & Lazarus, 1981). Consequently, many measures used to assess the effects of attempted or completed rape incidents in the above-mentioned studies do not necessarily include problems specific to sexual assault. Without research identifying the specific effects of rape, we are limited in understanding how this experience is similar to or distinct from other traumatic events.

In spite of the growing volume of research on rape (Koss, 1985; Russell, 1983), there are several reasons why we do not know more about its effects. Many aspects of the experience do not meet societies' criteria for the "typical" rape that is assumed to occur (Burt, 1980; Koss & Burkhart, 1989). Consequently, victims may not disclose their assault experience until years later (Williams, 1984; Williams & Holmes, 1982). Although rape is most often perpetrated by persons who are known to the victim (Koss & Burkhart, 1989; Koss, Dinero, Seibel, Cox, 1988; Russell, 1983; Williams, 1984), societal attitudes are more negative toward victims of acquaintance rape and view stranger rape as the more serious assault (Tetreault & Barnett, 1987). However, most research indicates that both acquaintance and stranger rape have a similar impact upon victims (Koss et al., 1988).

The lifetime prevalence of attempted and completed rapes (15 percent to 22 percent) is most likely underestimated because women often do not consider themselves as rape victims (Burt & Estep, 1981; Koss et al., 1988; Koss & Burkhart, 1989). Victims who are more severely abused also tend to receive less support than those who experienced less violent rape (Ruch & Chandler, 1983). When rape is disclosed to the authorities, the investigation of the allegations and prosecution of the perpetrator often results in the revictimization of the survivor (Burt, 1980).

Consequently, rape survivors often attempt to cope with the experience without the support of legal, medical, or mental health professionals. We need to understand more fully the social-psychological processes of rape and the pervasiveness of its aftermath for those whose assault is unreported and who do not seek or receive professional attention (Koss & Burkhart, 1989). Such information is important for researchers, and particularly so for the general public who, in the coping and healing process following rape, may prefer instead to seek support from a network of family and friends.

Most rape research focuses upon the initial effects of rape from 3 months to 1 year (Sales, Baum &-Shore, 1984). Since few studies have examined long-term effects, beyond 3–4 years postrape (Ellis, 1983; Girelli, Resick, Marhoefer-Dvorak, Hutter, 1986; Resick, 1983; Santiago, McCall-Perez, Gorcey, Beigel, 1985), the available empirical studies are limited to the assessment of the trauma of recent abuse. Many of the samples in current rape research do not include the highest risk groups such as women living in areas with high crime rates. While studies historically have included samples who are recruited while seeking help for their victimization (Burgess & Holmstrom, 1974; Girelli et al., 1986; Sales et al., 1984), college students are the most common subjects (Koss, 1985). There are few epidemiological studies that include multiethnic samples and examine ethnic differences in rape (Russell, 1986). Ethnic minorities are often underrepresented in research, even though African-American women have been described as most at risk for rape at some point in their lives (Amir, 1971; Hinderland & Davis, 1977; Katz & Mazur, 1979; Miller et al., 1978; National Crime Survey, 1975; Peters, 1976).

Inconsistencies have been noted in the questions asked to elicit a rape history (Koss, 1985). Earlier studies included one indirect question regarding sexual assault (Bureau of Justice Statistics, 1980). More current research indicates that behaviorally oriented questions that describe the use of coercion in sex on a continuum is more likely to reveal unacknowledged rape incidents (Koss, 1985). Some definitions include rape occurring in childhood (before age 18), along with those reported in adulthood (since age 18), and cite a lifetime prevalence rate (Koss, 1985; Russell, 1983). However, research on the effects of child sexual victimization has indicated that there are specific factors related to the manner in which children process attributions for their victimization (Finkelhor, 1984; 1988) that may be quite distinct from adult women. Rape experiences also need to be examined within a developmental context in order to avoid overlooking age-related issues that may also influence negative outcomes.

Finally, sexual assault does not affect all victims to the same degree. Research has yet to examine the mediating factors that minimize or exacerbate the most traumatic aspects of rape (Koss & Burkhart, 1989). Studies of cognitive processes have been used in other research on coping with stress (Cervantes & Castro, 1985; Friedrich, Urquiza, & Belke, 1985; Harter, Alexander, & Neimeyer, 1988). Internal mediators such as behavioral and characterological self-blame have been associated with a poor adjustment to rape (Meyer & Taylor, 1986). Among the specific problems noted are fear, anxiety, depression, problems in interpersonal relationships (Orzek, 1983; Resick, 1983), and self-perceptions as a victim (Meyer & Taylor, 1986).

In light of societal attitudes about rape, external mediators such as the supportive responses of the person(s) to whom the rape was disclosed should also be included in research. The influence of supportive persons may help to minimize the immediate effects of rape that range from anxiety, symptoms of Post-Traumatic Stress Disorder (Kilpatrick et al., 1982; Roth, Dye, & Lebowitz, 1988), sexual dysfunction (Becker et al., 1986; Kilpatrick et al., 1982), the dissolution of relationships (Cohen, 1988), mistrust of men, depression, flashbacks of the original trauma (Girelli et al., 1986; Resick, 1983; Santiago et al., 1985), suicide attempts (Kilpatrick et al., 1982), and nervous breakdowns (Kilpatrick, Best, & Veronen, 1984) years after the assault has occurred.

The support of families or friends can also facilitate the victim's understanding of her sexual assault. If victims do not disclose their assault to anyone, support systems are prevented from helping survivors deal with the trauma. Support in the disclosure process has been found to help child victims regain control of their lives and to lessen the lasting effects of sexual abuse (Wyatt & Mickey, 1987). More empirical documentation, however, about mediating processes such as attribution to victimization and the support of family, police, or other agencies and later outcomes is needed in research on adult victims.

Few studies have attempted to identify which of the many traumatic dimensions involved in rape are directly interconnected. For example, little is known about the effect of the victim's age at the time of the most recent abuse and its influences upon later outcomes. Younger victims tend to have higher levels of symptoms that are relatively short in duration, whereas relatively older victims have less severe symptoms (Cohen & Roth, 1987), but with more long-term effects. Current research does not clarify in cases of multiple occurrences of rape (Marhoefer-Dvorak et al., 1988), which of the ages of abuse were used in the analyses. It seems viable, however, to expect that the age of the most recent abuse might be important, because the effects initially experienced after a rape have been described as part of post-traumatic stress disorder, the rape crises syndrome, and the overall effects of sexual violence (Burgess, 1983; Cunningham, Pearce, & Pearce, 1988; Holmes & St. Lawrence, 1983; Rosenberg, 1986).

Studies have not examined the number of rapes per assault by one or more perpetrators for their effects upon the trauma of the sexual assault. The severity of attempted or completed rapes involving the use of physical violence, threats of death, or use of weapons to coerce victims, has been identified as contributing to women's psychological problems (Ruch & Leon, 1983). We need more research, however, examining the trauma to determine which specific aspects may have the greatest effect on later outcomes.

Similar to the research of Sales et al. (1984), coping strategies used to avoid future assaults have been described in the literature. Survivors of attempted rape typically have enrolled in a self-defense course, began therapy, and had extra locks and alarms installed. Survivors of a completed rape, however, have been less likely to engage in behavior which may provide protection from future assaults. A primary reason for not seeking preventive measures has been the perceived helplessness and extreme vulnerability to being revictimized due to the trauma of the assault (Russell, 1983). Additionally, there are the preconceptions of family and friends "that if they don't talk about the assault and try not to think about it, the victim will forget and recover" (Resick, 1983).

This study differs from previous research in several ways. The long-term effects of attempted and completed incidents of rape are assessed in a multiethnic community sample of women. A method of incorporating the effects of multiple incidents of rape is used in multivariate analyses, examining four traumatic aspects of the rape experience; specifically, the age when rape last occurred (recency of abuse), the severity of the incidents, the number of rapes per assault, and the victim's relationship to the perpetrator. The victim's attribution for rape is used as an internal mediator. To whom the victim disclosed her abuse, the support she received, the actions she took and whether the police or other agencies became involved are included as external mediators to assess which of these factors can heighten or lessen women's initial and lasting effects of rape.

The findings will hopefully be used to develop measures to more accurately assess the circumstances of multiple incidents of rape as well as its initial and lasting effects on women's sexual relationships and psychological adjustment years after rape has occurred.

Method

Sample Selection

Multistage stratified probability sampling with quotas was used to recruit comparable samples of African-American and White American women 18 to 36 years of age in Los Angeles County, for a larger study of women's sexual experiences. The age criteria included women who had an opportunity to develop a number of adult heterosexual relationships. The actual quotas used for the study were based upon the population of African-American women 18 to 36 years of age, with differing levels of education, marital status, and numbers of children. The inclusion of African-American and White American women in the sample was based upon their own ethnic identification[1] (see Wyatt, 1985 for further discussion).

The participants were located by random-digit dialing of 11,834 telephone prefixes in Los Angeles County, combined with four randomly generated numbers. Random-digit telephone dialing procedures identified 1,348 households in which a woman resided. Of those who met the demographic criteria, 709 agreed to participate and 266 refused, resulting in a 27 percent refusal rate.[2] The first 248 women meeting the desired quotas were interviewed: 126 African-American women and 122 White American women. Both samples were compared for women in Los Angeles County and were found to be comparable (Wyatt, 1985). Table 3-1 illustrates the comparability of the demographic characteristics of 55 participants who reported at least one attempted or completed rape at age 18 or older and were subsequently used in the analyses. It was not possible to match both samples on income level. However, the range extended from less than $5,000 to above $50,000 per year, with comparability between groups except at very low income levels. These discrepancies between groups were also found in Los Angeles County statistics for income by ethnicity (Wyatt, 1985).

Table 3-1

DEMOGRAPHIC CHARACTERISTICS OF AFRICAN-AMERICAN AND WHITE
AMERICAN WOMEN (N = 55)

	African-American Women (n = 31)		White American Women (n = 24)	
	No.	Percent	No.	Percent
Age Range				
18–26	13	24%	6	11%
27–36	18	33	18	33
Education				
Less than one year of high school	6	11	3	5
High school graduate	13	24	10	18
Some college	8	15	8	15
College graduate	3	5	2	14
Graduate/Professional	1	2	1	2
Marital Status				
Never married	12	22	18	15
Ever married	19	35	16	29
Children				
None	8	15	9	16
1 or more	23	42	15	27

Note: $p > .05$.

Procedure

Each participant was interviewed face to face at the location of her
choice by a trained female interviewer of the same ethnicity. Participants were reimbursed $20.00 for their time and up to $2.50 for
expenses. Interviews were usually conducted in two sessions and
ranged in total from 3 to 8 hours. At the completion of the interview,
referrals for mental health services were provided upon request (for
fewer than 5 percent of the sample).

Instrumentation

In an effort to obtain more specific information regarding a range
of women's sexual experiences and the effects on their intimate

relationships and psychological and sexual functioning, the Wyatt Sex History Questionnaire (WSHQ), a 478-item structured interview, was used to obtain both retrospective and current data regarding women's consensual and abusive sexual experiences. Before its use in research, it was initially pretested on two multiethnic groups (77 female volunteers and 16 pilot respondents). Questions were arranged chronologically from childhood to adulthood so that inconsistencies in data would be apparent. If inconsistencies were noted, immediate clarification from the respondent was possible. For example, if a woman reported first intercourse at age 19 and a sexual assault at the same age, a series of questions was asked about the circumstances of each event to ensure that they were not identical.

Reliability was established for certain portions of the questionnaire. Interreliability was established on a weekly basis among the four interviewers, averaging .90. When ten audio-tapes were randomly examined for accuracy of interviewers' written transcriptions of participants' responses, only two responses out of 4,780 items were noted to have been in error.

Several additional analyses were conducted to examine the reliability of the data. Participants were asked about their demographic characteristics during telephone recruitment and again during the interview between 1 to 9 months later. Pearson correlations ranged from .82 to 1.0.

Finally, 119 respondents were re-interviewed about current and past demographic characteristics 1 month to 2 years after the initial interview (Peters, 1984). Pearson correlations ranged from .65 to .98. Overall, participants' responses over time were consistent, strengthening the probability that the responses to other questions were consistent, as well.

At the end of the interview, which covered a range of sex-related topics, respondents were asked four questions about whether they had experienced any of several types of sexual abuse most commonly reported since age 18. If the respondent answered "yes" to any of these questions, she was asked a series of more detailed questions about each incident.

Definition of Rape

In this study, rape was defined as the involuntary penetration of the vagina or anus by the penis or another object. After this definition was read to each person, they were asked about sexual experiences that may have occurred without their consent. These experiences may have occurred since age 18 and involved a friend, a relative, or stranger.

The specific questions of interest to this study were:

> Since the age of 18, have you ever been raped?
> Since the age of 18, has anyone ever tried to rape you?

Regardless of a woman's uncertainty about whether a particular experience constituted sexual abuse, she was encouraged to describe it. This type of hesitancy was particularly common in cases of attempted or completed rapes committed by persons known to them. Consequently, the incident was sometimes not considered by these women to be a typical rape, as other studies have indicated (Burt, 1980). These incidents, however, were included in this study.

The approach used to assess the prevalence of types of sexual assault since age 18 differs from recent studies that use behavioral descriptions and exclude the term "rape" (Koss & Gidycz, 1985). This study defined incidents of attempted and completed rape and asked about the circumstances of each incident. Rape-related information was sought after rapport was well established, 1 to 2 hours into a structured interview. Discrepancies between the woman's and research definitions of rape and terms such as "anus" (a word about which 9 percent were unfamiliar), "vagina," and "other objects used for penetration" were clarified. We found it particularly useful to discuss the definition of rape before women described their experiences. After the completion of the interview, it was not uncommon for women to recontact the interviewer and report additional incidents, once they realized that what they experienced was rape.

Preparation of Data

While attempted and completed sexual assaults and their effects have been examined previously (Ruch & Leon, 1983), few studies have examined the effects of multiple incidents (Marhoefer-Dvorak, et al., 1988). Little attention has also been given to the cumulative impact of multiple experiences in data analyses. Consequently, a method of incorporating all incidents of sexual assault was developed on similar data (Wyatt & Mickey, 1988; Wyatt & Newcomb, 1989), and modified for this study Since age 18, 1 in 4 women reported at least one attempted or completed rape. The number of rape incidents ranged from 1 to 7 and 42 percent of women reported more than one attempted or completed sexual assault since age 18. When chi-square and Fisher's exact tests were used to assess differences between African-American and White women's responses to rape, a significant difference was found on only one item (Wyatt, 1988). Of those incidents where women attributed their assault to something about the perpetrator or the environment ("He was crazy and I was alone"), 76 percent were reported by African-American women as compared to 24 percent reported by their White peers (Fisher's exact test p <.05). However, since 61 percent of women attributed their victimization to something about themselves (internal attribution), the entire sample was used in these analyses and ethnic differences were not examined.

Four phases of data coding were required to accommodate multiple incidents of sexual assault. In the first phase, 25 variables were selected to represent three domains: Circumstances of Abuse, Internal and External Mediators, and the Outcomes. These were chosen to represent constructs identified as important in the rape literature, some of which had yet to be examined empirically. Four strategies were used to recode data on a per person basis. First, categorical data, unsuitable for parametric analyses, were reordered for 12 variables. In order to take all abuse incidents into consideration, a single code was generated for each item to represent the consistency in the severity or circumstance of the event. For example, based upon previous studies (Russell, 1983), incidents that were perpetrated by family members or that occurred in the home were given higher values to designate the most severe circumstances. Second, women's most severe incident was used in coding 4 variables. For example, a victim reported being assaulted on two separate occasions. In the first incident, she was raped two or more times by a perpetrator. In another incident she was raped by one perpetrator, on one occasion. Consequently, the first incident of multiple rapes was used in the analyses. Third, there were 5 variables coded for the presence or absence of an attribute. For example, whether the perpetrator's ethnicity was consistently different from or similar to the victim was coded as yes (1) or no (2). Finally, 4 variables received global ratings reached by two psychologists (with .90 reliability), assessing the consistency of responses over multiple incidents. For example, if a victim reported that those persons that she told about two incidents of assault were somewhat or very nonsupportive, respectively, coding on supportiveness of persons told overall was nonsupportive (see Appendix 3-1). This method of coding highlights women's most severe multiple rape incidents.

These variables were examined for skewedness. For 6 variables, categories were collapsed to ensure that the distributions were as normal as possible.

In the third phase, the associations between variables were examined in a correlation matrix. Eight variables were deleted because they failed to correlate with any others (p>.05). In the final phase, the remaining 18 variables were used to form four composite scores guided by factor analyses and their conceptual similarity. Five single variables were also used in subsequent analyses (see Appendix 3-1).

Consequently, the age of most recent rape, the severity of abuse (a composite score of the number of attempted or completed rape incidents and degree of physical coercion used), the maximum number of rapes per incident, and the proximity of the perpetrator to the victim (a composite score of the relationship of victim to perpetrator and the location of the rape) constituted the Circumstances of Abuse variables. The internal mediator was attribution for the rape incidents having occurred. However, since 61 percent of the women reported internal attributions, this variable was labeled self-blame. Supportive response to confiding was a composite score of to whom victims disclosed the rape, their response, and any possible action taken by them. For example, the lowest composite score on this variable would indicate disclosing abuse to no one and, consequently, no response was offered nor actions taken. The effects of assault appear to be greatest when they are not acknowledged or discussed (Russell, 1983). If a woman told her husband and was reprimanded, with no other support, she received the second lowest composite score. A high score would indicate that a woman disclosed to her husband, received support, and was accompanied by him to the police or a rape crisis center. Involvement of authorities consisted of whether or not police, mental health counselors, or rape treatment clinics were involved. Supportive responses to confiding and involvement of authorities were the external mediators. Finally, there were two Outcome Variables. Negative effects was a composite score of initial (i.e., heightened anxiety, fear, and sleeplessness (immediately postassault)) and lasting psychological effects (depression, fear, and relationship problems), lasting effects on women's sexual functioning (e.g., dislike for sexual acts perpetrated on them or disinterest in sex), and attitudes toward men (e.g., fear of men or the inability to select nonabusive partners). Adaptive lifestyle changes (e.g., changing locks on doors or taking a self-defense class) was the second Outcome Variable.

These variables were selected because of their relationship to one another. They best captured aspects of attempted and completed sexual assault experiences of interest in this study.

Analyses

Measured or observed variable simultaneous path analysis models are used to analyze the data (e.g., Bentler & Newcomb, 1986). A quasi-longitudinal study design based upon retrospective assessments allowed us to test the relationship between circumstances related to sexual abuse with later outcomes. Although latent variables would have been preferred in the path models (e.g., Bentler, 1980; Newcomb & Bentler, 1988), because of their ability to control or separate measurement error from true-score variation, the sample size was too small ($n = 55$) to yield stable estimates on multiple indicator factors (which would require almost tripling the number of variables included in the present path model). Univariate statistics for each of the individual variables are presented in Table 3-2.[3] Given the apparent normality of the data, the maximum likelihood method was used to estimate parameters in the path model, and the EQS computer program was used (Bentler, 1989).

Table 3-2

SUMMARY OF VARIABLE CHARACTERISTICS

Domain/Variable	Mean	Range	Variance	Skew	Kurtosis
Characteristics of Abuse					
Age of most recent abuse	22.85	17–35	19.18	1.07	0.46
Severity of abuse	3.28	2–6	.96	1.17	0.60
Maximum rapes per incident	1.02	0.2–2	0.32	0.82	−0.79
Proximity of perpetrator to victim	3.93	2–6	1.46	−0.35	−1.04
Mediational Process					
Internal attributions/self-blame	1.67	1–2	0.22	−0.72	−1.51
Supportive response/ confiding	8.33	3–12	4.97	−0.50	−0.93
Involvement of authorities	1.36	1–2	0.24	0.55	−1.73
Outcomes					
Negative effects	8.96	4–16	12.04	0.44	−0.89
Involvement of authorities	1.67	1–3	0.81	0.67	−1.4646

Results

These analyses link traumatic circumstances (abuse incidents) to internal and external mediators, which in turn lead to various outcomes. Based upon the conceptual nature of the variable, 9 variables were grouped into one of these three domains (see Table 3-2): 4 variables represent the Circumstances of Abuse domain, 3 variables reflect the Mediators domain, and 2 variables account for the Outcome domain.

The three domains of variables were expected to influence each other unidirectionally. The Circumstances of Abuse variables influenced the mediator variables, which in turn affected the Outcome variables as depicted in Figure 3-1. It is also possible that some of the Circumstances of Abuse variables may directly influence the Outcome variables over-and-above the intervening effects of the mediator variables (this is depicted by the dashed line in Figure 3-1).

Figure 3-1

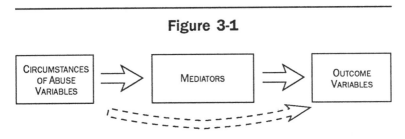

Path Diagram of relationship between Circumstances of Abuse, Internal and External Mediators, and Outcome variables.

There was no a priori theory regarding how the within-domain variables should be structurally related. In order to operationalize and test this conceptual model, all variables within each domain were allowed to correlate freely (or the residuals if they were predicted variables). Each variable in the Circumstances of Abuse domain was initially allowed to predict each variable in the Mediator domain. Similarly, variables in the Mediator domain were allowed to predict the 2 variables in the Outcome domain. This model was tested against the correlations of all variables as given in Table 3-3.

The initial model did not fully account for all of the covariation in the data ($p < .001$). Based upon selected Lagrangian Multiplier

Table 3-3

ZERO-ORDER CORRELATIONS BETWEEN ALL VARIABLES

Domain/Variable	I	II	III	IV	V	VI	VII	VIII	IX
Characteristics of Abuse									
I Age of most recent abuse	1.00								
II Severity of abuse	.29	1.00							
III Maximum rapes per incident	.03	.04	1.00						
IV Proximity of perpetrator	.26	.36	−.03	1.00					
Mediational Processes									
V Internal attrition/ self-blame	.47	.34	.13	.31	1.00				
VI Supportive response to confiding	−.17	−.45	−.01	−.06	−.34	1.00			
VII Involvement of authorities	.11	.02	.04	−.14	−.20	.15	1.00		
Outcome									
VII Negative effects	.33	.41	.37	.21	.33	−.20	.22	1.00	
IX Adaptive lifestyle changes	.16	−.04	−.03	−.38	.01	−.03	−.19	.05	1.00

Note: Any *r* > .26 is significant at the *p* < .05 level, two-tailed test (for a one-tailed test *r* > .22).

modification indices (Bentler & Chou, 1986), necessary paths were added between variables in the Circumstances of Abuse domain and variables in the Outcome domain, since this was the only area of the model that was not saturated with effects. Four such additional paths were necessary. The Wald test was used for deleting parameters (Bentler & Chou, 1986), and paths or correlations that were not needed (nonsignificant) were removed. This approach of overfitting and then deleting nonsignificant parameters was found by MacCallum (1986) to capture best the "true" model reflected in covariance structure models.

The resulting model fit the data well, (23, *n* = 55) = 13.28, *p* = .95, Bentler and Bonett (1980) normed-fit-index = .86. Only significant paths and correlations were retained in this final model. Standardized parameter estimates for this final path model are depicted graphically in Figure 3-2. Covariances are correlations and residual variables are variances.

Three pairs of variables in the Circumstances of Abuse domain were significantly correlated and retained in the analyses. Only the residual of internal attributions/self blame and involvement of authorities were significantly correlated in the Mediator domain. The residuals of the two variables in the Outcome domain were not significantly correlated ($p > .05$). Decomposition of direct, indirect and total effects for all predicted variables for this final model are presented in Table 3-4.

More consistent internal attributions/self-blame for each assault incident was significantly predicted from women who were older at the time of their most recent abuse and in connection with greater severity of abuse (including multiple sexual assaults and physical force used in the incidents). A supportive response from someone told about

Table 3-4

DECOMPOSITION OF EFFECTS FROM THE FINAL PATH MODEL

	Dependent Variables				
Predictors	Supportive Internal Attributions	Adaptive Response to Confiding	Involvement of Authorities	Negative Effects	Lifestyle Changes
Age of Latest Abuse					
Direct	.35	.00	.00	.00	.28
Indirect	.00	.00	.00	.08	.28
Total	.35	.00	.00	.08	.28
Severity of Abuse					
Direct	.25	−.46	.00	.31	.00
Indirect	.00	.00	.00	.06	.00
Total	.25	−.46	.00	.37	.00
Maximum Rapes Per Incident					
Direct	.00	.00	.00	.31	.00
Indirect	.00	.00	.00	.00	.00
Total	.00	.00	.00	.31	.00
Proximity of Perpetrator to Victim					
Direct	.00	.00	.00	.00	−.45
Indirect	.00	.00	.00	.00	.00
Total	.00	.00	.00	.00	−.45
Internal Attributions					
Direct	.00	.00	.00	.21	00
Indirect	.00	.00	.00	.00	.00
Total	.00	.00	.00	.21	.00
Supportive Response to Confiding					
Direct	.00	.00	.00	.00	00
Indirect	.00	.00	.00	.00	.00
Total	.00	.00	.00	.00	.00
Involvement of Authorities					
Direct	.00	.00	.00	.25	00
Indirect	.00	.00	.00	.00	.00
Total	.00	.00	.00	.25	.00

Figure 3-2

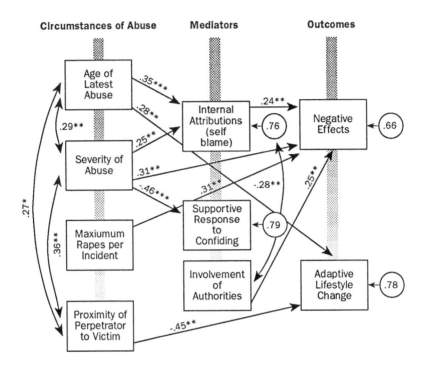

Path Model of Circumstances of Abuse, Internal and External Mediators, and Outcome Variables. Parameter estimates are standardized and residual are variances. Significance levels were determined by critical ratios (*p <.05; **p < .0l; ***p <.00l).

the abuse and some action taken were also significantly predicted from less severe sexual assault. Involvement from authorities such as police or other professionals trained to deal with rape was not predicted reliably by any variable in the Circumstances of Abuse domain.

Negative short- and long-term effects of abuse were significantly predicted from internal attributions/self-blame and more involvement from authorities, from the Mediator domain, and greater severity of abuse and more rapes per incident, from the Circumstances of Abuse domain. Finally, adaptive lifestyle change was not reliably predicted from any of the Mediators. It was, however, predicted from older age at most recent assault and more distant proximity of perpetrator to victim (abuse perpetrated away from home, by a stranger), both from the Circumstances of Abuse domain. Fully 39 percent of the variance in negative effects and 22 percent of the variance in adaptive lifestyle changes were accounted for by variables in the Circumstances of Abuse and Mediator domains.

The effects depicted in Figure 3-2 represent direct influences. Indirect influences can also be inferred through a mediating variable. For instance, older age at most recent abuse has both a direct influence on survivors making no lifestyle changes and an indirect effect on negative effects via the mediating influence of more consistent internal attributions/self-blame for each assault occurring.

Discussion and Implications of Findings

This study represents a beginning effort to identify internal and external mediators of four traumatic aspects of multiple rape incidence and to assess their effects upon women's initial and lasting effects and behavioral change. These data are retrospective and the outcome indices are not assessed by standardized measures. However, the results reflect a community sample of women's perceptions of their experiences and some of the strategies used to cope with rape, not always identified in other clinical or community samples (Roth et al., 1988; Russell, 1983). Although our sample size was sufficiently large to test this small 9-variable model, replication with a larger sample is necessary to validate the paths and effects we have found. With a larger sample and multiple indicators for each critical construct, particularly when used as internal and external mediators, latent-variable models can confirm these results and help mitigate the difficulty of measurement error that plagues all types of survey research. In spite of the variability in samples used in rape research, similar findings of other studies were noted in these results (Cohen & Roth, 1987; Meyer & Taylor, 1986; Ruch & Chandler, 1983; Sales et al., 1984). Self-blame for each sexual assault, the number of repeated rapes per incident, and the severity of attempted and completed acts of rape (e.g., physical coercion) predicted negative effects on women's overall adjustment, as well as negative initial and lasting attitudes toward sex and intimacy. However, this study also offered important documentation that the involvement of police and other agencies such as emergency rooms and counseling centers can also negatively impact the effects of rape years after its occurrence. Additionally, women who consistently blame themselves after each assault and involvement of authorities were also found to mediate the effects of other traumatic circumstances of rape.

When women blame themselves for sexual assault having occurred, they can be effected differently from victims of other trauma, such as auto accident survivors (Bulman & Wortman, 1977). Whatever the immediate gain in sense of control may be offset by the long-range consequences of self-blame on self-esteem (Koss & Burkhart, 1989). Attributions to victimization used in other traumatic circumstances, including "I should have known better," or "I should have seen it coming" only add to the trauma of sexual abuse by causing victims to feel even more responsible for the assault and powerless in intimate relationships.

Similar to previous findings (Ruch & Chandler, 1983), women in this study received little support for having been raped, even in the most severe circumstances, such as being beaten, having their lives threatened, or a weapon being used on them (Cohen & Roth, 1987). Indeed, ten women told no one about the incidents until years later. This finding is, however, consistent with other rape research (Williams, 1984; Williams & Holmes, 1982). Additionally, as the severity of abuse increases, so does self-blame and the fear of not being believed as a "typical victim" (Williams, 1984). The following describes the circumstance of a severe incident. The response she received when she disclosed her assault to someone known to her, as well as to the police, is a good example of why victims are reluctant to disclose:

> Respondent: On the advice of a girlfriend I let a man take me home from a party. We stopped at his apartment on some excuse. . . . He grabbed me, threw me on the bed—he had my girdle and panties off . . . and penetrated my body fast. I immediately started to fight. . . . He broke my cricoid cartilage [in my neck]. . . . [At that moment] I felt that my life was threatened and I stopped fighting. I didn't know where I was. I wandered the streets looking for a pay phone. A policeman asked me what I was doing. When I told [him] what had happened. . . . [The police] dismissed it

> [and] when I asked for help [he] said [he]
> couldn't help me. . . . He was going off duty
> and . . . would come back and take me home.
> He made a pass at me before he dropped me
> off.

Interviewer: Who did you tell?

Respondent: My girlfriend.

Interviewer: What did she say?

Respondent: See what men are like? That is all they
want—you should get something out of it—
money.

Interviewer: What effect did this incident have on you?

Respondent: I was very depressed, angry, resented men,
[had] brief periods of angry promiscuity . . .
took many showers and douches, changed
[my] hairdo and wanted to change myself. I
never go into parking lots, elevators, or hall-
ways. I became very militant and have a gun
at home—no one will ever assault me again.

This vignette illustrates physical and psychological trauma, as well as the degree of nonsupport from a confidant and police that may have exacerbated negative effects of abuse on future psychological and sexual functioning, as well as distrust of those who might have been supportive. The seriousness of the incident appeared to result in the potentially supportive confidant who blamed the victim for the rape. It was as if nothing so terrible would have occurred if the victim had not contributed in some fashion. In other words, there is a reluctance to accept the idea that a rape victim is blameless. Violent crimes like rape generally leave members in society feeling insecure and vulnerable to victimization. It is sometimes both a relief and a comfort to believe that victims may have precipitated incidents of sexual abuse so that those at highest risk feel less helpless and vulnerable.

As illustrated in the vignette, it was disconcerting to note that supportive agencies sometimes contributed to these women's difficulty in coping with rape. The involvement of police or other authorities was related to initial and lasting negative effects of adjustment to rape. On the average, the time lapse between the most recent abuse incident and the data collection (between 1980–1983) was 5½ years. Only 54 percent of the women reported the rape to the authorities, partly because at that time many had negative expectations about the way in which their assault would be viewed. Today, the possible involvement of authorities might be perceived differently. According to the Los Angeles County Homicide Division,[4] the standard procedure now begins with the choice of reporting a rape to a male or female officer. The victim is then assisted by the officer to the hospital to collect evidence and medical care. Counseling and referral information from rape crises centers is also offered to the victim before she is escorted home. This formalized procedure, however, was initiated only 6 years ago. The rape victims' anticipation of poor treatment contributes to their failing to report their abuse (Feild, 1978). Negative experiences like those in the vignette often influence a woman's intentions to involve authorities in subsequent incidents. Consequently, the cycle of unreported rapes continues, even with changes in policy toward the treatment of rape victims.

Additionally, women who were relatively older when their most recent assault occurred and those who did not know their assailants tended to make lifestyle changes to protect themselves from further victimization (Ellis, 1983).

If the abuse was perpetuated by an unknown person, victims attempted more often to regain control over their lives. They made changes involving self-protection (e.g., buying a gun, extra locks on the door, not being out after dark, etc.). The more unexpected type of abuse perpetuated by a boyfriend or husband seemed to create more of a sense of powerlessness: lifestyle changes were not as frequently made (Russell, 1983).

One of the most disturbing findings was that none of the internal or external mediators influenced lifestyle changes. Regardless of how blame was attributed for the incidents, the amount of support, or to whom they disclosed, lifestyle changes were not affected. There are several interpretations of this finding. The nonsignificant relationship between lifestyle changes and cognitive mediators may be due to small sample size. Another interpretation might be that behavioral efforts to prevent revictimization and to regain feelings of control were influenced more by the specific circumstances of the rape experiences than by the mediators selected for this study. Other mediators should be examined in future research to assess their relationship to lifestyle changes after sexual assault. This study, however, represents a beginning attempt to examine factors that mediate the initial and lasting effects of rape and provides information about specific effects of sexual assault that should be routinely assessed in rape research.

Those at most risk for the pervasive effects of sexual assault appear to be relatively older women (ages 27 to 36) whose abuse was recent. They tended to engage in the kind of self-blame that perpetuates the cycle of nondisclosure, especially if the perpetrator was known to them. These are not the women who are often described as most likely to be rape survivors (Koss & Burkhart, 1989), possibly because the preponderance of research today includes young college women. This pattern of nondisclosure could be problematic for women who do not seek professional help to cope with rape, but instead use their families and friends as a sole means of emotional support. In this study, only five women received counseling for their rape symptoms. Such women may not receive information about the damaging effects of self blame on their healing process. Similarly, family members may not understand the importance of their support and the avoidance of victim blaming in the disclosure process. If women anticipate that they will be blamed, they may not disclose their abuse at all and instead may merge into the population of survivors who experience intimacy, relationship, and sexual problems with little understanding of their etiology.

We as professionals have to assume part of the responsibility for these victims remaining invisible, unless we continue to press for changes in societal attitudes and public sensitivity to support rape victims and their efforts to cope with this trauma, even if they do not seek professional help.

Although supportive networks have had a history of insensitivity for many, the message for today should be that they can and deserve to receive better treatment.

Notes

1. The term "African-American" refers to women of African descent whose parentage also includes a variety of other ethnic and racial groups found in America. Caucasian women additionally included women of Jewish heritage. These women spent at least 6 of the first 12 years of their childhood in the United States.

2. The 27 percent refusal rate excludes 335 women who terminated telephone contact before information regarding their demographic characteristics could be obtained. The estimated rate of refusal, including those who terminated phone contact before their eligibility could be assessed, as well as those who did not answer when called but who might have been eligible was 33 percent. However, if the 335 women who

terminated contact were considered, the refusal rate would increase to 45 percent.

3. Univariate and multivariate estimates of distribution indicated that these data were essentially normal and hence suitable for path analysis. Inspection of these statistics reveals that the data are normally distributed in terms of both skew and kurtosis. The largest kurtosis was on involvement of authorities (−1.73) and the highest skew was on severity of abuse (1.17), which are not very large. Confirming this conclusion regarding the normality of the data, the normalized multivariate kurtosis estimate was found to be fairly normal (−2.26).

4. Telephone interview with Detectives Ron Phelps and Steve Laird, Rape Special Section of Robbery and Homicide, Los Angeles County Police.

References

Amir, J. 1971. *Patterns in Forcible Rape.* Chicago: University of Chicago Press.

Becker, J., L. Skinner, G. Abel, & J. Cichon. 1986. Level of postassault sexual functioning in rape and incest victims. *Archives of Sexual Behavior* 15:37–49.

Bentler, P.M. 1980. Multivariate analysis with latent variables: Causal modeling. *Annual Review of Psychology* 31:419–56.

———. 1989. *Structural Equations Programs.* Los Angeles: BMDP Statistical Software Inc.

Bentler, P.M., and D.G. Bonett. 1980. Significance tests and goodness of fit in the analysis of covariance structures. *Psychological Bulletin* 88:588–606.

Bentler, P.M., and C.P. Chou. 1986. *Statistics for Parameter Expansion and Construction in Structural Models.* Paper presented at the American Educational Research Association meeting, San Francisco.

Bentler, P.M., and M.D. Newcomb. 1986. Personality, sexual behavior, and drug use revealed through latent variable methods. *Clinical Psychology Review* 6:363–85.

Bulman, R.J., and C.B. Wortman. 1977. Attributions of blame and coping in the "real world": Severe accident victims react to their lot. *Journal of Personality and Social Psychology*, 35:351–63.

Bureau of Justice Statistics Dec. 1980. *Criminal Victimization in the United States, 1978.* Washington, DC: U.S. Department of Justice.

Burgess, A. 1983. Rape trauma syndrome. *Behavioral Sciences and the Law* 1:97–113.

Burgess, A., and L.L. Holmstrom, 1974. Rape trauma syndrome. *American Journal of Psychiatry* 131:981–86.

Burt, M.R. 1980. Cultural myths and supports for rape. *Journal of Personality and Social Psychology* 38:217–30.

Burt, M.R., and R.E. Estep. 1981. Apprehension and fear: Learning a sense of sexual vulnerability. *Sex Roles* 8:511–22.

Cervantes, R.C., and F.G. Castro. 1985. Stress, coping, and Mexican-American mental health: A systematic review. *Hispanic Journal of Behavioral Sciences* 7:1–73.

Cohen, L.J. 1988. Providing treatment and support for partners of sexual-assault survivors. *Psychotherapy* 25:94–98.

Cohen, L.J., and S. Roth. 1987. The psychological aftermath of rape: Long-term effects and individual differences in recovery. *Journal of Social and Clinical Psychology* 5,: 525–34.

Cunningham, J., T. Pearce, and P. Pearce. 1988. Childhood sexual abuse and medical complaints in adult women. *Journal of Interpersonal Violence* 3:131–44.

Ellis, E. 1983. A review of empirical rape research: Victim reactions and response to treatment. *Clinical Psychology Review*, 3:473–90.

Feldman-Summers, S., P. Gordon, and J. Meagher. 1979. The impact of rape on sexual satisfaction. *Journal of Abnormal Psychology*, 88:101–05.

Feild, H.S. 1978. Attitudes toward rape: A comparative analysis of police, rapists, crisis counselors, and citizens. *Journal of Personality and Social Psychology* 36:156–79.

Finkelhor, D. 1984. *Child Sexual Abuse: New Theory and Research*. New York: Free Press.

————. 1988. The trauma of child sexual abuse: Two models. In G. Wyatt and G. Powell (eds.), *The Lasting Effects of Child Sexual Abuse* (pp. 61–82). Newbury Park, CA: Sage Publications.

Friedrich, W., A.J. Urquiza, and R. Belke. 1985. Behavior problem in sexually abused children. *Journal of Pediatric Psychology*. 11:47–57.

Girelli, P. Resick, P. S. Marhoefer-Dvorak, and C. Hutter. 1986. Subjective distress and violence during rape: Their effects on long-term fear. *Victims and Violence* 1:35–46.

Hammen, C., T. Marks, A. Mays, and R. DeMayo 1985. Depressive self blames: Life stress and vulnerability to depression. *Journal of Abnormal Psychology* 94:308–19.

Harter, S., P.C. Alexander, and R.A. Neimeyer. 1988. Long-term effects of incestuous child abuse in college women: Social adjustment, social cognition, and family characteristics. *Journal of Consulting and Clinical Psychology* 56:5–8.

Hinderland, M.J., and B.L. Davis. 1977. Forcible rape in the United States: A statistical profile. In D. Chappell, P. Geis and G. Geis (eds.), *Forcible Rape: The Crime, the Victim and the Offender*, pp. 87–114. New York: Columbia University Press.

Holmes, M., and J. St. Lawrence. 1983. Treatment of rape-induced trauma: Proposed behavioral conceptualization and review of the literature. *Clinical Psychology Review* 3:417–33.

Kanner, A.D., J.C. Koyne, C. Schaefer, and R.S. Lazarus. 1981. Comparison of two modes of stress measurement: Daily hassles and uplifts versus major life events. *Journal of Behavior Medicine* 4(1):1–40.

Katz, S., and M.A. Mazur. 1979. *Understanding the Rape Victim: A Synthesis of Research Findings*. New York: John Wiley and Sons.

Kilpatrick, D.G., C.L. Best, and L.J. Veronen. 1984. *Mental Health Consequences of Criminal Victimization: A Random Community Survey.* Presented at APA, Toronto, Ontario, Canada.

Kilpatrick, D.G., L.J. Veronen, and P.A. Resick. 1982. Psychological sequelae to rape: Assessment and Treatment strategies. In D.M. Doleys, R.L.P. Meredith, and A.R. Ciminero (eds.), *Behavioral Medicine: Assessment and Treatment Strategies* (pp. 473–97). New York: Plenum Publishing Co.

Koss, M.P. (1985). The hidden rape victim: Personality, attitudinal, and situational characteristics. *Psychology of Women Quarterly* 8:193–212.

Koss, M., and B. Burkhart. 1989. A conceptual analysis of rape victimization. *Psychology of Women Quarterly*, 13:27–40.

Koss, M., T. Dinero, C. Seibel, and S. Cox. 1988. Stranger and acquaintance rape: Are there differences in the victim's experience? *Psychology of Women Quarterly* 12:1–24.

Koss, M.P., and C.A. Gidycz. 1985. Sexual experiences survey: Reliability and validity. *Journal of Consulting and Clinical Psychology* 42:162–70.

MacCallum, R. 1986. Specification searches in covariance structure analyses. *Psychological Bulletin* 100:107–20.

Marhoefer-Dvorak, S., P. Resick, C.K. Hutter, and S.A. Girelli. 1988. Single- versus multiple-incident rape victims: A comparison of psychological reactions to rape. *Journal of Interpersonal Violence* 3(2):145–60.

Meyer, B., and S. Taylor. 1986. Adjustment to rape. *Journal of Personality and Social Psychology* 50(6):1226–34.

Miller, J., D. Moeller, A. Kaufman, P. Awasto, D. Pathak, and J. Christy. 1978. Recidivism among sexual assault victims. *American Journal of Psychiatry* 135:1103–04.

National Crime Panel Survey Report 1975. *Criminal Victimization Surveys in the Nation's Five Largest Cities.* U.S. Department of Justice, Law Enforcement Assistance Administration, National Criminal Justice Information and Statistics Service, US. Government Printing Office, Washington, DC.

Newcomb, M.D., and P.M. Bentler. 1988. *Consequences of Adolescent Drug Use: Impact on the Lives of Young Adults.* Beverly Hills, CA: Sage.

Orzek, A. 1983. Sexual assault: The female victim, her male partner, and their relationship. *The Personnel and Guidance Journal* 62:143–46.

Peters, J.J. 1976. Children are victims of sexual assault and the psychology of offenders. *American Journal of Psychotherapy* 30:393–421.

Peters, S.D. 1984. *The Relationship Between Childhood Sexual Victimization and Adult Depression Among Afro-American and White Women.* Unpublished doctoral dissertation, UCLA.

Resick, P. 1983. The rape reaction: Research findings and implications for intervention. *The Behavior Therapist*, 6:129–32.

Rosenberg, M. 1986. Rape crisis syndrome. *Medical Aspects of Human Sexuality*, 10:65–71.

Roth, S., E. Dye, and L. Lebowitz. 1988. Group therapy for sexual-assault victims. *Psychotherapy* 25:82–93.

Ruch, L., and S. Chandler. 1983. Sexual assault trauma during the acute phase: An exploratory model and multivariate analysis. *Journal of Health and Social Behavior* 24:174–85.

Ruch, L., and J. Leon. 1983. Sexual assault trauma and trauma change. *Women and Health* 8:5–21.

Russell, D. 1983. The prevalence and incidence of forcible rape and attempted rape of females. *Victimology: An International Journal* 7:81–93.

Russell, D. 1986. *The Secret Trauma: Incest in the Lives of Girls and Women*, pp. 157–173. New York: Basic Books.

Sales, E., M. Baum, and B. Shore. 1984. Victim readjustment following assault. *Journal of Social Issues* 40:117–136.

Santiago, J., F. McCall-Perez, M. Gorcey, and A. Beigel. 1985. Long-term psychological effects of rape in 35 rape victims. *American Journal of Psychiatry* 142:1336–40.

Tetreault, P.A., and M.A. Barnett. 1987. Reactions to stranger and acquaintance rape. *Psychology of Women Quarterly* 11:353–58.

Williams, J.E., and K.A. Holmes. 1982. In judgment of victims: The social context of rape. *Journal of Sociology & Social Welfare* 9:154–69.

Williams, L.S. 1984. The classic rape: When do victims report? *Social Problems* 31:459–67.

Wright, C.N. 1985. *A Prospective Study of Stress and Depression in Black Females.* Unpublished doctoral dissertation, UCLA.

Wyatt, G.E. 1985. The sexual abuse of Afro-American and White American Women in childhood. *Child Abuse and Neglect* 9:507–19.

———. 1988. *The Prevalence and Socio-cultural Context of Afro-American and White American Women's Sexual Abuse.* Presented at the American Psychological Association Convention, Atlanta, Georgia.

Wyatt, G.E., and M.R. Mickey. 1987. Ameliorating the effects of child sexual abuse. *Journal of Interpersonal Violence* 2:403–14.

———. 1988. The support of parents and others as it mediates the effects of child sexual abuse: An exploratory study. In G. Wyatt and G. Powell (eds.), *The Lasting Effects of Child Sexual Abuse* (pp. 211–26). Newbury Park: Sage Publications.

Wyatt, G.E., and M. Newcomb. 1989. *Internal and External Mediators to Women's Child Sexual Abuse.* Manuscript under editorial review.

Appendix 3-1

Coding Procedures for 25 Variables Used Initially for Data Analysis Strategies

1. Items with Categorical Responses	Coding Range
1. Location of abusea (3-point scale)	(1) public place (2) home of perpetrator (3) home of subject
2. Relationship of perpetrator to victim[b] (6-point scale)	(1) stranger (2) casual acquaintance

(3) acquaintance
(4) friend
(5) relative/father
(6) husband/boyfriend

3. Whom victim first told of abuse[c]
   (5-point scale)

   (1) husband/boyfriend
   (2) family member
   (3) friend/co-worker
   (4) persons not in social
   network—includes police
   (5) no one

4. Short-term physical effects[d]
   (3-point scale)

   (1) none
   (2) minor effects
   (3) major effects

5. Short-term emotional effects[d]
   (4-point scale)

   (1) none
   (2) awareness of and
   preoccupation with abuse
   (3) negative feelings
   (4) depression

6. Short-term effects on sex life[c]
   (2-point scale)

   (1) none
   (2) some

7. Short-term effects on lifestyle[c]
   (3-point scale)

   (1) adaptive changes
   (2) less adaptive changes
   (3) none

8. Action taken by person told[n]
   (4-point scale)

   (1) took some action
   (2) comforted, provided
   emotional support
   (3) no action taken
   (4) respondent was blamed
   or reprimanded

9. Lasting emotional effects[c]
   (4-points scale)

   (1) none
   (2) minimal effects
   (3) moderate effects
   (4) severe effects

10. Lasting effects on sex life[c]
    (3-point scale)

    (1) adaptive changes
    (2) less adaptive changes
    (3) no changes

11. Lasting effects on sex life[d]
    (3-point scale)

    (1) adaptive changes
    (2) less adaptive changes
    (3) no changes

12. Success of community or personal
    support[b] (3-point scale)

    (1) professional
    (2) family, friends
    (3) none

II. Quantitative Variables for Whom the Most Extreme Response Was Selected for Multiple Incidents

1. Age at which abuse occurred (latest abuse)

   age of earliest—age of
   most recent abuse

2. Number of perpetrators[d] (2-point scale)

   one, two, or more

3. Number of abuse incidents[e] (3-point scale)

   (1) attempted rape
   (2) one rape
   (3) two or more rapes

4. Age of perpretrator[f] (4-point scale)

   (1) teenager (19 or younger)
   (2) young adult (20–24)
   (3) adult (24–54)

(3) older person (55 or older)

III. Dichotomous Variables	Coding
1. Ethnicity of perpetrator[f] (2-point scale)	same as victim—cross ethnic
2. Perpetrator drinking?[f] (2-point scale)	(1) no drinking (2) drinking in at least one incident
3. Victim drinking?[f] (2-point scale)	(1) no drinking (2) drinking in at least one incident
4. Involvement of agencies or police[d] (2-point scale)	(1) involved in at least one incident

(2) not involved in any incidents

5. Attribution to victimization[d] (3-point scale)   (1) mostly internal (self-blame)

(2) mixed (some internal and external incidents)

(3) mostly external (attribution given to perpertrator, family, or environment)

IV. Global Ratings on All Incidents

Worst Effect Collected	Range of Codes
1. Reason for not telling[f] (3-point scale)	(1) mostly internal (2) mixed (3) mostly external
2. Supportiveness of person told[b] (4-point scale)	(1) very supportive responses (2) moderate support, combination of somewhat supportiveness, neutral response or respondent didn't know (3) mixed or neutral combination of all neutrals, some supportive and some nonsupportive, or victim didn't tell (4) nonsupport; all responses nonsupport
3. Effects on attitudes toward men[c] (4-point scale)	(1) no effects (2) mild, some effects but not lasting (3) moderate effects (4) severe effects
4. Degree of physical force used[e] (2-point scale)	none—some

[a]Used in composite score, Proximity of Abuse

[b]Used in composite score, Supportive Response to Confiding.

[c]Used in composite score, Negative Effects.

[d]Used as a single item

[e]Used in composite score, Severity of Abuse.

[f]Deleted from further analysis because no association with other variables.

Chapter 4

Studying the Long-Term Effects of Sexual Abuse: The Trauma Symptom Checklist (TSC) Scales[1]

Diana M. Elliott
Rosemead School of Psychology
Biola University

John Briere
Department of Psychiatry and the Behavioral Sciences
University of Southern California School of Medicine

■

*This chapter is a synthesis and expansion of two recent papers (Briere &
Runtz, 1989; Elliott & Briere, 1990). Reprint requests may be sent to
Diana M. Elliott at Rosemead School of Psychology, 13800 Biola Avenue,
La Mirada, CA 90639-0001.*

■

Recent research has documented an association between childhood
molestation and subsequent psychological problems in adulthood.
Among the long-term correlates of a sexual abuse history are "post-
traumatic stress" symptoms such as nightmares, flashbacks, dissocia-
tion, and sleep disturbance (Briere & Runtz, 1987; Herman, 1981;
Lindberg & Distad, 1985; Putnam, 1988), alterations in mood, such as
depression and anxiety (Bagley & Ramsay, 1986; Jehu, Gazan, &
Klassen, 1984-85; Peters, 1988; Stein, Golding, Siegal, Burnam, &
Sorenson, 1988), interpersonal dysfunction (Bagley & Ramsay, 1986;
Briere & Zaidi, 1989; Courtois, 1979; Elliott & Gabrielson, 1990;
Finkelhor, Hotaling, Lewis, & Smith, 1989), and sexual problems
(Briere & Runtz, 1990; Courtois, 1979; Elliott, 1990; Gold; 1986;

Maltz, 1988). Increased awareness of the affect of child abuse has undoubtedly increased clinical effectiveness in work with child victims, as well as focusing public attention on the magnitude of the problem. Further, research on the long-term effects of abuse has been an important factor in the identification and treatment of adults who were abused as children.

Although the preponderance of research in this area indicates negative long-term sequelae of abuse, the measurement systems used in these studies have been of variable quality. Most instruments employed in such investigations have been either ad hoc scales, often lacking reliability and or/validity, or measures originally developed without reference to child abuse and thus potentially less sensitive to abuse-specific symptomatology.

In a "National Symposium on Assessing the Impact of Child Sexual Abuse," the invited participants frequently described problems inherent in the use of generic assessment instruments as measures of abuse effects and called for the development of new, more abuse-relevant scales (e.g., Berliner, 1987; Conte, 1987; Finkelhor, 1987). The "Trauma Symptom Checklist" described in this chapter reflects this growing interest in instruments specifically designed to assess child abuse effects.

Measurement of Postabuse Trauma

Abuse impact measures may be divided into "construct" versus "symptom" approaches. The former attempts to relate abusive childhood experiences to clinical phenomena already thought to exist in the general population, such as "Hysteria" or "Depression." Such constructs represent hypotheses about underlying processes that are thought to produce certain symptoms or problems, and that are assumed to be present when these symptoms occur. Although the construct approach has real value (for example, it may allow us to examine the relationship between existing psychological disorders and key childhood traumas such as incest), it may be problematic or misleading if either (a) the construct in question is a poor one (i.e., does not represent a "real phenomenon"), or (b) sexual abuse effects do not directly correspond to the specific pattern of disturbance associated with the construct in question.

In contrast to the "construct" approach, the "symptom" perspective restricts itself to observable or reportable problems, such as sexual dysfunction or periods of depersonalization, and examines their variation between abused and nonabused subjects. Given our incomplete understanding of abuse effects, this method allows the actual data to describe the exact pattern of abuse-related symptomatology. Such symptom-items are either interpreted individually or are summed with similar items to form content homogeneous scales (e.g., "anxiety" or "somatic preoccupation"). The only instance in which such scales might include diverse or multidimensional symptomatology would be when certain patterns of problems have been empirically shown to covary with sexual abuse such that a summary score would reflect the overall extent of postabuse trauma.

In an early example of the "symptom" approach, Briere and Runtz (1987) devised a Crisis Symptom Checklist (CSC), which was found to discriminate relatively well between adult clinical subjects with histories of childhood sexual abuse and those with no such history. Unfortunately, the CSC was somewhat limited in terms of (a) the number of symptoms it addressed (twenty-four items), (b) its failure to assess the *extent* of symptomatology because each item was dichotomously scored as present or absent, and (c) the absence of specific subscales (e.g., "Anxiety" or "Depression").

The intent of the present chapter is to describe two subsequent revisions and extensions of the CSC: the Trauma Symptom Checklist 33 (TSC-33) and the Trauma Symptom Checklist 40 (TSC-40). These scales were designed to be brief, abuse-oriented instruments of reasonable reliability and validity that can be used in clinical research as measures of traumatic impact, perhaps most notably in the area of long-term child abuse effects. The TSC-33 consists of thirty-three symptom items, each of which is rated for frequency of occurrence on a four-point scale. These items are summed to produce a total score and five symptom subscales (Anxiety, Depression, Dissociation, Post-Sexual Abuse Trauma-hypothesized [PSAT-h], and Sleep Disturbance).

Recently, the TSC-33 was expanded by seven items to form the TSC-40 (see Appendix 4-1). Five items were added to the two sexual symptom items found in the TSC-33 to form a new "Sexual Problems" subscale. In addition, two items were added to the Sleep Disturbance subscale to increase its reliability. Finally, in order to improve the content validity of the PSAT-h subscale, an additional item from the new Sexual Problems Subscale ("bad thoughts or feelings during sex") was added to the PSAT-h. In order to allow discrimination between the regular PSAT-h and this augmented version, the resultant subscale was renamed the Sexual Abuse Trauma Index (SATI).

This chapter reports on the psychometric characteristics of the TSC-33 in a clinical sample of adult women (Briere & Runtz, 1989), and the TSC-40 in a large, nonclinical sample of professional women (Elliott & Briere, 1990). Additionally, data is presented from six other studies that used the TSC scales in discriminating a history of sexual abuse or to correlate specific characteristics of sexual abuse to adult symptomatology (Alter-Reid, 1989; Bagley, 1989; Briere, Evans, Runtz, & Wall, 1988; Cole, 1986; Magana, 1990; Williams, 1990).

Table 4-1
TSC-33 AND TSC-40 SCALE AND SUBSCALE CHARACTERISTICS

| Subscale | No. of Items | | Alpha | | TSC-40 Subscale Composition (item nos.) |
	TSC-33	TSC-40	Clinical Sample[a]	Non-clinical Sample[b]	
Anxiety	9	9	.72	.66	1, 4, 10, 16, 21, 27, 32, 34, 39
Depression	9	9	.72	.70	2, 3, 9, 15, 19, 20, 26, 33, 37
Dissociation	6	6	.75	.64	7, 14, 16, 25, 31, 38
PSAT-h[c]	6		.72	.59	5, 7, 13, 21, 25, 29, 31
SATI[d]		7		.62	5, 7, 13, 21, 25, 29, 31
Sexual Problems[d]		7		.73	5, 9, 11, 17, 23, 20, 35, 40
Sleep Disturbance[c]	6		.66	.73	2, 8, 13, 19
Sleep Disturbance[d]		6		.77	2, 8, 13, 19, 22, 28
TSC-33 Total score		33		.89	1–16, 18–21, 24–27, 30–34, 36–39
TSC-40 Total score		40		.90	1–40

[a] Clinical sample from Briere & Runtz, 1989; [b] Nonclinical sample from Elliott & Briere, 1990; [c] TSC-33; [d] TSC-40.

Sample Characteristics and Subscale Reliability

In their initial validation study, Briere and Runtz (1989) administered the TSC-33 to a sample of 195 Canadian women seeking treatment at a crisis intervention center. The average age of the women in this sample was 27.4 years, and the modal relationship status was single (42 percent). Subjects were categorized as having a sexual abuse history if they described sexual contact (ranging from fondling to intercourse) on or before the age 16 with someone five or more years older. On the basis of this definition, 133 women had childhood histories of sexual victimization.

Analysis of the internal consistency of the five TSC-33 subscales indicated reasonable reliability, with an average subscale alpha of .71 and an alpha of .89 for the total TSC-33 (see Table 4-1). The Sleep Disturbance subscale had relatively lower reliability (a=.66), probably caused by the smaller number of items in this subscale.

The revised version of the Trauma Symptom Checklist (TSC-40) was administered to a national, stratified sample of profession women (n=2,833, Elliott & Briere, 1990). The average age of the women in this sample was 41.7 years, and the modal relationship status was married (66 percent). Most of the subjects held a master's degree or higher (82 percent), and earned more than $45,000 per year (73 percent). Based on the definition of abuse utilized by Briere and Runtz (1989), 761 women (26.9 percent) were designated as sexual abuse survivors.

Analysis of the internal consistency of the six TSC-40 subscales in the Elliott and Briere (1990) study demonstrated adequate reliability, with an average subscale alpha of .69 and an alpha of .90 for the total TSC-40. The data suggested that those changes to the TSC-33 found in the TSC-40 were relatively successful. The Sleep Disturbance scale appeared to have benefitted from the addition of two items, yielding an alpha of .77 (an improvement over the shorter version in both the Briere and Runtz clinical sample [a=.66] and Elliott and Briere's nonclinical sample [a=.73]). The new Sexual Problems subscale also appeared to be reasonably reliable (a=.73). Although the Sexual Abuse Trauma Index had lower internal consistency (a=.62) relative to other subscales (reflective, in part, of the intentional heterogeneity of items it contains), it was nevertheless an improvement over the PSAT-h in the nonclinical sample (a=.59). Finally, the total TSC-40 score, like the TSC-33, was shown to be highly reliable (a=.90).

Interestingly, with the exception of the Sleep Disturbance subscale, all of the subscales in the nonclinical sample displayed slightly lower internal consistency than they did in the original clinical group of women. As indicated by Anastasi (1988), cross-sample fluctuations in alpha coefficients are not unusual for psychological tests. The coefficient is affected by the range of scores in a given group, with more heterogenous samples usually resulting in higher reliability estimates. In the current instance, subscale scores were considerably more heterogenous in the clinical sample (mean subscale standard deviation of 4.56) than in the nonclinical sample of professional women (mean standard deviation of 2.67 for the same subscales).

Validity

As indicated in Table 4-2, twenty-three of the TSC-33 items discriminated between abused and nonabused subjects in the clinical sample (Briere & Runtz, 1989), assuming a minimal univariate probability level of $p<.05$. Thirty-six of the TSC-40 items discriminated between abused and nonabused subjects in the nonclinical sample (Elliott, 1990), assuming a minimal univariate probability level of $p<.01$. (The probability of chance findings was set at a more stringent level in the nonclinical sample because of the considerably larger sample size and thus greater statistical power to detect actual differences.)

The results of the univariate tests for the subscales and the total score for both the clinical and nonclinical samples are reported in Table 4-3, along with data from three additional studies (Bagley, 1989; Briere et al, 1988; Cole, 1986). These data suggest that the Trauma Symptom Checklist subscales and total scores discriminate well between abused and nonabused clients. Transformation of F values, using the normal distribution procedure outline by Wolfe (1986), suggested that the average sexual abuse survivor in the validation sample had a higher TSC-33 score than approximately 70 percent of the nonabused clinical subjects (Briere & Runtz, 1989). Application of this statistic to Elliott and Briere's sample similarly indicated that the typical sexual abuse survivor had a higher TSC-40 score than approximately 67 percent of her nonabused peers.

In addition to the findings in Briere and Runtz's clinical sample and Elliott and Briere's nonclinical group, five other studies have examined the performance of the TSC in discriminating abused subjects.

Table 4-2

TSC-40 ITEM DIFFERENCES BETWEEN SEXUALLY ABUSED AND NONABUSED SUBJECTS

		Clinical Sample[a]			Nonclinical Sample[b]	
No. Item		No Abuse	Abuse	F (1,193)	No Abuse	Abuse	F (1,283)
1	Headaches	0.97	1.49	9.31**	1.05	1.10	2.35
2	Insomnia	1.26	1.56	3.10	0.79	0.95	25.02**
3	Weight loss	0.81	0.84	0.04	0.19	0.22	2.08
4	Stomach problems	0.94	1.30	4.29*	0.61	0.77	25.01**
5	Sexual problems	0.29	1.11	23.64**	0.47	0.67	43.00**
6	Isolation	1.81	2.00	1.43	0.87	1.10	46.64**
7	"Flashbacks"	0.71	1.44	17.98**	0.36	0.55	48.82**
8	Restless sleep	1.27	1.97	18.10**	0.99	1.13	18.02**
9	Low sex drive	1.44	1.33	0.27	1.10	1.29	25.65**
10	Anxiety attacks	0.87	0.91	3.48	0.61	0.77	25.73**
11	Sexual overactivity	0.05	0.32	7.93**	0.13	0.20	15.45**
12	Loneliness	1.90	2.00	0.37	0.87	1.09	45.82**
13	Nightmares	0.68	1.42	20.52**	0.41	0.54	28.41**
14	"Spacing out"	0.65	1.20	10.68**	0.62	0.77	25.89**
15	Sadness	1.94	2.09	1.04	1.02	1.18	33.12**
16	Dizziness	0.37	0.76	9.14**	0.29	0.36	10.12**
17	Dissatisfying sex life	—	—	—	0.96	1.15	25.34**
18	Temper problems	0.76	1.20	7.81**	0.76	0.86	12.75**
19	Early morning awakenings	0.98	1.26	2.30	0.76	0.86	8.67**
20	Crying	0.87	1.16	3.49	0.25	0.33	14.96**
21	Fear of men	0.52	1.60	41.92**	0.15	0.29	44.96**
22	Not feeling rested	—	—	—	1.21	1.35	21.15**
23	Unenjoyable sex	—	—	—	0.49	0.69	50.37**
24	Getting along with others	0.48	0.91	8.90**	0.57	0.66	13.77**
25	Memory problems	0.73	1.09	6.26*	0.75	0.89	22.79**
26	Hurt self	0.26	0.68	9.12**	0.07	0.15	37.36**
27	Fear of women	0.15	0.55	13.49**	0.06	0.13	33.24**
28	Waking in the night	—	—	—	0.88	1.00	13.08**
29	Bad thoughts or feelings during sex	—	—	—	0.09	0.20	41.71**
30	Passing out	0.00	0.12	4.91*	0.02	0.03	4.31
31	Unreality	0.50	1.12	14.70**	0.21	0.29	14.87**
32	Excessive washing	0.06	0.44	9.27**	0.03	0.05	3.13
33	Inferiority	1.52	1.92	5.86*	0.70	0.92	51.84**
34	Tension	1.74	1.94	1.57	0.82	1.00	29.88**
35	Sexual confusion	—	—	—	0.32	0.51	51.56**
36	Hurt others	0.34	0.62	5.23*	0.10	0.15	11.30**
37	Guilt	1.61	1.94	3.93*	0.86	1.07	41.78**
38	Out of body experiences	0.39	0.70	4.50*	0.12	0.19	17.50**
39	Trouble breathing	0.42	0.70	4.18*	0.17	0.26	20.73**
40	Sexual feelings when you shouldn't have them	—	—	—	0.22	0.32	23.85**

[a] Clinical sample from Briere & Runtz, 1989; [b] Nonclinical sample from Elliott, 1990; * $p<.05$; ** $p<.01$.

Table 4-3

TSC-33 AND TSC-40 SCALE AND SUBSCALE DIFFERENCES BETWEEN SEXUALLY ABUSED AND NONABUSED ADULT SUBJECTS FROM FIVE STUDIES

		Abused		Nonabused		ANOVA	
		X	(SD)[a]	X	(SD)	F	df
Briere & Runtz (1989)							
Crisis intervention	Anxiety	9.95	(5.07)	6.03	(3.73)	29.58**	1,193
center, outpatients,	Depression	12.19	(6.32)	10.24	(5.79)	4.23*	
females only	Dissociation	6.31	(4.11)	3.34	(3.33)	24.73**	
(abused n= 133;	PSAT-h	7.78	(3.82)	3.41	(2.89)	63.48**	
nonabused n= 62)	Sleep Dist.	6.2	(3.38)	4.19	(2.86)	16.55**	
TSC-33		39.97	(15.83)	27.26	(11.93)	38.69**	
Elliott & Briere (1980)							
Working	Anxiety	4.74	(2.95)	3.80	(2.66)	65.61**	1,2832
professionals	Depression	6.98	(3.39)	5.74	(3.25)	79.39**	
nonclinical,	Dissociation	3.05	(2.20)	2.35	(2.06)	62.57**	
females only	PSAT-h[b]	3.23	(2.30)	2.35	(1.98)	101.20**	
(abused n=761;	SATI[c]	3.43	(2.51)	2.44	(2.10)	110.04**	
nonabused	Sexual Prob.[c]	5.02	(3.40)	3.77	(2.99)	90.63**	
n=2,202)	Sleep Dist.[b]	3.49	(2.23)	2.95	(2.12)	34.81**	
Sleep Dist.[c]		5.84	(3.06)	5.03	(3.03)	39.94**	
TSC-33		20.80	(9.98)	16.75	(9.13)	104.04**	
TSC-44		26.02(	12.05)	20.91	(11.11)	112.36**	
Bagley (1989)							
Community	TSC-33	23.22		16.26		23.04**	1,344
sample, females							
(abused n=116;							
nonabused n=229)							
Briere et al. (1980)							
Crisis	Anxiety	9.65		5.73		20.03**	1,75
intervention	Depression	14.10		10.10		15.21**	
center,	Dissociation	6.83		2.80		24.62**	
outpatients,	PSAT-h	7.80		2.93		44.62**	
males and	Sleep Dist.	6.88		4.35		16.98**	
females	TSC-33	43.80		28.98		26.98**	
(abused n=40;							
nonabused n=40)							
Cole (1986)							
University	Anxiety	4.49		3.30		2.76	1,212
students,	Depression	6.64		3.66		5.14*	
nonclinical,	Dissociation	3.43		2.60		3.30	
males	PSAT-h	3.15		2.31		5.23*	
and females	Sleep Dist.	3.79		3.03		6.34**	
(abused n=113;	TSC-33	19.85		16.00		6.58**	
nonabused n=114)							

[a] SD's only available on two studies; [b] TSC-33; [c] TSC-40; * p<.05; **p<.01

These are (a) two studies of sexual and physical abuse effects among volunteer subjects (Alter-Reid, 1989; Cole, 1986), (b) a study that evaluated the combined effects of childhood molestation and adult sexual intimacies within a client-therapist relationship (Magana, 1990), (c) a stratified random sample of Canadian women (Bagley, 1989), and (d) a study that evaluated sex differences in the effects of sexual abuse on clinical subjects (Briere et al., 1988).

In Cole's (1986) study of university students, the majority of subscales and the total TSC-33 score discriminated sexually abused from nonabused subjects, with the two remaining subscales (Anxiety and Dissociation) showing trends in the same direction. Other analyses indicated that the TSC was also a predictor of physical abuse within this college student sample.

In Alter-Reid's (1989) study of seventy volunteers, women with a history of both sexual and physical abuse reported significantly higher levels of Post Sexual Abuse Trauma and overall distress on the TSC-33 than did either women with a history of sexual abuse in isolation or women with no history of sexual abuse (sexual combined with physical abuse: X=47.00; sexual abuse in isolation: X=32.74; no sexual abuse: X=23.05, $p<.001$). Consistent with the results of Cole's study, Alter-Reid found that the TSC was also a significant predictor of physical abuse apart from the presence of a sexual abuse history.

Magana's (1990) study was composed of a clinical sample of twenty-nine abused women, ten of whom had experienced combined childhood sexual abuse and sexually inappropriate behavior within the context of a client-therapist relationship. Although no control group was used in this study, the means reported on the TSC subscales and total score for sexual abuse survivors were comparable to those of survivors in other clinical samples. Women who experienced revictimization by a therapist had significantly higher TSC-33 scores than did adult survivors who had not been revictimized by a therapist (X=51.10 and 40.54, respectively, $p<.05$).

Bagley's (1989) community study of 345 randomly selected Canadian women revealed that the TSC-33 was more effective than the Middlesex Hospital Questionnaire, the Center for Epidemiological Studies in Depression (CESD) scale, or Coopersmith's self-esteem inventory in identifying former sexual abuse survivors (abused X=23.22; nonabused X=16.26, $p<.01$). Bagley concluded that the pattern of correlations among the TSC-33 subscales and the other measures of psychological distress suggested reasonable concurrent validity for the TSC.

Briere et al. (1988) examined the joint effects of gender and sexual abuse history on TSC-33 scores in a sample of crisis center outpatients. No sex differences were found for subscale scores or for the total TSC-33, both in terms of the total sample and within the sexual abuse group. There were, however, significant differences between sexually abused and nonabused subjects, as indicated in Table 4-3.

The findings in these studies are congruent with most other research in the area of long-term psychological impacts of childhood sexual abuse. Women who were molested as children generally report more anxiety, depression, dissociation, sexual problems, sleep disturbance, and posttraumatic symptoms than do their nonabused peers. The strength of these associations, and their presence in both clinical and more high-functioning nonclinical samples, suggest the ubiquity of abuse-related symptomatology in the general population. Thus, these data not only support the validity of the TSC with regard to sexual abuse but also reinforce the findings of other studies that childhood sexual victimization is commonly associated with later psychological distress.

Performance of the New TSC-40 Subscales

The Sexual Problems subscale of the TSC-40 appears to be especially predictive of sexual abuse history. This is consistent with the existing body of research indicating that sexual disturbance is a significant part of the symptomatology seen in adult women with a history of sexual abuse. Interestingly, although this new subscale discriminates well between sexually abused and nonabused women, the correlation between the TSC-33 (which has no Sexual Problems subscale) and the TSC-40 was .99, as reported in the Elliott and Briere (1990) study. This suggests that although sexual problems are an important element of post-sexual abuse symptomatology, they tend to covary with those aspects previously measured by the TSC-33.

The performance of the Sexual Abuse Trauma Index (formerly the PSAT-h) supports its use as a summary measure of the traumatic effects of sexual abuse. This measure was the most predictive among the Trauma Symptom Checklist subscales of sexual abuse history in three of the four studies listed in Table 4-3. Based upon a comparison of effect size estimates, Elliott and Briere (1990) concluded that this measure was essentially equivalent to the total TSC score in terms of its responsiveness to a history of sexual abuse.

Clinical versus Nonclinical Samples

Not surprisingly, clinical subjects tend to have higher scores on TSC scales than do nonclinical individuals. The three studies sampling clinical populations (Briere et al. 1988; Briere & Runtz, 1989; Magana, 1990) were markedly higher on subscale and overall scores, irrespective of abuse history, than were the three studies sampling nonclinical populations (Bagley, 1989; Cole, 1986; Elliott & Briere, 1990). Subscale means for the three clinical samples were remarkably similar to one another, as were those among the three nonclinical samples. The mean TSC-33 score for the clinical samples was 41.37 for abused women and 27.65 for their nonabused clinical peers. The mean TSC-33 score among the nonclinical samples for abused and nonabused women was 20.97 and 16.67, respectively. The average TSC score among *abused* women from nonclinical samples was lower than the average TSC score of *nonabused* women from clinical samples, suggesting that subjects' scores should be compared to appropriate clinical or nonclinical norms, rather than considered in isolation. Summary data on the TSC for abused women in clinical and nonclinical samples are found in Table 4-4.

Relation to Abuse Characteristics

If the Trauma Symptom Checklist is truly a measure of the impact of victimization, it might be expected to covary as a function of the specific aspects of abuse (Briere & Runtz, 1988). Because of the passage of time, and the probable effects of other intervening experiences (including other forms of victimization), however, correlations between the characteristics of the molestation and outcome measures are often small but statistically significant (Browne & Finkelhor, 1986).

Within Briere and Runtz's clinical subsample of abuse survivors, 61 percent were victims of incest and 77 percent had experienced anal, oral, or vaginal penetration as a child. The mean age that molestation began in the clinical sample was 8.0 years, and the mean duration of abuse was 5.9 years. The characteristics of the abuse were somewhat less severe within Elliott and Briere's nonclinical subsample of

Table 4-4

TSC-33 Scale and Subscale Means for
Sexually Abused Subjects

	Clinical					
	Altar-Reid (1989) $n=47$	Briere et al. (1989) $n=40$	Briere & Runtz (1989) $n=133$	Magana (1989) $n=29$	Williams (1990) $n=531$*	MEAN CLINICAL $n=771$
Anxiety	—	9.65	9.95	11.80	9.04	9.30
Depression	—	14.10	12.19	13.82	11.30	11.69
Dissociation	—	6.83	6.31	9.10	6.79	6.77
PSAH-h	7.85	7.80	7.78	9.70	7.33	7.53
Sleep Disturbance	—	6.88	6.21	6.30	5.35	5.62
TSC-33	43.98	43.80	39.97	45.82	37.05	38.55

*77% of all Williams's subjects were in treatment at the time of the study. Most of the remaining subjects were involved in self-help groups for survivors. Only 7% had never been in treatment.
— Data not available

sexually abused women. In this study, 61 percent of the adults molested as children reported intrafamilial abuse, and 24 percent had been anally, orally, or vaginally penetrated at some point during the molestation. The average age at first molestation was 9.3 years, and the duration of abuse ranged from one day (32 percent of the women reported a one-time incident of abuse) to fourteen years.

A third study examining the performance of the TSC-33 in relation to characteristics of abuse was completed on a probability, primarily clinical sample of 531 survivors (77 percent were in treatment at the time of the study; Williams, 1990). This group was predominantly Caucasian (92 percent), and female (88.5 percent), with a mean age of 36 years. Williams used a broader definition of sexual abuse than either Briere and Runtz or Elliott and Briere, including noncontact (i.e., exposure or solicitation) and a maximum cutoff age of 18 years. Physical force was used during the molestation of approximately 65 percent of the victims. Vaginal or anal penetration occurred at some point during the molestation of 26 percent of the survivors, and the modal length for the abuse was longer than six years.

In both the clinical and nonclinical samples, some abuse characteristics were significantly correlated with Trauma Symptom Checklist

Table 4-4 (continued)
TSC-33 Scale and Subscale Means for Sexually Abused Subjects

	Nonclinical		
Bagley (1989) n=116	Cole (1986) n=113	Elliot & Briere (1990) n=781	MEAN NONCLINICAL n=1010
—	4.49	4.74	4.71
—	6.64	6.98	6.96
—	3.43	3.05	3.10
—	3.15	3.23	3.22
—	3.79	3.49	3.53
23.22	19.85	20.80	20.97

scale and subscale scores, although the size of the association was typically small. Most notably related to symptomatology were compounded abuse (physical and sexual abuse in combination) and the duration of and frequency with which the abuse occurred (see Table 4-5). The subscale most strongly associated with abuse characteristics was the Sexual Abuse Trauma Index (SATI), suggesting that this subscale may indeed be an indicator of a form of abuse-related posttraumatic stress. Interestingly, and unlike Briere et al. (1988), Williams found sex differences for each of the TSC subscales and total score of the TSC-33. In each instance, males had significantly lower scores than females (TSC-33 total score: males X=31.18; females X=37.88, p<.01).

Conclusions

Although the aforementioned studies used a discriminant approach to validating the Trauma Symptom Checklist, the authors of this scale did not intend it to be used as a "litmus test" for the presence or absence of a sexual abuse history. Some subjects in both the clinical and nonclinical groups reported low levels of symptomatology despite

Table 4-5

Correlation of TSC-33 and TSC-40 Scale and Subscales with Abuse Characteristics Within Sexual Abuse Subsamples

	Parental Incest		Duration			Frequency		
	CS[a]	NCS[b]	CS[a]	PCS[c]	NCS[b]	CS[a]	PCS[c]	NCS[b]
Anxiety	−.04	.07	−.08	.14*	.09*	−.01	.15*	.11*
Depression	.06	.05	.13	.15*	.06	.18*	.17*	.09*
Dissociation	−.06	.12*	.00	.15*	.10*	.01	.16*	.06
PSAT-hd	.06	.11	.15*	.18*	.12*	.19	.20	.10
SATle	.11	.11*	.10*	.04	.05	.07		
Sexual Prob.e	.09	.06	.10*	.04	.05	.07		
Skeeo Dist.d	.08	.04	.12	.16*	.07	.06	.14*	.06
Sleep Dist.e	.04	.06	.05*	.00	-.03	.07		
TSC-33	.02	.10*	.05	.18*	.10*	.08	.19*	.12*
TSC-40	.10*	.09*	.11*	.03	.04	.12*		

[a] CS = Clinical sample, from Briere & Runtz, 1989; [b] NCS = Nonclinical sample, from Elliott & Briere, 1990; [c] PCS = Primarily clinical sample, from Williams, 1990; [d] TSC-33; [e] TSC-40; * $p<.05$.

having been sexually abused as a child, whereas other subjects were more highly symptomatic but denied a sexual abuse history.

The Trauma Symptom Checklist scales were created to assess the specific pattern of disturbance manifested by various types of trauma victims. The studies reported here provide support for the success of this endeavor in terms of evaluating the specific long-term effects of sexual molestation. Such data indicate an important aspect of the Trauma Symptom Checklist: Although probably of limited use as a way of identifying or "verifying" former victims of child abuse, it may be helpful in determining the extent or pattern of posttraumatic impact on a given individual or group of individuals. Certain forms of abuse may produce elevated Depression (e.g., frequent or compounded abuse), whereas another aspect of victimization may result in greater Sexual Problems (e.g., parental incest). It is likely that as new abuse parameters are investigated—for example, the victims's attribution of blame or guilt—these too will differentially influence TSC subscales.

Further research is indicated regarding the effectiveness of this measure in the assessment of other forms of trauma. In both clinical

Table 4-5 (continued)

CORRELATION OF TSC-33 AND TSC-40 SCALE AND SUBSCALES WITH ABUSE CHARACTERISTICS WITHIN SEXUAL ABUSE SUBSAMPLES

Penetration		No. of Abusers			Compounded Abuse	
CS[a]	NCS[b]	CS[a]	PCS[c]	NCS[b]	CS[a]	NCS[b]
.06	.01	−.13	−.24*	.03	.13	.07
−.06	.01	.15*	.15*	.01	.17*	.09*
.17*	.04	−.08	.28*	.08*	.13	.15*
.21*	.02	.02	.26*	.09*	.09	.14*
−.02	.00	.06	.24*	.04	.19*	.05
.08	.02	.01	.25*	.04	.16*	.12*

and nonclinical samples, TSC scores appear to increase in the presence of both physical and sexual abuse, suggesting that scores on this instrument may be elevated by various forms of victimization. Thus, it is possible that the Trauma Symptom Checklists are responsive to a variety of traumatic life experiences, only one of which is sexual abuse. Such variability should be investigated in future studies, wherein a variety of childhood and adulthood stressors could be ascertained and associated with TSC scores.

Note

1. A third instrument assessing abuse effects, The Trauma Symptom Checklist for Children (TSC-C; Briere, 1989) has been developed, and appears to display reasonable psychometric properties upon preliminary analysis (Lanktree & Briere, 1990). The instrument is not discussed in this chapter, however, given its use as a measure of more short-term reactions to abuse among child victims, with the focus of this chapter being the lasting effects of abuse among adult survivors.

References

Alter-Reid, K. 1989. *The long-term impact of incest: An investigation of traumagenic factors and effects in four types of childhood abuse.* Unpublished manuscript.

Anastasi, A. 1988. *Psychological testing* (6th ed.). New York: Macmillan.

Bagley, C. 1989. *Utility of the Trauma Symptom Checklist in Screening for Young Women Who Experienced Serious Sexual Abuse in Childhood.* Unpublished manuscript.

Bagley, C., and R. Ramsay. 1986. Disrupted childhood and vulnerability to sexual assault: Long-term sequels with implications for counseling. *Social Work and Human Sexuality* 4:33–48.

Berliner, L. April 1987. *Response paper.* Presented at the National Symposium on Assessing the Impact of Child Sexual Abuse, Huntsville, AL.

Briere, J. 1989. *The Trauma Symptom Checklist for Children (TSC-C).* Unpublished psychological test.

Briere, J., D. Evans, M. Runtz, and T. Wall. 1988. Symptomatology in men who were molested as children: A comparison study. *American Journal of Orthopsychiatry* 58:457–461.

Briere, J., and M. Runtz. 1990. Differential adult symptomatology associated with three types of child abuse histories. *Child Abuse and Neglect* 14:357–64.

———. 1987. Post Sexual Abuse Trauma: Data and implications for clinical practice. *Journal of Interpersonal Violence* 2:367–79.

———. 1988. Symptomatology associated with childhood sexual victimization in a non-clinical adult sample. *Child Abuse and Neglect* 12:51–59.

———. 1989. The Trauma Symptom Checklist (TSC-33): Early data on a new scale. *Journal of Interpersonal Violence,* 4:151–63.

Briere, J., and L.Y. Zaidi. 1989. Sexual abuse histories and sequelae in female psychiatric emergency room patients. *American Journal of Psychiatry* 146:1602–606.

Brown, A., and D. Finkelhor. 1986. Initial and long-term effects: A review of the research. In D. Finkelhor, *A Sourcebook on Child Aexual Abuse* (pp. 143–179). Beverly Hills, CA: Sage.

Cole, C B. 1986, May. *Differential Long-Term Effects of Child Sexual and Physical Abuse.* Paper presented at the National Conference on Sexual Victimization of Children, New Orleans, LA.

Conte, J. 1987, April. *Response paper.* Presented at the National Symposium on Assessing the Impact of Child Sexual Abuse, Huntsville, AL.

Courtois, C. 1979. The incest experience and its aftermath. *Victimology: An International Journal,* 4:337–47.

Elliott, D. M. 1990. *The effects of Childhood Sexual Experiences on Adult Functioning in a National Sample of Professional Women.* Unpublished doctoral dissertation, Rosemead School of Psychology, La Mirada, CA.

Elliott, D. M., and J. Briere. 1990, April. *Predicting Molestation History in Professional Women with the Trauma Symptom Checklist (TSC-40).* Paper presented at the annual meeting of the Western Psychological Association, Los Angeles.

Elliott, D. M. and D.L. Gabrielson. 1990, August. *Impaired Object Relations in Professional Women Molested as Children.* Paper presented at the annual meeting of the American Psychological Association, Los Angeles, CA.

Finkelhor, D. 1987, April. *Response paper.* Presented at the National Symposium on Assessing the Impact of Child Sexual Abuse, Huntsville, AL.

Finkelhor, D., G. Hotaling, I. Lewis, and C. Smith. 1989. Sexual abuse and its relationship to later sexual satisfaction, marital status, religion, and attitudes. *Journal of Interpersonal Violence*, 4:379–99.

Gold, E.R. 1986. Long-term effects of sexual victimization in childhood: An attributional approach. *Journal of Consulting and Clinical Psychology*, 54:471–75.

Herman, J.L. 1981. *Father-Daughter Incest.* Cambridge, MA: Harvard University Press.

Jehu, D., M. Gazan, and C. Klassen. 1984–85. Common therapeutic targets among women who were sexually abused in childhood. *Journal of Social Work and Human Sexuality* 3:25-45.

Lanktree, C.B., and J. Briere. 1990, August. *Early data on the Trauma Symptom Checklist for Children (TSC-C).* Paper presented at the annual meeting of the American Psychological Association, Boston.

Lindberg, F.H., and L.J. Distad. 1985. Post-traumatic stress disorders in women who experienced childhood incest. *Child Abuse and Neglect* 9:329–34.

Magana, D. 1990. *The Impact of Client-Therapist Sexual Intimacy and Child Sexual Abuse on Psychosexual and Psychological Functioning.* Unpublished doctoral dissertation, University of California, Los Angeles.

Maltz, W. 1988. Identifying and treating the sexual repercussions of incest: A couples therapy approach. *Journal of Sex and Marital Therapy* 14:145–63.

Peters, S. 1988. Child sexual abuse and later psychological problems. In G. E. Wyatt and G. J. Powell (eds.), *Lasting Effects of Child Sexual Abuse*, pp. 101–117. Newbury Park, CA: Sage.

Putnam, F.W. 1988. *Diagnosis and Treatment of Multiple Personality Disorder.* New York: Guilford.

Stein, J.A., J.W. Golding, J.M. Siegal, M.A. Burnam, and S.B. Sorenson. 1988. Long-term psychological sequelae of child sexual abuse: The Los Angeles Epidemiologic Catchment Area Study. In G. E. Wyatt and G. J. Powell (eds.), *Lasting Effects of Child Sexual Abuse*, pp. 135–154. Newbury Park, CA: Sage.

Williams, M.B. 1990. *Child Sexual Abuse and Post-Traumatic Stress Disorder: The Enduring Effect.* Unpublished doctoral dissertation, Fielding Institute, Santa Barbara, CA.

Wolfe, F.M. 1986. *Meta-analysis: Quantitative for methods for research synthesis.* Sage University Paper Series on Quantitative Applications in the Social Sciences, No. 07-001. Beverly Hills, CA: Sage.

Appendix 4-1

TRAUMA SYMPTOM CHECKLIST 40 (TSC-40)

How often have you experienced each of the following In the last two months?

		Never			Often
1	Headaches	0	1	2	3
2	Insomnia (trouble getting to sleep)	0	1	2	3
3	Weight loss (without dieting)	0	1	2	3
4	Stomach problems	0	1	2	3
5	Sexual problems	0	1	2	3
6	Feeling isolated from others	0	1	2	3
7	"Flashbacks" (sudden, vivid, distracting memories)	0	1	2	3
8	Restless sleep	0	1	2	3
9	Low sex drive	0	1	2	3
10	Anxiety attacks	0	1	2	3
11	Sexual overactivity	0	1	2	3
12	Loneliness	0	1	2	3
13	Nightmares	0	1	2	3
14	"Spacing out" (going away in your mind)	0	1	2	3
15	Sadness	0	1	2	3
16	Dizziness	0	1	2	3
17	Not feeling satisfied with your sex life	0	1	2	3
18	Trouble controlling your temper	0	1	2	3
19	Waking up early in the morning and can't get back to sleep	0	1	2	3
20	Uncontrollable crying	0	1	2	3
21	Fear of men	0	1	2	3
22	Not feeling rested in the morning	0	1	2	3
23	Having sex that you didn't enjoy	0	1	2	3
24	Trouble getting along with others	0	1	2	3
25	Memory problems	0	1	2	3
26	Desire to physically hurt yourself	0	1	2	3
27	Fear of women	0	1	2	3
28	Waking up in the middle of the night'	0	1	2	3
29	Bad thoughts or feelings during sex	0	1	2	3
30	Passing out	0	1	2	3
31	Feeling that things are "unreal"	0	1	2	3
32	Unnecessary or over-frequent washing	0	1	2	3
33	Feelings of inferiority	0	1	2	3
34	Feeling tense all the time	0	1	2	3
35	Being confused about your sexual feelings	0	1	2	3
36	Desire to physically hurt others	0	1	2	3
37	Feelings of guilt	0	1	2	3
38	Feeling that you are not always in your body	0	1	2	3
39	Having trouble breathing	0	1	2	3
40	Sexual feelings when you shouldn't have them	0	1	2	3

Chapter 5

The Efficacy of Psychological Interventions with Recent Rape Victims

Barbara Anderson
Ellen Frank
University of Pittsburgh

■

This work was supported in part by Grants MH-29262 and MH-30915 from the National Institute of Mental Health.

■

The early descriptive studies of the psychological response to rape victimization indicated that while some rape victims made a relatively rapid and complete recovery from the initial trauma, others had more prolonged difficulties (Burgess & Holmstrom, 1986; Queen's Bench Foundation, 1975). Furthermore, these studies suggested that most victims continued to experience some residual fears and problems many months, and even years, after the assault.

At least three empirical studies of rape victims appear to contradict these early descriptions (Stewart, Hughes, Frank, Anderson, Kendall, & West, 1987). Each of the major assessment studies (Frank, Turner, & Stewart, 1980; Kilpatrick, Veronen, & Resick, 1979a; Resick, Calhoun, Atkeson, & Ellis, 1981) has found greatly elevated symptom levels in recent victims and highly significant differences between victims and matched control subjects at initial assessment. When studied over a period of one year, subjects tend to show marked improvement. Indeed, a cursory reading of the repeated-assessment only studies (Kilpatrick et al., 1979b; Resick, et al., 1981), in that scores on standardized assessment instruments for depression, fear, anxiety, and social adjustment were used as outcome measures, would suggest that recovery from rape occurs within a few months and is largely a function of the passage of time. However, in her summary of the empirical studies of rape trauma, Ellis (1983) identifies three sequential reactions to a rape experience; a short term, an intermediate, and a long-term reaction. She describes the short-term reaction as involving a wide range of global traumatic symptoms, including somatic complaints, sleep disturbance, nightmares, fear, suspiciousness, anxiety, major depression, and difficulties in social functioning. It is this global traumatic reaction that is reflected in the initial score elevations on measures of depression, fear, anxiety and social adjustment seen in all empirical studies (Atkeson, Calhoun, Resick, & Ellis, 1982; Calhoun, Atkeson, & Resick, 1982; Ellis, Atkeson & Calhoun, 1981; Frank & Stewart, 1982, 1983, 1984a; Kilpatrick, Veronen, & Resick, 1979a; Veronen & Kilpatrick, 1980). These same empirical studies provide evidence for existence of an intermediate reaction, seen between three months and one year post assault, which involves depression, social dysfunction, sexual dysfunction, and rape-specific anxiety rather than the more diffuse anxiety observed earlier. Finally, these empirical investigations document a long-term reaction that is still observed at one year and beyond, involving anger, diminished capacity to enjoy life, hypervigilance to danger, and continued sexual dysfunction.

Over the course of the last ten years, we have been concerned with the psychological status and possible treatment needs of recent victims of sexual assault. Our primary concern has been to determine what form of intervention would facilitate most rapid and most complete recovery from both the global short-term reaction to rape and from the intermediate and long-term reactions to rape. During the first six years of this program of research we studied the impact of two well-described, time-limited psychotherapeutic treatments, Cognitive Behavior Therapy and Systematic Desensitization, on psychological and psychosocial parameters in the aftermath of a sexual assault experience. In order to document that impact we carried out careful assessments using well-validated, standardized measures of those parameters. This systematic approach to assessment, treatment, and follow-up yielded valuable information on the reactions and recovery of recent rape victims; however, it also pointed to unresolved issues with respect to the relationship between treatment intervention and recovery from the short-term global reaction to rape and from the intermediate and long-term reactions.

Subjects assigned to both Cognitive Behavior Therapy and Systematic Desensitization showed highly significant improvement by three months on all assessment measures employed in our study (i.e., depression, fear, self-esteem, anxiety, and social adjustment). However, we failed to observe significant differences between these treatment interventions when the two groups of treated subjects were compared (Frank, Anderson, Stewart, Dancu, Hughes, & West, 1988). Furthermore, although our treated subjects did appear to show somewhat earlier and more complete recovery from the initial reaction than untreated subjects assessed with the same measures in other studies (Calhoun et al., 1979; Kilpatrick et al., 1979a), these differences did not appear to be large enough to warrant a recommendation that those regularly engaged in service to victims provide a course of Cognitive Therapy or Systematic Desensitization for all clients.

However, we, as well as others (Coates & Winston, 1983; Forman, 1983), remained reluctant to conclude that treatment is not indicated for rape victims. Although subjects entered into each of the active treatment modalities studied for recent victims (Frank & Stewart, 1984; Frank et al., 1988; Kilpatrick, 1984) appeared to have achieved approximately the same mean levels of symptom remission in approximately the same period of time as subjects exposed to repeated assessment alone, Kilpatrick's (Kilpatrick et al., 1979a) and Calhoun's (Atkeson et al., 1982) delayed-assessment subjects and our delayed-treatment seekers (Stewart et al., 1987) provided evidence of a subgroup who did not recover from the short-term reaction within that period of time. Both Kilpatrick et al. (1979a) and Atkeson et al. (1982) found lower levels of symptoms at each assessment point for subjects who had been exposed to repeated assessment as compared to subjects exposed to their first assessment at that time. Although some of the changes observed in the repeated-assessment subjects may be accounted for by the subjects' adaptation to the assessment measures, these results suggested that merely having contact with clinicians or assessors produced some additional improvement over what would be expected solely as a result of the passage of time. Indeed, Calhoun et al. (1982) and Kilpatrick (1984) have noted that subjects found the assessment process to be therapeutic.

At least one additional line of evidence from our own work tends to confirm the view that some victims remain symptomatic despite the passage of time. We compared sexual assault victims who sought treatment within one month of their assaults to victims who delayed seeking treatment anywhere from two months to nearly three and one-half years after their assaults (Frank et al., 1988). Although the delayed-treatment seekers entered the treatment protocol four months later, on the average, than the immediate-treatment seekers, their initial symptomatology was higher than that of the subjects assessed within a few weeks of the assault. However, when comparisons were made between end-of-treatment scores, there were no differences between the groups on absolute levels of symptomatology, suggesting that structured behavioral treatments are associated with comparable levels of symptom reduction whether they are instituted within a few weeks of an assault experience or many months later. Finally, there is evidence to suggest that untreated subjects differ from those who receive treatment in terms of the percentage who continue to experience symptoms of the intermediate and long-term reactions in terms of their level of social adjustment. (Resick et al., 1981). This evidence has led us to question whether a brief, intensive intervention that focuses specifically on rape reactions might not facilitate a rapid recovery from the initial global reaction and prevent or minimize the extent of the intermediate and long-term reactions. Thus, over the last four years of our program of research we investigated the efficacy of a brief, intensive Psychoeducational Intervention (PEI) directed specifically at the concerns of recent rape victims against a placebo condition, Psychological Support (PS). This chapter describes these two treatment interventions and reports on the efficacy of these interventions with recent sexual assault victims. In addition, we compare Cognitive Behavior Therapy (CBT) and Systematic Desensitization (SD) treated groups with the PEI and PS treated groups in order to examine whether a particular treatment modality is associated with greater treatment gains over a one-year period.

Treatment Interventions

A full description of Cognitive Behavioral Therapy and Systematic Desensitization as used in our program can be found in Frank and Stewart (1984).

Psychoeducational Intervention (PEI)

The brief history of rape victim research has included relatively few systematic assessment studies and even fewer assessment and treatment studies of recent victims. Those studies which have been reported (Kilpatrick et al., 1979b; Calhoun et al., 1982; Frank et al. 1984; Frank et al., 1988) have shown few, if any, differences among treatment interventions or between subjects who were treated and subjects who were seen for repeated assessment only. It has become clear that highly potent nonspecific factors may have accounted for this failure to find differences among subjects.

In each case, in addition to assessment or assessment and treatment, research staff provided subjects with reassurance, support, and information, and represented a constant and nonjudgmental resource to which subjects could turn. In order to understand their individual contribution to recovery, we believed it was essential to separate the psychological support elements from the information provision elements. We have designed an active intervention, Psychoeducational Intervention, which includes information about rape reactions and how to manage them, offered in a supportive environment.

Our psychoeducational intervention is designed to help the victim understand why the rape myths exist and why operating from the basis of those myths will be nonadaptive for her. The intervention is also directed toward (1) enabling the victim to construct a world view that includes the possibility of victimization but does not assume the certainty of victimization, (2) enabling her to view her crisis responses as well within the bounds of normal crisis responses, (3) enabling her to understand and perhaps even to shape the reactions of significant others to knowledge of the assault, and perhaps most important, (4) enabling her to gain control over some of the most distressing short-term reactions and thus prevent, if possible, the serious life disruptions that are a common consequence of the initial global reaction.

Elements of the Psychoeducational Intervention (PEI): Session One

The psychoeducational intervention begins with a discussion of rape response as a crisis response. Each subject is given an opportunity to explore the fact that in all crises we respond with both our minds and our bodies, so that there are uncomfortable emotions associated with a crisis response as well as uncomfortable physiological responses. The counselor also briefly explores the idea that recovery following a crisis response is a process and that an important aspect of recovery is being able to observe that process as it is occurring. At this very early point in the intervention, an effort is made to get the subject to describe briefly her feelings and physiologic reactions so that a comparison can be made between the immediate impact of the assault and how the subject feels by the end of this first session. It is anticipated that this technique will enable her to see that the process of recovery has already begun to occur.

The second element of the first PEI session is relaxation training. Having already established that we respond physiologically as well as psychologically to crises, the counselor can make a natural transition to the usefulness of being able to gain a measure of control over some of the physiologic responses that the rape victim experiences. The subject is informed that since many of these physiologic responses are anxiety responses and since it is impossible to be both anxious and relaxed at the same time, relaxation training can play an important role in the subject's gaining control over at least the physiologic part of her crisis response.

Subjects are taught progressive muscle relaxation using Jacobson's procedure (Jacobson, 1983; 1970). Relaxation training consists of teaching the subject to alternately tense and relax various muscle groups until a state of relaxation or calmness is achieved. Each subject is introduced to relaxation training by being told that she is going to be taught how to relax herself through tensing and relaxing various muscle groups. Following this explanation, the therapist demonstrates how the muscles are to be tensed and relaxed in the exact sequence that they will be used in the training. Muscles in the upper part of the body are relaxed first, gradually working down to the lower extremities.

Once the subject understands the procedure, she is instructed to lie on the couch or relaxation chair, close her eyes, and try to assume the most comfortable position possible. She is then instructed to allow her thoughts to ramble through her mind and to try not to focus on any one thing in particular. Finally, she is instructed not to try to force herself to relax, but to let it happen as it will. After waiting three minutes, the therapist begins the relaxation exercises. Throughout the exercises, the therapist constantly instructs the subject on how to tense and relax each muscle group while continually suggesting a state of calmness and serenity. Once the exercises are completed, each subject is asked to remain relaxed for a period of five minutes. The therapist checks the subject's level of relaxation by lifting and releasing the arm; the freeness with which the arm descends is an indication of the level of relaxation. Following the five-minute period, the therapist counts backwards from 10 to zero and the patient is instructed to open her eyes on the count of 0. Any questions that the subject might have concerning the procedure are answered at this time. An audiotape recorder is used to record the entire training process, and the resulting audiotape is given to the subject to take home so that she can continue to practice relaxation on her own. Subjects are instructed to practice the exercises at home twice daily, once in the morning and once at night. Periods when the subject has privacy are recommended as ideal times.

Session Two

The second PEI session is ideally scheduled within three to four days of the first. It begins with a review of the relaxation procedure prior to presentation of any new elements. The first new element of the second PEI session focuses on reactions that subjects can anticipate in themselves and others in the aftermath of rape. This is accomplished through a combination of techniques including discussion of her own experiences and viewing of brief videotape segments of a group of subjects from our earlier studies who describe some of the reactions which they experienced. The topics covered include: (1) depressive symptoms, what they are, how long they last, and the fact that they are normal responses to a crisis situation; (2) fear and anxiety responses, techniques for dealing with those responses (including the relaxation techniques the subject has just learned), and ways in that one can learn to live with minimal levels of fear and anxiety; (3) changes in social adjustment, including those that the subject may be experiencing at school or work, in her functioning at home or with friends and relatives, or in her dating and sexual relationships; and (4) alterations in her self-concept. As this final area is later connected with the discussion of myths and realities of sexual assault, many of the ideas that come up in this discussion are temporarily set aside until the next element of the psychoeducational intervention.

Following the discussion of reactions the subject can anticipate in herself, the counselor moves on to talk with the subject about responses that can be anticipated in significant others. Again, using brief segments of videotapes, including one of a mother of a victim, another of a boyfriend of a victim, and a third of a female friend of a victim, the counselor and subject explore why significant others may act the way they do, and why one might anticipate responses that, on the surface, are difficult to understand. The counselor then discusses with the subject what kinds of responses from significant others have thus far been helpful and unhelpful to her. The counselor also discusses ways in which the subject can let others know what her needs are so that she can obtain the kind of support that she feels she needs, and what she might do in the event that the expected or desired social support is not forthcoming. Finally, the counselor explores how the subject might identify those network members who are supportive and maximize her contacts with them. Where appropriate, the counselor and subject review videotape segments which indicate that the subject might anticipate a future point in time at which those who have not been supportive may become supportive.

The third element of the second PEI session focuses on separating the myths from the realities of rape. It begins by giving subjects a worksheet through which they can explore the truth or falsehood of a variety of statements about rape. This list of statements was drawn from the true/false quiz used as part of the educational package developed under the auspices of the National Center for the Prevention and Control of Rape on the topic of acquaintance rape. This quiz covers a broad spectrum of both stranger and acquaintance rape myths. Once the subject has filled out the worksheet, the counselor offers a set of statistics based on our studies and others on the characteristics of victims, the characteristics of assailants, the frequency of acquaintance versus attack rapes, and so forth. She then asks the subject to compare these data with the myths about rape.

The final component of the second PEI session involves the teaching of thought-stopping, a behavioral technique that we believe has a particularly positive effect on the recovery of recent victims. We begin this section by discussing the fact that part of the process of recovery does involve thinking about the assault and events surrounding the assault and coming to terms with them. However, for many victims, at least early in the recovery process, these thoughts are too overwhelming, and they may engulf them with negative emotions. In that case, the most effective and adaptive strategy may be thought-stopping. Subjects are specifically instructed in thought-stopping procedures. They are taught how to cue themselves to stop thoughts and how to switch to a pleasant or relaxing thought as a substitute.

At the end of the session the counselor asks the subject to record on a special recording sheet (1) symptoms that she experiences in the intervening days, (2) what strategies she used to cope with those symptoms, and (3) the helpfulness of that particular strategy as to whether it seemed to reduce, have no effect, or intensify the symptom.

Session Three

The third session of the psychoeducational intervention begins with a review of the homework assignment just described. The first new element of the third PEI session focuses on potential triggers for postrape symptomatology. The counselor asks the subject to review a worksheet listing activities in which she may or may not have engaged over the course of the last few days and asking whether any of those triggered symptoms related to the assault. These include activities that may represent reminders of the assault, such as waiting for a bus or being home alone. This list also includes flashbacks, nightmares, interactions with her advocate or the police, watching television, listening to people tell jokes, having sex, being with strangers, being with someone related to the assailant, and so on. Having filled out the worksheet the subject then has an opportunity to discuss whether any of these events have occurred for her and whether or not they triggered symptoms. Like other aspects of the psychoeducational intervention, this is an anticipatory treatment technique that enables subjects to be prepared for situations that may trigger symptoms for them.

The final element of the third PEI session focuses on the process of recovery. Although some suggestions have been made about the recovery process at the very outset of the first day, the counselor now focuses more specifically on how long it typically takes to recover, what kinds of changes the subject can expect to take place, and what kinds of things may not change for a very long time. Finally, the counselor spends some time talking about what things may actually improve over a prerape baseline. This provides her with an opportunity to discuss the fact that, for many women, the process of recovery from sexual assault gives them a greater sense of control over their lives and a more profound sense of self-esteem than they had at any point prior to the assault.

Session Four

At the outset of the final PEI session the counselor again reviews the relaxation procedures with the subject. The first new element of the final psychoeducational session focuses on disclosing the assault. It is our experience that, by this time subjects will have disclosed their experience to a number of individuals in their social network. Since some subjects may not have disclosed the assault to anyone other than the rape crisis center staff and the research staff, and some may have persons remaining in their network about whom they have questions as to whether they should disclose the assault, the counselor takes the subject through a decision-making process in which she can evaluate the risks and benefits of disclosing the assault to those who do not yet know about it.

The final element of this last psychoeducational intervention session involves explaining the concept of gradual desensitization to feared situations and connecting that technique to the relaxation training with which the psychoeducational intervention began. The counselor has already inquired about how the relaxation practice has proceeded over the intervening days. The counselor now takes the subject through the relaxation procedure in order to observe any difficulties the subject may be having with it. She then explains that, once a relaxed state has been achieved, it is possible for the subject to gradually approach areas of her life or her environment that have become anxiety-provoking since the assault. The counselor introduces the concept of a hierarchical approach to a feared situation. Using one example of a fear-producing situation from the subject's life, the counselor helps the subject break the example down into a series of hierarchical steps that might be used to approach the feared situation. The sample of hierarchy construction is done on paper so that the subject has a copy of her in-session work to take home and to use as an example for any gradual desensitization that she might attempt on her own.

For those subjects who were sexually active at the time the assault occurred, the counselor suggests that, if the subject has had difficulty in returning to her normal sexual activities, the hierarchical approach may be especially helpful. For those subjects who were not sexually active at the time of the assault, the counselor indicates that sexual activity may represent a fear-producing situation in the future. The counselor suggests that the subject keep the desensitization materials on hand so that should she experience such fears in the future, she will be able to apply a hierarchical approach to those fears.

Psychological Support (PS)

It is generally recognized that in psychological and physical therapies as well as psychoeducation, a better outcome is obtained if the intervention is presented by an individual who is supportive and encouraging toward the subject. In our own research, when rape victims were asked to identify the people to whom they turned for support after the rape, one third of the treatment decliners (assessment-only subjects) and over three quarters of the treatment acceptors indicated that their counselor was one of the people to whom they returned for postrape support and that the counselor's support was important to them in coping with the assault (West & Frank, unpublished data). Since psychological support is an element in the Psychoeducational Intervention modality as well as assessment-only modalities, in order to control for the therapeutic effects of support alone it was necessary to compare PEI subjects to a group of subjects who were assigned to Psychological Support only.

At least two major research studies that have recently been completed that have employed a psychological support modality without active psychotherapy in order to study the differential effects of imipramine, placebo, and psychotherapy in the treatment of depression. The NIMH Treatment of Depression Collaborative Research Program (Elkin, Parloff, Hadly, and Autry, 1985) and the Maintenance Therapies in Recurrent Depression Study (Frank, Kupfer, & Perel, 1989; Frank et al., in press) provided extremely useful guidelines for the development of our Psychological Support modality. In spite of the fact that these studies involved the investigation of pharmacologic as well as psychotherapeutic interventions and employed a medical model oriented toward biological disease, elements from their manuals for the nonpsychotherapy conditions (Fawcett & Epstein, 1980; Kupfer, Frank & O'Donnell, 1981) proved appropriate for our Psychological Support protocol with minor modifications.

In order to avoid any form of psychotherapy or specific rape education in the Psychological Support (PS) modality, the counselors received specific training in Psychological Support with clear instructions about the interventions that were and were not allowed based on our awareness of rape-specific issues and on the work of Fawcett and Epstein (1980) and Kupfer et al. (1981).

In the four Psychological Support sessions, the counselor focused each session on current rape-related symptoms and the subject's response to those symptoms. No specific problem areas or treatment goals were defined for the subject, but she was given support in terms of her own efforts to set goals and deal with symptoms. She was also given encouragement to expand on rape-related symptoms as they arose. When the subject perceived a symptom decrease, the clinician noted the changes and provided psychological support for the subject's ability to bring about these changes.

Fawcett and Epstein (1980), in their document entitled "Clinical Management-Imipramine-Placebo Administration Manual," describe the interpersonal processes permitted in the Clinical Management Condition, which we have used with minor revisions. These revisions are related to differences outlined previously between the two treatment approaches and theoretical orientation of the two studies employing these methods.

Conduct of the psychological support modality

1. *General Therapeutic Rapport.* The PS clinician makes every attempt to convey acceptance to the subject and to place her at ease as much as possible. It should be kept in mind that the subject's engagement with the study will rely heavily on the relationship established with the clinician.

2. *Psychological Support.* Psychological support is provided by the PS clinician throughout the course of intervention. The support may be especially necessary in the early phase of the study when the subject is likely to develop doubts that the intervention will help. If the subject mentions various interpersonal or work-related problems, support is given, keeping in mind that an improvement in rape-related symptoms will probably help the patient deal with these types of problems.

3. *Optimism and Hopefulness.* Each subject is approached by the PS counselor with the assumption that the rape-related symptoms can be lessened by use of this modality

and the subject's efforts to cope with the assault will be enhanced.

4. *Reassurance and Encouragement.* Subjects are expected to need encouragement to continue with the PS intervention and to maintain adherence to the research protocol. Crises may occur in which the subject requires even more reassurance and encouragement to continue. Unless the subject is withdrawn from the study (due to suicidal risk or other potentially dangerous behavior), she is encouraged to continue the assigned condition. It is important that the subject understand that an initial failure to improve does not lead to the assumption that improvement will not be forthcoming, and that many recent victims experience a brief period of worsening before sustained improvement begins.

5. *Enhancing Expectations of Positive Outcome.* It is particularly important that, in the first session, the subject is informed about the considerable evidence that suggests that support can be useful in reducing symptomatology and coping with rape. If necessary, this information is reviewed in subsequent sessions.

   Frequently, subjects will ask what they can do to help themselves recover from their rape-related symptoms. Short of psychotherapeutic intervention, it is possible to give simple advice to the subject, such as increased physical activity through walking, age-appropriate exercise, or the performance of physical work. Subjects may also request advice concerning certain decisions or attempts to engage in certain activities during this period. Simple advice of this type is permitted within the context of the PS framework, and the PS clinician keeps notes on any such advice.

6. *Ventilation and Abreaction.* Subjects usually want to describe their rape-related feelings in a somewhat perseverative fashion and share their experience of fears and doubts. Within the limited time context of the PS sessions, subjects should be permitted to do this to the extent that it is thought to be of help in sustaining the supportive relationship. In the context of PS, however,

detailed attempts to clarify the patient's feelings or to focus on certain aspects of these feelings, in the present or past, should be avoided.

Interpersonal processes not permitted in the PS condition:

1. *Clarification of subjects' feelings* toward others or toward the PS clinician is avoided.
2. *The interpretation of interpersonal events*, styles of interpersonal relating, suppressed feelings, or distorted cognitive sets is avoided in the PS sessions.
3. *Focusing on specific psychological themes, especially cognitive distortions.* Focusing, definition, and clarification of psychological themes in the subject's current rape-reaction and in her life is not permitted, especially as these may take the form of distorted cognitions.
4. *No behavioral instructions* or routines are permitted beyond simple advice or general advice concerning physical or general activity such as instructions that the subject should be going out more, and so on, as she shows improvement. Specific behavioral routines to practice at home or elsewhere are avoided.
5. *Psychological explanations of the behavioral or psychodynamic origins of rape-related stress* are avoided in the PS sessions with subjects. Also, interpretations relating to recent losses, secondary gain and other psychological mechanisms are avoided.
6. In general, *any involved interpersonal transaction that goes beyond support and general advice* is avoided in the PS condition in order not to overlap with the psychotherapeutic conditions.
7. *Transference and counter transference explanations*, clarifications, and/or interpretations are to be avoided.

Method

Study Design

Subjects were referred to the investigators by Allegheny County Center for Victims of Violent Crime or Pittsburgh Action Against

Rape between September 1978 and October 1988. Both of these centers provided medical and legal advocacy to those women who required it, but crisis counseling was kept to a minimum with potential research subjects until such time as they had declined participation in our research protocol. Within a week to ten days of making contact with one of these rape crisis centers, each potential subject was asked by her crisis center advocate whether she would be willing to be contacted by a counselor from a research project at the University of Pittsburgh that offered assessment and treatment to women who had experienced a sexual assault. If a potential subject agreed, she was contacted by one of the clinicians associated with the project who met with her and explained the nature of the research protocol. All participating subjects signed a consent form outlining the requirements of their participation. During the first six years of the project, women were randomly assigned to either Cognitive Behavior Therapy (CBT) or Systematic Desensitization (SD). In the latter part of the research program, women were randomly assigned to either Psychoeducational Intervention (PEI) or Psychological Support (PS) modalities.

Assessment Measures

Over the course of our ten years of research, we came to conceptualize postrape symptomatology as a variant of post-traumatic stress disorder. This shift was reflected in changes in both the treatment protocols we carried out and in the assessment measures we employed. However, two assessment measures remained constant over the course of this program of research: the Beck Depression Inventory (Beck, Ward, Mendelsohn, Mock, & Erbaugh, 1961), a twenty-one-item self-report measure of depressive symptoms, and a modified version of the Veronen–Kilpatrick Fear Survey Schedule (Kilpatrick et al., 1979b), a 120-item self-report inventory of general and rape-related fears. In addition, biographic and psychiatric history data along with information on the assault incident were gathered using the Demographic, Assault, and Psychiatric History Interview Schedule (DAPHIS), a structured interview guide designed by project staff.

Subjects

Of the approximately 532 referrals from rape crisis centers to whom the study was presented, 51.3 percent agreed to participation. Although psychological assessment data could not be obtained on nonparticipants, none of their demographic characteristics and none of the variables characterizing their rape experiences differed significantly from those of the subjects who agreed to enter the study.

Since the present chapter concentrates on the efficacy of the four treatment interventions, demographic, rape situational, and psychiatric history variables are examined among the four groups. These

Table 5-1

DEMOGRAPHIC CHARACTERISTICS OF CBT–SD TREATMENT COMPLETERS AND PEI–PS TREATMENT COMPLETERS

	CBT–SD Treatment Completers (n=60)	PEI-PS treatment completers (n=88)
Age (in years)	23.3 ± 7.4	25.4 ± 9.0
	%	%
Race		
Caucasian	81.4	69.0
African-American	18.6	31.0
Religion		
Roman Catholic	40.4	51.2
Protestant	42.1	26.7
Other	17.5	22.1
Education		
High school or less	49.2	44.8
Post high school	50.8	55.2
Marital status		
Single	84.8	86.2
Married	15.2	13.8
Living arrangements		
Parents	45.0	37.9
Mate[a]	13.3	10.3
Roommate	6.7	10.3
Alone	12.7	18.4
Other	13.3	27.6
Annual income		
Under $10,000	33.4	32.5
$10,000–$20,000	27.1	35.0
Over $20,000	27.8	32.5
Employment status		
Unemployed	46.7	49.4
Employed	53.3	50.6

[a]Includes marital partners and other males living with subjects by consensual agreement.

variables are presented in Tables 5-1, 5-2, and 5-3, respectively. Within the two groups (CBT vs. SD and PEI vs. PS treatment completers), there were no significant differences between those subjects assigned to CBT or SD and those assigned to PEI or PS on any

Table 5-2

FREQUENCY OF SELECTED RAPE SITUATION CHARACTERISTICS FOR CBT–SD AND PEI–PS TREATMENT CENTERS

	CBT–SD Treatment Completers (n=60)	PEI–PS Treatment Completers (n=88)
	(%)	(%)
Location		
Victim's home	26.7	36.8
Vehicle	26.7	13.8
Actor's home	20.0	13.8
Street	11.7	9.2
Other	15.0	26.4
Relationship of actor to victim		
Known	50.9	58.6
Unknown	49.2	41.4
Weapon employed by actor		
Yes	41.7	34.9
No	58.3	65.1
Victim beaten or tortured		
Yes	40.0	41.9
No	60.0	58.1
Victim's life threatened		
Yes	47.5	48.2
No	52.5	51.8
Victim's family or friends threatened		
Yes	13.6	8.2
No	86.4	91.8
Victim attempted to defend self		
Yes	67.2	67.4
No	32.8	32.6
Nature of actor's approach		
Blitz[a]	40.7	56.3
Con[b]	59.3	43.7

[a]Burgess and Holmstrom (1986) define a "blitz" rape as one in which there is no preparation for the assault and no participation on the part of the victim.
[b]Burgess and Holmstrom (1986) define a "con" rape as one during which there is some enticement of the victim in which she is finally assaulted.

Table 5-3

FREQUENCIES OF SELECTED PSYCHIATRIC HISTORY CHARACTERISTICS OF
CBT–SD AND PEI–PS TREATMENT COMPLETERS

	CBT–SD Treatment Completers (*n*=60)	PEI–PS Treatment Completers (*n*=60)
	(%)	(%)
Previous psychiatric treatment		
Yes	35.0	44.8
No	65.0	55.2
Suicidal ideation		
Never	33.3	28.7
Prerape only	31.7	34.5
Postrape only	16.7	19.5
Pre- and postrape	18.3	17.2
Suicide attempts		
Never	76.7	67.8
Prerape only	20.0	27.6
Postrape only	3.3	3.4
Pre- and postrapes	0.0	1.2

demographic, psychiatric history, or rape situation variable. The two cohorts of treatments completers were generally similar in terms of demographic features, rape situation, and psychiatric history variables.

Results

In the first six years of our program of research, subjects requesting treatment were assigned to Cognitive Behavior Therapy or Systematic Desensitization (SD) on a random basis, (Frank et al., 1988). Of recent sexual assault victims (i.e., presenting within 1 month of the assault), 50 were assigned to CBT, and 49 were assigned to SD. Of those, 34 CBT subjects and 26 SD subjects completed treatment. The rate of treatment completion did not differ for the two groups. In the last four years of the research program, subjects requesting treatment were randomly assigned to Psychoeducational Intervention (PEI) or Psychological Support (PS). Of recent rape victims, 69 were assigned to PEI, and 63 were assigned to PS. Of those, 48 PEI subjects and 40 PS subjects completed treatment. The rate of treatment completion did not differ for the two groups.

Efficacy of PEI and PS Treatment Interventions

Since there were no significant differences between those subjects assigned to PEI and those assigned to PS on any demographic, psychiatric history, or rape situation variable, analyses of variance with repeated measures (i.e., initial, end-of-treatment) were computed separately for each self-report measure. Analysis of depression and fear scores showed significant differences across assessment periods [$F(1,71)=65.48$, $p< .0001$; $F(1,77)=42.12$, $p< .0001$] for each measure respectively (see Table 5-4).

There were no significant differences between those subjects who received PEI and those who received PS, nor were there any significant treatment modality x assessment period interactions, suggesting that both treatment interventions were associated with comparable levels of symptom reduction.

We then examined whether these treatment gains remained at three months, since there is a notion in the literature that rape-related target symptoms are not stable until three months postrape. Once again, analysis of depression and fear scores showed significant differences across assessment periods [$F(1,55)=75.00$, $p<.0001$; $F(1,62)=61.05$, $p<.0001$] for each measure respectively. There were no significant differences between those subjects who received PEI and those who received PS, nor were there any significant treatment modality x assessment period interactions, again suggesting that both treatment interventions were associated with comparable levels of symptom reduction at the three month assessment point.

Finally, using a cross-sectional approach, we examined follow-up scores on depression and fear at six months and at one year post assault. There were no significant differences between the two groups on either of these measures at either time point (see Table 5-4).

Efficacy of "Short-Term Therapy" Versus "Brief Intervention" Protocols

As we pointed out earlier, recent victims who were randomly assigned to either Cognitive Behavior Therapy (CBT) or Systematic Desensitization (SD), although showing highly significant pre–post improvement, did not evidence any significant differences in the extent of that improvement. We were also unable to demonstrate any significant differences between the Psychoeducational Intervention and Psychological Support modality in terms of levels of improvement. We thus became interested in the question of whether more intensive treatments like CBT or SD were associated with better functioning at three months, six months, or one year than were the brief interventions represented in PEI and PS.

As noted, there were no differences between the two treatment modalities within each protocol with respect to demographic, rape situation, or psychiatric history variables, nor were there any differences in initial or end-of-treatment symptomatology. Therefore, we combined CBT and SD subjects together to form the "short-term therapy" group, and PEI and PS subjects were combined to form the "brief intervention" group. Analyses of variance with repeated measures were computed separately for the self-report measures of depression and fear. Analyses of the depression and fear scores showed significant differences across the baseline and assessment periods [$F(1,115)=185.33$, $p<.0001$; $F(1,121=137.25)$, $p<.0001$)] for each measure respectively (see Table 5-5). There were no significant differences between those subjects who were members of the short-term therapy versus the brief intervention protocol, nor were there any significant Treatment Protocol x Assessment Period interactions, suggesting that both treatment protocols were associated with comparable levels of symptom reduction.

Table 5-4
ASSESSMENT SCORES FOR "SHORT-TERM" AND "BRIEF" PROTOCOL SUBJECTS

	"Short-Term" Treatment (n=60)		"Brief" Treatment (n=88)	
Initial Assessment				
Beck Depression Inventory	20.2	(10.0)	20.7	(10.1)
Modified Fear Survey	309.1	(71.2)	308.7	(84.9)
Three-Month Assessment				
Beck Depression Inventory	7.0	(6.1)	10.1	(9.8)
Modified Fear Survey	229.4	(71.2)	233.6	(79.7)
Six-Month Assessment				
Beck Depression Inventory	7.8	(9.6)	11.5	(10.8)
Modified Fear Survey	222.3	(75.8)	236.6	(86.5)
One-Year Assessment				
Beck Depression Inventory	6.1	(7.0)	8.5	(8.8)
Modified Fear Survey	203.8	(63.3)	212.7	(78.7)

Table 5-5

ASSESSMENT SCORES FOR SUBJECTS ASSIGNED TO PSYCHOEDUCATIONAL INTERVENTION AND PSYCHOLOGICAL SUPPORT

	PEI (n=49)		PS (n=39)	
Initial Assessment				
Beck Depression Inventory	19.4	(10.1)	22.1	(10.0)
Modified Fear Survey	306.2	(87.0)	312.0	(83.1)
Post Treatment				
Beck Depression Inventory	11.5	(6.1)	13.4	(9.8)
Modified Fear Survey	261.3	(93.6)	261.6	(93.4)
Three-Month Assessment				
Beck Depression Inventory	10.7	(9.2)	9.4	(10.7)
Modified Fear Survey	237.2	(76.5)	229.0	(84.7)
Six-Month Assessment				
Beck Depression Inventory	11.3	(10.9)	11.8	(10.9)
Modified Fear Survey	240.4	(63.3)	231.1	(87.4)
One-Year Assessment				
Beck Depression Inventory	9.2	(7.9)	7.9	(9.7)
Modified Fear Survey	213.0	(71.2)	211.8	(88.0)

Finally, using a cross-sectional approach because of subject attrition, we examined follow-up scores on depression and fear at six months and one year post assault. There were no significant differences between the two groups on either of these measures at either time point.

Clinical Significance of Depressive Symptomatology

Since the literature has suggested that depression is not an incidental phenomenon within a population of recent rape victims (Atkeson et al., 1982; Frank, Turner, & Stewart, 1979; Frank & Stewart, 1984a), and since the consequences of major depressive disorder have the potential to be even greater than those of debilitating fear and anxiety (which typically do not lead to attempted or completed suicide), we have continued to pursue our interest in depressive symptomatology. In order to assess the extent to which improvement observed in our research subjects could be considered clinically significant, we examined the number of treated subjects in each protocol who fell into two severity categories on the Beck Depression Inventory: (1) nondepressed group (i.e., subjects having a total score less than 16) and (2) depressed group (i.e., subjects having a total score of 16, or greater) at each assessment point.

There were no differences between treatment modalities for each protocol at any assessment point, suggesting that PEI was as effective as PS and CBT was as effective as SD in reducing depressive symptomatology. The following analyses then compared the two protocols with treatment modalities combined.

There were no significant differences between the two protocols with respect to the number of subjects who aggregated in each of these two groups at initial assessment as indicted by chi-square analyses (see Table 5-6). At the three-month assessment, however, the two groups of treatment completers were statistically different from each other $(X^2(1) = 6.273, p=.01)$. Only 10 percent of the CBT–SD treated subjects were still moderately to severely depressed, whereas 28 percent of the PEI–PS treated subjects fell within that depressed category. There was a trend for this same pattern of results at six months post assault (14 percent of CBT–SD subjects vs. 28 percent of PEI–PS subjects); $X^2(1)=2.813, p=.09$. There were no significant differences between the two groups at the one-year assessment period.

Table 5-6

PERCENTAGES AND NONDEPRESSED SUBJECTS

	"Short-Term" Treatment	"Brief" Treatment
Initial Assessment	56.7%	62.8%
Depressed	43.3	37.2
Three-Month Assessment*		
Depressed	10.0	27.9
Nondepressed	90.0	72.1
Six-Month Assessment**		
Depressed	14.3	28.6
Nondepressed	84.7	71.4
One-year assessment		
Depressed	10.0	21.1
Nondepressed	90.0	78.9

*$p<.01$; **$p<.09$

Discussion

The present study is limited, as are all studies of posttraumatic symptomatology, by our lack of information about the symptom status of subjects immediately prior to the traumatic event. This state of affairs, coupled with the notion that clinically and statistically significant improvement of most rape-related symptoms occurs spontaneously in the two to three months following an assault, has important implications for treatment efficacy studies. As Kilpatrick and Calhoun (1988) have pointed out, one such implication for treatment studies implemented during this time period is the necessity of including a no-treatment control group. Since we (Frank et al., 1988) have maintained that to randomly assign subjects referred to us from rape crisis centers to a no-treatment or waiting-list control group is ethically indefensible, we could not demonstrate, on the basis of our original protocol data, that Cognitive Behavior Therapy or Systematic Desensitization are superior to no intervention. Taking note of this limitation in the more recent protocol, we compared an active rape-specific intervention, Psychoeducational Intervention, against a "placebo" condition, Psychological Support. This placebo intervention was modeled after placebo conditions used in other controlled treatment trials. That is, a placebo has the shape of the active treatment, it takes place in the same environment as the active treatment, it is offered along with the same level of psychological support as the active treatment, and it is associated with the same positive expectations on the part of its recipient as the active treatment, but it lacks other characteristics of the active treatment. We believe that such a placebo allowed us to control for the effects of a supportive environment and positive expectations on the part of subjects in assessing the efficacy of the other intervention being studied as well as being ethically defensible. However, we were unable to demonstrate the efficacy of the active intervention. In addition, we could not demonstrate any significant differences between the two protocols (i.e., short-term therapy vs. brief intervention) with respect to mean levels of symptomatology, suggesting that both protocols were associated with significant pre–post changes as well as with comparable levels of symptom reduction for many recent rape victims. However, it appears that the percentage of subjects who are still depressed at three months is greater in the brief-treatment protocol than in the short-term therapy protocol. This clinical approach suggests that focusing on mean levels of symptomatology, especially with respect to depressive symptomatology, may mask a subgroup of women for whom more intensive intervention is indicated. These findings are in some respects comparable to the outcome of the National Institute of Mental Health Treatment of Depression Collaborative Research Program (TDCRP), after which our placebo condition was modeled (Elkin, Shea, Watkins, et al., 1989). This was a multisite collaborative study that investigated the effectiveness of cognitive therapy and interpersonal therapy, for the treatment of outpatients with major depressive disorder. Two hundred and fifty patients were randomly assigned to one of four sixteen-week treatment conditions: interpersonal therapy, cognitive behavior therapy, imipramine hydrochloride plus clinical management, or placebo plus clinical management. Their results indicated that subjects in all treatment conditions showed a significant reduction in depressive symptoms and improvement in functioning. They were also unable to demonstrate any evidence of greater effectiveness of either of the psychotherapies compared to each other, nor was there any evidence that either of the psychotherapies was significantly less effective than the imipramine condition, at termination from treatment. However, when the sample was dichotomized on initial level of severity of depressive symptoms and impairment in functioning, significant differences among treatments were present only for the subgroup of patients who were more severely depressed and functionally impaired. The findings suggested some evidence for the effectiveness of interpersonal psychotherapy for this group and strong evidence of the effectiveness of imipramine plus clinical management. In contrast, there were no significant differences among the three active interventions or the placebo condition for the less severely depressed and functionally impaired group.

For the most part it appears, then, that the minimum requirements of a supportive therapeutic environment are associated with comparable levels of symptom reduction in recent rape victims as with more active interventions. Such a negative finding, in terms of the lack of significant treatment differences, has practical implications for those individuals, usually rape crisis workers, who typically are the first individuals to offer psychological support to recent rape victims. First, the basic principles of psychological support can be readily implemented by crisis support workers. Second, depending on the specific needs of rape victims, elements of the psychoeducational intervention modality can be implemented accordingly.

However, we remain disinclined to suggest that active treatment interventions do not have a role in the treatment of rape victims. First of all, we see the victim's reactions as the outcome of a complex set of interactions. These involve: (1) what the victim brings to the assault (including her past psychiatric history, her personal coping style, and her social network); (2) the nature of the assault itself; (3) the dynamic relationship between the nature of the assault and both her coping style and her network's postrape response (both of which may be affected by the nature of the assault); (4) the global traumatic reaction that follows an assault; (5) the extent to which that global reaction creates permanent or relatively permanent changes in the victim's life and in her behavior; and, finally, (6) the effect of any interventions employed on both the global reaction and on the stress associated with any major life changes that may have resulted from that reaction. In this model the individual with a history of good psychological functioning, an adaptive coping style, and a social network that is supportive in its postrape response, who experiences a rape in which brutality and fear for loss of life are minimal, might be expected to experience a relatively mild and short-lived initial reaction from which she is able to recover without active treatment intervention, without the development of serious secondary life disruptions (moving, job loss, etc.), and, perhaps, with minimal or absent development of the typical intermediate and long-term reactions. On the other hand, the individual with a history of recurrent depressions, a nonadaptive coping style, and/or a social network that is unsupportive in its postrape response, who then has an assault experience in which she is conned into letting "workmen" enter her apartment and is then raped by several assailants, would be expected to show a severe short-term reaction. This global traumatic reaction renders her unable to concentrate and fearful of remaining in her apartment for even brief periods of time. In all likelihood, this individual would lose her job, choose to change her residence, and develop a serious intermediate reaction (primarily depressive symptoms and sexual dysfunction). Neither her level of employment nor the nature of her residence return to prerape levels. Even if traditional treatment is instituted, and certainly if it is not, according to the model, this individual would continue to show symptoms of the long-term reaction described by Ellis (1983), particularly diminished capacity to enjoy life and continued sexual difficulties.

This model is one of a complex disequilibrium and requires a multifaceted approach if one is to arrive at conclusions that could ultimately lead to reducing the short- and long-term distress associated with rape experience. In addition, the model suggests that active treatment may be beneficial if initiated early for some rape victims. For other women who either present later or for whom the symptoms do not dissipate over time even with early intervention, it suggests that later treatment can facilitate the recovery process. Thus the question regarding the role of early treatment may not be "Does treatment work?" Possibly, a more productive question is "Is it possible to identify good and poor treatment responders and do they respond differently to different types of treatment?" (Kilpatrick & Calhoun, 1988).

In some respects, it is the late-treatment seekers we have studied who provide the best evidence for the efficacy of short-term therapy with rape victims (Frank et al., 1988). Their initial scores on both self-report and interview measures suggested that they were experiencing a trauma syndrome at least as severe as that evidenced by the early-treatment seekers. In fact, their self-report scores indicated significantly higher levels of symptomatology than those reported by the early-treatment seekers even though, on average, they entered the treatment protocol four months later. However, when offered the same systematic behavioral treatments, these subjects showed similar symptom reduction over a comparable time period on all measures, as well as comparable improvement in social adjustment. The late-treatment seekers, like the assessment-only subjects studied by Kilpatrick et al. (1979b) and Atkeson et al. (1982), cannot be considered an experimental control for the early-treatment seekers. Any comparisons made between the two groups must be viewed in the light of a quasi-experimental design and interpreted with caution. The late-treatment seekers do, however, clearly represent a subgroup of rape victims whose symptoms have stabilized at a very high level. Their improvement in either CBT or SD was both statistically and clinically significant, suggesting that these short-term behavior therapies are effective treatments for rape trauma.

Finally, Koss and Burkhart (1988) have suggested that interventions administered immediately post assault may be too early and too brief to facilitate the therapeutic process of rape resolution for some rape victims. They point out that many women do not seek professional psychotherapy until many months or years after the assault; however, few empirical studies are available to describe reactions beyond the one-year period. Thus, it may be that the primary role of both clinicians and researchers in the treatment of rape victims is the identification and management of chronic, post traumatic responses to a nonrecent assault.

It has been well documented that a pattern of psychological responses, rape trauma syndrome, can occur in the aftermath of sexual assault. It is still an empirical question as to whether active treatment interventions facilitate the process of recovery, especially in the period immediately post assault. Comprehensive and integrative models should be a goal of future research, so that it is possible to distinguish individuals who would benefit from early treatment, to assess the differential severity of the rape trauma symptoms over the course of the recovery period, and to ascertain those factors related to etiology, prognosis, or treatment of rape trauma syndrome. Such an integrated approach is essential for enhancing our understanding of the psychological sequelae of sexual assault so that the needs of the victims can be addressed effectively and efficiently.

References

Atkeson, B.M., K.S. Calhoun, P.A. Resick, and E.M. Ellis. 1982. Victims of rape: Repeated assessment of depressive symptoms. *Journal of Consulting and Clinical Psychology* 50(1):96–102.

Beck, A.T., C.H. Ward, M. Mendelsohn, J. Mock, and J. Erbaugh. 1961. An inventory for measuring depression. *Archives of General Psychiatry* 4: 561–71.

Burgess, A.W., and L.L. Holmstrom. 1974a. Rape trauma syndrome. *American Journal of Psychiatry* 131:981–86.

———. 1986. *Rape: Crisis and Recovery.* West Newton, MA: Awab, Inc.

Calhoun, K.S., B.M. Atkeson, and P.A. Resick. 1982. A longitudinal examination of fear reaction in victims of rape. *Journal of Counseling Psychology* 29: 655–61.

Coates, D., and T. Winston. 1983. Counteracting the deviance of depression: Peer support groups for victims. *Journal of Social Issues* 39(2):169–194.

Elkin, I., M.B. Parloff, S.W. Hadley, and J.H. Autry. 1985. NIMH Treatment of Depression Collaborative Research Program: Background and research plan. *Archives of General Psychiatry* 42:305–16.

Elkin, I., M.T. Shea, J.T. Watkins, S.D. Imber, S.M. Sotsky, J.F. Collins, D.R. Glass, P.A. Pilkonis, W.R. Leber, J.P. Docherty, S.J. Fiester, and M.B. Parloff. 1989. NIMH Treatment of Depression Collaborative Research Program: General effectiveness of treatments. *Archives of General Psychiatry* 46:971–82.

Ellis, E.M. 1983. A review of empirical rape research: Victim reactions and response to treatment. *Clinical Psychology Review* 3, 473–90.

Ellis, E.M., B.M. Atkeson, and K.S. Calhoun. 1981. An assessment of the long-term reaction to rape. *Journal of Abnormal Psychology* 90(3):263–266.

Fawcett, J., and P. Epstein. 1980. *Clinical management—imipramine—placebo administration manual.* Unpublished manuscript. NIMH Psychotherapy of Depression Collaborative Research Program.

Forman, B.D. 1983. Assessing the impact of rape and its significance in psychotherapy. *Psychotherapy: Theory, Research and Practice* 20:595–19.

Frank, E., B. Anderson, B.D. Stewart, C. Dancu, C. Hughes, and D. West. 1988. Efficacy of cognitive behavior therapy and systematic desensitization in the treatment of rape trauma. *Behavior Therapy* 19:403–20.

Frank, E., D.J. Kupfer, and D.M. Perel. 1989. Early recurrence in unipolar depression. *Archives of General Psychiatry,* 46, 397–400.

Frank, E., D.J. Kupfer, and D.M. Perel, C.L. Cornes, D.Jarrett, A. Mallinger, M. Thase, A.B. McEachran, and V.J. Grochoanski. (In press). Three year outcome for maintenance therapies in recurrent depression. *Archives of General Psychiatry.*

Frank, E., and Stewart, B.D. 1984. Depressive symptoms in rape victims: A revisit. *Journal of Affective Disorders* 7:77–85.

———. 1984. Physical aggression against women: Treating the victims. In B.A. Blechman (ed.), *Behavior Modification with Women,* (pp. 245–72) New York: Guilford Press.

———. 1982. The treatment of depressed rape victims: An approach to stress-induced symptomatology. In P. Clayton (ed.), *Treatment of Depression: Old Controversies and New Approaches,* pp. 309–30. New York: Raven Press.

———. 1983. Treating depression in victims of rape. *The Clinical Psychologist* 36(4):95–98.

Frank, E., S. Turner, and B. Duffy. 1979. Depressive symptoms in rape victims. *Journal of Affective Disorders* 1(4):269–77.

Frank, E., S. Turner, and B.D. Stewart. 1980. Initial response to rape: The impact of factors within the rape situation. *Journal of Behavioral Assessment* 2(1):39–53.

Jacobson, E. 1970. *Modern Treatment of Tense Patients.* Springfield: Charles C. Thomas Press.

———. 1983. *Progressive Relaxation.* Chicago: University of Chicago Press.

Kilpatrick, D.G. 1984. *Treatment of fear and anxiety in victims of rape.* National Center for the Prevention and Control of Rape, NIMH, Final Report Grant No. MH29602.

Kilpatrick, D.G., and K.S. Calhoun. 1988. Early behavioral treatment for rape trauma: Efficacy or artifact? *Behavior Therapy* 19(3):421–27.

Kilpatrick, D.G., L. Veronen, and P.A. Resick. 1979a. Assessment of the aftermath of rape: Changing patterns of fear. *Journal of Behavioral Assessment* 88:101–05.

————. 1979b. The aftermath of rape: Recent empirical findings. *American Journal of Orthopsychiatry* 49:658–69.

Koss, M.P., and B.R. Burkhart. 1988. A Conceptual analysis of rape vistimization. *Psychology of Women Quarterly* 13:27–40

Kupfer, D.J., and E. Frank, and S. O'Donnell. 1981. Medication Clinic Manual (unpublished manual).

Queen's Bench Foundation. 1975. *Rape Victimization Study*. San Francisco: Queen's Bench Foundation.

Resick, P.A. K.S. Calhoun, B.M. Atkeson, and E.M. Ellis. 1981. Social adjustment in victims of sexual assault. *Journal of Consulting and Clinical Psychology* 49(5):705–12.

Stewart, B.D., C. Hughes, E. Frank, B. Anderson, K. Kendall, and D. West, 1987. The aftermath of rape: Profiles of immediate and delayed treatment seekers. *The Journal of Nervous and Mental Disease* 175(2):90–94.

Veronen, L.J., and D.G. Kilpatrick. 1980. Reported fears of rape victims: A preliminary investigation. *Behavior Modification* 4:383–96.

Chapter 6

The Social Support of Survivors of Rape: The Differences Between Rape Survivors and Survivors of Other Violent Crimes and Between Husbands, Boyfriends, and Women Friends

Timothy Baker
University of Pennsylvania

Louise Skolnik
Adelphi University

Rob Davis & Ellen Brickman
Victim Services Agency of New York City

■

This article was prepared under grant #R01Mh40352 from the National Institute of Mental Health. We gratefully acknowledge the assistance of Malcolm Gordon, Project Officer at NIMH, in formulating this project, and of Carol Cohen, Kristen Cowal, Cynthie Gordon, and Eve Pomerentz, for their role in our data collection.

■

With the publication of "The Rape Trauma Syndrome" by Burgess and Holmstrom in 1974, a major portion of the study in the field of rape turned away from the perpetrator toward the survivor and her recovery. Their work was followed and built upon by such researchers as Atkeson, Calhoun, Resick, and Ellis (1982), who focused on anxiety and depression; Kilpatrick, Veronen, and Resick (1981), who looked at classically conditioned fear responses; and Foa (in press), who focused on post-traumatic stress disorder and models of intervention. Current rape-related posttrauma studies are expanding on Horowitz's (1976) response syndrome work, applying it to the importance of intrusive imagery (Brett & Ostroff, 1985), the impact of style of rape (Silverman, Kalick, Bowie, & Ebril, 1988), the information processing of trauma (Hartman & Burgess, 1988) and the convergence of psychological and biological components (van der Kolb, 1984; Kolb, 1987). Additionally, studies indicate that people worry about their safety in general, and about being raped in particular. Gordon and Riger (1989) reported that fear of rape was central to the day-to-day concerns of about one-third of the women studied.

One of the areas that has been identified as important to the recovery of the rape survivor has been the support she receives from others. In her report to the American Psychiatric Association, Elaine Hilberman (1976) noted, "Rape is a crisis for the significant other family members and friends, who also need emotional support.... The victim's social network must be sensitized to the meaning of the rape so that they are able to give honest support to the victim." Failure to receive this needed support can result in what Symonds (1980) referred to as the "second injury" to the survivors. According to Warner (1980), 50 to 80 percent of raped women separated from their husbands and boyfriends following the attack.

In the early work, "Crisis Intervention with Victims of Rape," Sutherland-Fox and Scherl (1972) made special note of the fact that the survivor's anxiety usually diminished significantly after she had talked with a relative or friend about the assault. In "Rape: The Husband's and Boyfriend's Initial Reaction," Burgess and Holmstrom (1979) reported two main components of the man's reaction; (1) his own response to the rape—his feeling of being personally victimized that often led to his wanting to go after the assailant, and "if only" feelings; and (2) his interaction with the raped women—whether the couple could discuss the rape, how they dealt with the woman's new phobias, and the resumption of sexual relations.

Both experimental work and empirical and clinical "real-world" findings have demonstrated that people do not always respond to crime victims in universally positive ways. Symonds (1980) notes the reluctance of society to accept the innocence of the crime victim. This reluctance has been explained by Lerner and Miller (1978) in terms of the observer's need to maintain a belief in a just world, where innocent people are not randomly victimized.

Most of the knowledge about negative supportive reactions to survivors of rape and sexual assault is derived from clinical impressions, rather than empirical research. These clinical impressions consistently suggest that rape survivors often encounter a great deal of negative, as well as positive, behavior from those closest to them—romantic partners, family members and close friends (Holmstrom & Burgess, 1979; McCahill, Meyer, & Fischman, Foley, 1979; 1985). Significant others may become withdrawn or may criticize the victim (Holmstrom & Burgess, 1979); may blame her for the rape (Stone, 1980; White & Rollins, 1981); may distress her by their focus on their own anger and desire for revenge (Burgess & Holmstrom, 1979; Emm & McKenry, 1988); may obsess over the details of the sexual activity involved (Emm & McKenry, 1988); and may discourage her from discussing the rape (Burge, 1983). The most striking aspect of all of these responses is that they represent not merely a lack of supportiveness, but a type of active negative support.

One of the areas tested in previous studies is the effect of the sex of the observer on attributions about rape. Some studies have found no effect (Acock & Ireland, 1983; Jones & Aronson, 1973; Selby, Calhoun & Brock, 1977; Thornton, 1977; Krahe, 1988). Others, however, have found that males attribute more responsibility, blame or fault to rape survivors for their plight than do females (Cann, Calhoun, & Selby, 1979; Deitz, Littlman, & Bentley, 1984; Krulewitz, Nash, & Payne, 1977; Thorton, Robbins & Johnson, 1981). Thus, where sex differences are observed, they are consistently in the direction of more survivor-blaming by males.

The support of significant others has also been included as part of the work of several other authors as noted at the end of the reference section. In addition, two papers have been published thus far from the study discussed in this paper. Baker et al. (1989) have written on the fear of AIDS by survivors of rape, and Brickman (1990) has focused on social support and adjustment to criminal victimization.

Conceptual Overview

This study's theoretical frame of reference is predicated on an ecosystems model derived from General Systems Theory and related ecological concepts. General Systems Theory is predicated on the view that all entities—physical, biological, and social—comprise "a complex of elements standing in interaction" (von Bertalanffy, 1952,

p. 199). Because a system is an "organized complexity," its whole is greater than the sum of its parts, and any part is perceived contextually as different from when it is analyzed separately (Rubin, 1973, p. 211). Within a system, all of the components, or subsystems, are interconnected as are the systems and the larger entities—or suprasystems—of which the system is a part. Boundaries separate a system from the external environment (i.e., other persons, institutions, the physical environs). Thus, the rape survivor, herself a biopsychosocial system, is part of larger social systems—for example, woman and husband, woman and boyfriend, woman and friendship network. These systemic units are, themselves, part of suprasystems such as the extended family and the neighborhood.

Several General Systems Theory concepts may serve to illuminate the survivor–significant-other relationship, and the degree and nature of support afforded the survivor. One of these is the idea of the living system as an open system. The boundaries of this open system are porous, allowing it to have a dynamic exchange of energy, information, resources, and so on, with the environment (von Bertalanffy, 1968). The system's capacity for growth is directly related to the degree and nature of interchange with the environment. Rubin (1973) explains:

> The conception of the person as an open system means that it is insufficient to view the person as a self-contained person. The open system idea emphasizes that the person is in ongoing transaction with his environment. . . . Therefore. . . it is essential to the understanding of behavior to take into account the context and dynamic processes occurring in interpersonal transactions.

Open systems, therefore, receive inputs from the environment, process this material (throughput), and feed back outputs to the environment (Jancill, 1969). Thus the quality of the input from the significant other as received and processed by the survivor at a sensory, perceptual, and cognitive level will have an impact on and be reflected in thoughts, feelings, and actions (Hartman & Burgess, 1988). Similarly, the inputs regarding rape from societal institutions (the media, criminal justice system, peer group, etc.) received by the significant other may affect that person's response to the event and his or her capacity to be supportive to the survivor (Brownmiller, 1985).

Moreover, the ecological metaphor applied to human interactions implies that the relationship between the survivor and the significant other is not linear. The individual and environment are in a reciprocal, interdependent relationship in which each affects the other. Thus, the survivor and significant other each "shape, change, or otherwise influence the other over time" (Meyer, 1988, p. 278).

General Systems Theory also proposes that a moving steady state characterizes the open system. While incorporating and processing environmental inputs, and while adapting and evolving, the system is generally able to maintain its balance (von Bertalanffy, 1968). However, this state of equilibrium within disequilibrium is tenuous and can be disrupted when traumatic life events and transitions occur. Inputs are too overwhelming and dissonant to be processed and responded to in a positive, functional manner. Rape is such an event. The transition to survivor "requires the restructuring of one's life space. . . . The environment can support or interfere with life transitions, but more than that, it can itself be a source of stress. . . . Relatives, friends or neighbors may be absent, or present but unrespon- sive, so that isolation or conflict results" (Germain and Gitterman, 1980, p. 7). The transition to being a significant other of a survivor also may involve a steady state upset that will affect the capacity of the significant other to support the survivor.

Furthermore, the life transition stress and the disequilibrium engendered by the rape trauma can induce negative person-environ- ment relationships for both the survivor and the significant other in which there my be a "sense of being in jeopardy, and such negative, often disabling feelings as anxiety, guilt, rage, helplessness, despair and lowered self-esteem" (Germain & Gitterman, 1987, p. 490).

Hypotheses

The present study focuses on two key elements concerning the support that rape survivors receive from people who are significant to them:

1. Are there differences between the amount of support, both positive and negative, that the rape survivor re- ceives from her significant others as compared with survivors of other violent crimes? and

2. Are there differences between the amount of support, both positive and negative, the survivor receives from significant others dependent upon the nature of the the

relationship—that is, whether they are female friends, or husbands, or boyfriends?

It is predicted that because of the complex meaning which the crime of rape has in our society, there will be more negative responses from the significant others toward the rape survivor as compared with the survivors of other violent crimes. And too, it is predicted that because rapes is a unique crime with regard to the survivor being of one sex and the perpetrator being of another, there will be a difference regarding the amount and type of support given based on the sex of the significant other and on the nature of the relationship between the survivor and the male significant others.

Method

Subjects

The data for this paper comes from a larger study of survivors of rape conducted for the National Institute of Mental Health by Victim Services Agency of New York City and Adelphi University. Participants in the study were 233 adult (over age 18) women; 58.8 percent were survivors of rape and 41.2 percent were survivors of other violent crimes. All were interviewed within eight weeks of the crime. Although some of the survivors knew their assailants, domestic abuse cases (i.e., where the perpetrator was a family or household member or current romantic partner) were not included in the study.

The sample was predominantly (59.8 percent) black; whites and Hispanics made up 25.8 percent and 8.7 percent of the sample, respectively. A large portion of the sample was of low socioeconomic status; 49.1 percent reported an annual family income of less than $10,000; 35.7 percent received public assistance; and 53.2 percent had no more than a high school education. Research participants ranged in age from 18 to 84; the median age was 29. Thirty-four percent of the sample had a person designated as a "significant other" participate in the study; 25.3 percent of the "significant other" were male, of which 30.0 percent were husbands and 70.0 percent were boyfriends.

Materials

The portions of the research protocol that were used for the present paper were the information concerning the nature of the crime—that is, whether it was rape or another violent crime—and the nature of the relationship between the survivor and the significant other—that is, whether this other respondent was a woman friend, or husband, or a boyfriend. It should be noted that thus far the only male significant others named by survivors have been ones with whom they had a romantic relationship. The measurement of social support was taken from the Crime Impact Social Support Inventory (CISSI). The CISSI is a forty-two-item list of responses and behaviors that a significant other could display after a crime. The survivors were asked to rate the frequency of each behavior on a 5-point scale (response options were "Never," "Rarely," "Sometimes," "Frequently," and "Always," with "Never" coded as 0 and "Always" as 4. The significant others had a similar set of questions asked of them, modified to indicate that the answers were to be reflective of their own (and not the survivor's) actions. Four of the items on the scale were taken from Barrera et al.'s *Inventory of Socially Supportive Behavior* (1981), others are variations on items from that scale, and the remainder were based on the crime survivor literature and clinicians' input about reactions of significant others as reported by survivors.

The CISSI was designed for this project. Its development was guided by previous research findings and clinical knowledge suggesting that support after a crisis is not a unidimensional phenomenon, with negative supportiveness representing merely a lack of positive supportive behavior. Instead, we suggested that positive supportive behavior and negative supportive behavior are two separate dimensions, which may be simultaneously displayed by the same significant other. Thus, the CISSI included questions about both positive (e.g., "My significant other expressed interest and concern in my well-being") and negative (e.g., "My significant other indicated that I should have fought back more") behaviors. The positive subscale was computed by summing the responses on the positive questions; the negative subscale was computed by summing the responses on the negative questions. Both were divided by the number of questions in that category responded to. If the respondent did not reply to at least 80 percent of the questions, the variable was treated as missing data.

Analysis of the CISSI data appears to confirm the existence of these two dimensions. While the full forty-two-item CISSI has a reliability index (alpha) of .79, the negative and positive subscales each yield an alpha of .89, suggesting the cohesiveness of these dimensions. These finding suggest the validity of using the positive and negative subscales as separate variables.

Procedures

Survivors were recruited through outreach to Victim Services Agency clients (who had sought counseling or other services after the crime) and through letters sent by the New York City Police Department to recent survivors, informing them of the project. Once a survivor had agreed to participate, she was asked to identify a significant other whom she could ask to take part. Initially, the survivor was asked if she was in a romantic relationship, if she had told her partner about the crime, and if she felt comfortable asking the partner to participate. If she answered "no" to any of these questions, she was asked to name "someone else that you're close to, whom you turn to for support," and, if she was willing, to ask that person to participate. Survivors and significant others were interviewed separately, at agency offices in their neighborhoods.

Interviews were conducted by a female interviewer. With the exception of the standardized psychological scales, the interview was orally administered; if the subject was unable to read the scales, these, too, were orally administered. At the conclusion of the interview, which was sixty to ninety minutes long, subjects were thanked for their participation, given a stipend, and reminded that there would be two follow-up interviews later in the year.

Findings

The data from the study are reported in the subsequent tables broken into four categories:

1. positive social support as reported by the survivors;
2. positive social support as reported by the significant others;
3. negative social support as reported by the survivors; and
4. negative social support as reported by the significant others.

The mean scores for the total sample as well as for the subsamples divided by the two types of crime (rape and other violent crimes) and the three types of relationship (husband, boyfriend, and female friend) are presented at the top of each table.

To test the two hypotheses presented above, four three-way analyses of variance were run for the positive and for the negative CISSI, each as reported by survivor and by the significant other. In each, the CISSI score is the dependent variable, and the type of crime and the type of relationship are the independent variables. There were significant differences found between the three relationship type groups and the two type of crime groups based on age. The F score of the differences between the three relationship groups and age was 6.721, significant at the .001 level. It was 63.193 for the differences between the rape and the other violent crime groups, significant at beyond the .001 level. The variable of age was, therefore, included as a covariate in the analysis.

The mean total score of the positive items on the Social Support Inventory as reported by the survivor are shown in Table 6-1, along with those scores for the several groups divided by type of crime and type of relationship.

Overall, survivors of both rape and other violent crimes reported that they experienced positive responses from their significant other about midway between "sometimes" and "frequently" (M=2.40). This

Table 6-1

Mean Positive Social Support Score
as Reported by the Survivor

	Husband	Boyfriend	Female	Total
Rape	2.08	2.67	2.32	2.36
Other crime	3.00	2.77	2.34	2.45
Total	2.54	2.72	2.33	2.40

Anova Results of Positive Social Support Scores
as Reported by the Survivor

	F	Sig. of F
Covariate		
Age of victims	.067	.796
Main effects		
Type of crime	.087	.769
Type of relationship	1.306	.277
Two-Way interactions		
Crime and relationship	.647	.527

Table 6-2

MEAN POSITIVE SOCIAL SUPPORT SCORE AS REPORTED BY THE SIGNIFICANT OTHER

	Husband	Boyfriend	Female	Total
Rape	2.80	2.84	2.81	2.81
Other crime	2.23	2.85	2.48	2.56
Total	2.61	2.84	2.70	2.72

ANOVA RESULTS OF POSITIVE SOCIAL SUPPORT SCORES AS REPORTED BY THE SIGNIFICANT OTHER

	F	Sig. of F
Covariate		
Age of the SO	.375	.542
Main effects		
Type of crime	2.553	.115
Type of relationship	.550	.579
Two-way interactions		
Crime and relationship	.500	.609

ran from a low of 2.08 from husbands of rape survivors to 3.00 from husbands of other crime survivors.

Table 6-2 presents the mean scores on the positive items on the CISSI as reported by the significant other.

The significant others generally felt that they exhibited positive responses more than the survivors did. Whereas the survivors reported a mean rate of 2.40, the significant others reported a mean rate of 2.72. The rates went from 2.23 for the husbands of survivors of other crimes to a rate of 2.85 for the boyfriends of survivors of other crimes. It might be noted that not only was there a much lower range of scores for the significant others as compared with those of the survivors, but the positive responses of husbands of the survivors of other violent crimes was lower when reported by the husbands as compared with those reported by the survivor.

As can be noted in Tables 6-1 and 6-2, there is no significant difference concerning either type of crime or type of relationship on the Positive Social Support Inventory as reported by the survivor or the significant other. The same is not true with regard to negative social support, particularly with regard to the reports of the significant other.

Tables 6-3 and 6-4 present the mean scores on the negative CISSI items as reported by the survivor and the significant other, respectively.

Of note is the fact that the negative responses are considerably lower than those for positive responses. Also, the differences between the responses of the survivors and of the significant others is, as might be expected, in the opposite direction, with the significant others seeing themselves as less negative than the survivor. The mean score for the survivors was .75, with a low of .34 for husbands of survivors of other violent crimes to a high of 1.40 for the boyfriends of survivors of rape. As reported by the significant other, the mean score was .62, with a low of .25 and a high of 1.08 for the same groups as noted by the survivors.

As can be noted in Table 6-3, the negative support exhibited by boyfriends of survivors of rape is over one and one half times greater than those of the husbands of survivors of rape and over 75 percent greater than female friends of survivors of rape. Thus, although there

Table 6-3

**MEAN NEGATIVE SOCIAL SUPPORT SCORE
AS REPORTED BY THE SURVIVOR**

	Husband	Boyfriend	Female	Total
Rape	.52	1.40	.78	.87
Other crime	.34	.37	.66	.59
Total	.43	.93	.73	.75

**ANOVA RESULTS OF NEGATIVE SOCIAL SUPPORT SCORES
AS REPORTED BY THE SURVIVOR**

	F	Sig. of F
Covariate		
Age of victims	4.591	.035
Main effects		
Type of crime	1.516	.222
Type of relationship	.842	.435
Two-way interaction		
Crime and relationship	3.649	.031

Table 6-4

MEAN NEGATIVE SUPPORT SCORE AS REPORTED BY THE SIGNIFICANT OTHER

	Husband	Boyfriend	Female	Total
Rape	.59	1.08	.74	.78
Other crime	.25	.47	.32	.35
Total	.43	.78	.60	.62

ANOVA RESULTS OF NEGATIVE SUPPORT SCORES AS REPORTED BY THE SIGNIFICANT OTHER

	F	Sig. of F
Covariate		
Age of the SO	13.250	.001
Main effects		
Type of crime	11.328	.001
Type of relationship	1.711	.189
Two-way interaction		
Crime and relationship	4.477	.001

was no significant difference found with regard to the main effects of either the type of crime or the type of relationship, the two way interaction of type of crime and type of relationship is significant ($F=3.649$, $p=.031$).

This relationship is even stronger when the negative support scores as reported by the significant others are entered into the ANOVA (see Tables 6-3 and 6-4). Here, there is not only a highly significant two-way interaction, but the differences between the rape group and the group of survivors of other violent crimes are even greater ($F=11.328$, $p=.001$).

Discussion and Implications

In testing the hypotheses, it was found that there were no significant differences on the positive supportive measure between the rape survivors and the survivors of other violent crimes. However, the two groups were significantly different with regard to negative support. Rape survivors were found to receive considerably more negative support from their significant others than do nonrape survivors. These differences are stronger when the self-reports of the significant others are examined. This finding suggests that rape elicits stronger negative responses from significant others than do other violent crimes and is consonant with the perception of such authors as Brownmiller (1985) who have focused on the nature of this difference. That rape is a crime that has strong impact on the significant other and on the survivor-significant-other dyad is reflected in this finding. The disequilibrium in the steady states of both the survivor and the significant other has induced a life-transition stress that has upset their reciprocal, adaptive transactions. This is reflected in the mutual perception of negatively supportive behaviors on the part of the significant other. The strength of the relationship between the self-report of the significant other on this measure and the type of crime suggests that the crime has strong impact on the significant other leaving him or her with a sense of inadequacy and/or guilt. The fact that the correlation is lower when taken from the report of the survivor, herself, also suggests the possibility that her defenses may blunt the effects of the negative support that the significant other is exhibiting.

No significant differences were found in the levels of positive support with regard to the sex of the significant other or the nature of the romantic relationship (husband or boyfriend.) There were also no significant differences between the males and females on the negative supportive dimension. However, when the differences between the relationship types taken in conjunction with the type of crime were considered, significant differences appeared when looking at the measure taken from the self-reports of the significant others. As can be noted, the boyfriends of rape survivors reported almost three times more negative activities than did husbands, and almost twice as much as female friends.

This finding is both consistent with and contradictory to what was found in other research. As was referred to previously, where differences were found, men were always more negative than women. Further, according to such authors as Burgess and Holmstrom (1974) and Moss, Frank, and Anderson (1990), husbands were more negative than boyfriends. The current study's findings suggest the opposite regarding the type of romantic relationships. Here the husbands exhibited fewer negative behaviors than did female friends and indeed showed far less (rather than more) negative supports than did boyfriends. It is possible that the difference is reflective of the geographic locations of the three studies (New York as compared with

Boston and Pittsburgh) or of some other intervening variable(s) (e.g., longevity of relationship, presence or absence of children). Further clarification of this issue is necessary.

The study has implications for both treatment and further research. Most basically, it suggests that in designing clinical interventions, rape cannot be viewed as being the same as other violent crimes. Consideration must be given to its unique dimensions and responses, differences that are possibly related to cognitive and affective societal inputs (myths, fears, survivor-blaming) received by both the survivor and the significant other prior to and after the rape. Survivors of rape may be in more or in a different form of disequilibrium because of these negative, emotionally charged systemic inputs and the resulting negatively supportive outputs. Thus treatment needs to focus on the survivor and the significant other, and the transactions between the two. Assessing the significant other's perceptions of and responses to the rape might assist in comprehending the survivor's current and potential adjustment. This study suggests that the assessment should include direct contact with the significant other as well as with the survivor. In addition, the differences in the findings when the survivor is asked to report on the nature of the relationship, as compared with when the significant other is asked, suggest that it is necessary for the clinician to ask both the survivor and the significant other about this relationship.

A cognitively oriented, psychoeducational approach, one that would alter inaccurate, emotionally based inputs and promote coping, is one intervention to be considered. It might be combined with additional supportive help designed to buttress the significant other so that he or she can then support the survivor. Because the survivor and significant other are in disequilibrium related to a severe life-transition stress—that is, are in crisis—the individuals would probably be especially responsive to therapeutic interventions (Parad, 1965).

Despite the fact that this and other studies' findings regarding the differences in husbands' and boyfriends' responses require further clarification, no researcher has indicated that treatment be reserved for one romantic partner category or the other. In order to serve these significant others, research is needed to determine which relationship category (husbands or boyfriends), if any, is most vulnerable following a rape. This finding also highlights the need for the clinician to assess and treat each situation as being unique.

Other potentially contributing elements warrant examination. Is locale a significant intervening variable? What of the length of the relationship, the presence and ages of children, the living arrangement, and so on. These variables need to be examined as to their impact on adjustment and/or their serving as possible intervening variables between the type of relationship and adjustment. It may even be that one or more of these variables rather than the type of relationship accounts for the differences found in this study as compared with others.

There remain additional questions to be explored. Clinical interventions need to be tested and treatment issues looked at. Should the significant other and the survivor be treated together or separately, and at what point in the helping process? Should the significant other receive individual and/or group treatment? What therapeutic approach, if any, appears to be the most effective in this regard?

Furthermore, this study focused on male, romantic significant others. Women, however, are affectively connected with others in their life space. What of these persons responses to an impact on the survivor? Are there differences regarding the positive and negative support offered by parents, siblings, or friends, both male and female.

Viewing the survivor and significant other as systems in reciprocal interaction suggests that in treating the rape survivor as well as the significant other, the assessment process must focus on relationship dynamics as they pertain to the rape trauma. For example, do the survivor and significant other speak about the rape? When and how did the significant other learn about the rape? How have normal interactional patterns been disrupted? How do these factors relate to the levels of positive and negatively supportive behavior and the survivor's recovery?

In conclusion, this study reinforced the view that positive and negative support appear to be discrete phenomena, that rape is not the same as other violent crimes in terms of supportive responses on the part of significant others, and that boyfriends are more negatively supportive than female friends and particularly husbands. While there is a need for further research to clarify differences with the findings of previous studies and to define intervening variables, the findings of this and other studies suggest the need for clinical interventions with the significant others and for demonstration projects to test the effectiveness of these interventions.

References

Acock, A.C. and N.K. Ireland. 1983. Attributions of blame in rape cases: Impact of norm violation, gender and sex-role attitudes. *Sex Roles* 9(2):179–93.

Atkeson, B.M, K.S. Calhoun, P.A. Reisch, and E.M. Ellis. 1982. Victims of rape: repeated assessment of depression symptoms." *Journal of Consulting and Clinical Psychology* 50(1):96–102.

Baker, T., A. Burgess, E. Brickmann, and R. Davis. (1990). Rape victims' concerns about possible exposure to HIV infection. *Journal of Interpersonal Violence* 5(1):49–60.

Barrera, E. 1981. Preliminary developments of a scale of social support: Studies in college students." *American Journal of Community Psychology*, 9:435–47.

Brett, E.A. and Ostroff, R. 1985. Imagery and post-traumatic stress disorder: An overview. *American Journal of Psychiatry*, 142:417–24.

Brownmiller, S.D. 1985. *Against Our Will: Men, Women, and Rape*. New York: Simon & Schuster.

Brickman, Ellen (1990). *Social Support and Adjustment to Criminal Victimization*. Doctoral Dissertation, Columbia University.

Burge, S. 1983. Rape: Individual and family reactions. Figley and McCubbin (eds.) *Stress and Family Vol. II: Coping with Catastrophe*. New York: Brunner/Mazel.

Burgess, A.W. and L.L. Holmstrom. 1974. Rape Trauma Syndrome. *American Journal of Psychiatry* 131(3), 196–202.

———. 1979. Rape: The husband's and boyfriend's initial reaction. *The Family Coordinator* 28(2):321–30.

Cann, A., L.G. Calhoun, and J.W. Selby, 1979. Attributing responsibility to the victim of rape: influence of information regarding past sexual experience. *Human Relations* 32: 57–67.

Deitz, S.R., M. Littman, and B.J. Bentley. 1984. Attribution of responsibility for rape: the influence of observer empathy, victim resistance and victim attractiveness. *Sex Roles* 10(3–4):261–80.

Emm, D. and P.C. McKenry. 1988. Coping with victimization: The impact of rape on female durvivors, male dignificant others and parents. *Clinical Psychology Review* 3(4):473–90.

Foa, E., B. Olasov, and G. Steketee. 1987. "Treatment of rape victims." NIMH monograph series, state of the art workshop on sexual assault.

Foley, T. 1985. Family responses to rape and sexual assault. In A.W. Burgess (ed.) *Rape and Sexual Assault: A Research Handbook*. New York: Garland.

(Fox) Sutherland, S. and D.J. Scherl. 1970. Patterns of response among rape victims. *American Journal of Orthopsychiatry* 40(3):503–11.

Germain, C.B., and A. Gitterman. 1980. *The Life Model of Social Work Practice*. New York: Columbia University Press.

———. 1987. "Ecological Perspective." In *Encyclopedia of Social Work*, 18th Ed., Vol. 1, Silver Spring, MD: National Association of Social Workers, pp. 488–99.

Gordon, M.T., and S. Riger. (1989). *The Female Fear*. New York: Free Press.

Hartman, Carol R. and Ann W. Burgess. 1988. Information processing of trauma. *Journal of Interpersonal Violence* 3(4):443–57.

Hilberman, Elaine (1976). *The Rape Victim*. Washington, DC: American Psychiatric Association.

Holmstrom, L., and A. Burgess. 1979. Rape: The husband's and boyfriend's initial reactions. *The Family Coordinator* 28(2):321–30.

Horowitz, M.J. 1976. *Stress Response Syndromes*. New York: Jason Aronson.

Janchill, Sister Mary Paul. 1969. Systems concepts in casework theory and practice. *Social Casework* 50(2):74–82.

Jones, C., and E. Aronson. 1973. Attribution of responsibility to a rape victim as a function of respectability of the victim. *Journal of Personality and Social Psychology* 26:415–19.

Kilpatrick, D.G., L.J. Veronen, and C.L. Best. 1981. Effects of the rape experience. *Journal of Social Issues* 37(4):105–22.

Kolb, L.C. 1987. A neuropsychological hypothesis explaining post-traumatic stress disorders. *American Journal of Psychiatry* 144:989–95.

Krahe, B. 1988. Victim and observer characteristics as determinants of responsibility attributions to victims of rape. *Journal of Applied Social Psychology* 18(1):50–58.

Krulewitz, J., J. Nash, and E. Payne. 1977. Sex differences in attributions about rape, rapists and rape victims. Paper presented at the meeting of the American Psychological Association.

Lerner, M.J., and D.T. Miller. 1978. Just world research and the attribution process: looking back and ahead. *Psychological Bulletin* 85:1030–51.

McCahill, T.W., L.C. Meyer. and A.M. Fischman. 1979. *The Aftermath of Rape*. Lexington, MA: Heath.

Meyer, Carol H. 1988. The eco-systems perspective. In Rachelle A. Dorfman (ed.) *Paradigms of Clinical Social Work*. New York: Brunner/Mozel, pp. 275–94.

Moss, M., E. Frank, and B. Anderson. 1990. The effects of marital status and partner support on rape trauma. *American Journal of Orthopsychiatry* 60(3):379–91.

Parad, H. (ed). 1965. *Crisis Intervention: Selected Readings*. New York: Family Service Association of America.

Rubin, Gerald K., 1973. General systems theory: An organismic conception for teaching modalities of social work Intervention. *Smith College Studies in Social Work* 43(3):206–19.

Selby, J.W., L.G. Calhoun, and T.A. Brock. 1977. Sex differences in the social perception of rape victims. *Personality and Social Psychology Bulletin* 3:412–15.

Silverman, D.C., S.M. Kalick, S.I. Bowie, and S.D. Ebrile. 1988. Blitz rape and confidence rape: A typology applied to 1000 consecutive cases. *American Journal of Psychiatry* 145:1438–41.

Stone, K. 1980. *The Second Victims: Altruism and the Affective Reactions of Affiliated Males to Their Partner's Rape.* Ann Arbor, MI: University Microfilms International.

Sutherland, S. and D.J. Scherl. 1970. Crisis intervention with victims of rape. *Social Work* 17(1):37–42.

Symonds, M. 1980. The "second injury" to the victims. *Evaluation and Change* (special issue) 36–38.

Thornton, B. 1977. Effect of rape victim's attractivenss in a jury simulation. *Personality and Social Psychology Bulletin* 3:666–69.

Thornton, B., M.A. Robbins, and J.A. Johnson. 1981. Social perceptions of the rape victim's culpability: The influence of respondent's personal-environmental causal attribution tendencies. *Human Relations* 34:225–37.

van der Kolb, B.A. (ed.). 1984. *Post-Traumatic Stress Disorder: Psychological and Biological Sequelae.* Washington, DC: American Psychiatric Press.

von Bertalanffy, Ludwig. 1968. *General Systems Theory: Foundations, Development and Applications.* New York: Genge Braziller.

———. 1952. *Problems of Life.* New York: Harper Torchbooks.

White, P.N. and J.C. Rollins. 1981. Rape: A family crisis. *Family Relations* 30:103–09.

Other Rape Studies in which Support Was Included

Becker, J., G. Abel, and L. Skinner. 1979. The impact of sexual assault on the victim's sexual life. *Victimology* 4:229–235.

Feldman-Summers, S., et al. 1981. Factors related to intentions to report rape. *Journal of Social Issues* 37(4):53–70.

Ledray, L. 1980. *Impact and Treatment of Rape Victims and Their Families.* Rockville, MD: NIMH.

Libow, J.A. and D.W. Doty. 1979. An exploratory approach to self-blame and self-derogation by rape victims. *American Journal of Orthopsychiatry* 49(4):670–79.

Medea, A. and K.V. Thompson. 1974. *Against Rape.* New York: Farrar, Straus and Giroux.

Miller, W.R., A.M. Williams, and M.H. Bernstein. 1982. The effects of rape in marital and sexual adjustment. *American Journal of Family Therapy* 10(1):51–58.

Norris, I., and S. Feldman-Summers .1981. Factors related to the psychological impact of rape on the victim. *Journal of Abnormal Psychology* 90(6):562–67.

Notman, M., and C.C. Nadleson. 1980. "Psychodynamic and life-state considerations in the response to rape." In L. McCombie (ed.) *Rape Crisis Intervention Handbook.* New York: Plenum Press.

Popiel, D.A., and E.C. Susskind. 1985. The impact of rape: social support as a moderator of stress. *American Journal of Community Psychology* 13(6):645–76.

Ruch, L.O., and S.M. Chandler. 1983. Sexual assault trauma during the acute phase: an exploratory model and multivariate analysis. *Journal of Health and Social Behavior* 24:174–85.

Stone, K. 1980. *The Second Victims: Altruism and the Affective Reactions of Affiliated Males to Their Partner's Rape.* Ann Arbor, MI: University Microfilms International.

Warner, C.G. (ed). 1980. *Rape and Sexual Assault.* Germantown, MD: Aspen.

White, P.N., and J.C. Rollins. 1981. Rape: A family crisis. *Family Relations* 30:103–09.

Part 2

Victim
Populations

■

Chapter 7

Sexual Assaults on College Campuses: Peer to Peer Harassment

Arlene McCormack,
University of Lowell

Jeanne L. Azarovitz
Lisa A. Eddy
Laurinda A. Michaud
Kathryn J. Pailes
University of Lowell

■

The authors would like to thank the students who helped collect the data for this study: Thomas Allardi, Susan Bigwood, Ellen Bryant, Tim Bryant, Peter Casserly, June Evans, Gerard Frater, Michael Gogos, Lori Gourley, Thomas Healy, Kelly Logue, Kimberly Miranda, Michele Parsons, John Pignato, Lisa Robert, Daniel Sandberg, Gia Sdoia, and David Wexler.

■

Studies in the field of women and educational attainment repeatedly cite the sexual harassment of female students as an impediment to learning and achievement (Betz & Fitzgerald, 1987; Decker, 1989; Dziech & Weiner, 1984; Hornig, 1984; McCormack, 1988; Pryor, 1985; Reilly, Lott, & Gallogly, 1986). While formal definitions of what exactly constitutes sexual harassment vary to some degree, all such definitions refer to sexually oriented practices that are unwelcomed by the student. Such practices are viewed as creating an intimidating academic environment, interfering with academic performance, and/ or preventing the recipient's full and equal enjoyment of educational opportunities. According to the Council of Graduate Departments of Psychology (Council of Graduate Education, 1980), sexual harassment is defined as the use of one's authority to coerce another individual into sexual relations or to punish the other person for his or her refusal. Sexual harassment also includes any deliberate, repeated, unsolicited oral or written comment, statement, anecdote, gesture, or physical contact of a sexual nature that is offensive and unwelcomed. Using such definitions, it is estimated that between 20 and 30 percent of women students experience sexual harassment on American campuses, that between 20 and 25 percent of women are harassed by faculty members, and that 15 percent of women are raped (Carmody, 1988; Kauffman, 1988; Marhoff & Forrest, 1983).

Although most of the studies on the sexual harassment of students focus on faculty-to-student harassment, there is an increasing focus on peer-to-peer sexual harassment, including date or acquaintance rape. Such recognition is increasing as educational administrators recognize that they are morally and perhaps legally obligated to curb violence committed by one student against another. Indeed, in 1988, the American Council on Education reminded its members that courts could hold them responsible for allowing a hostile or offensive environment if they failed to establish and enforce policies against sexual harassment (Carmody, 1988; Kauffman, 1988).

Given the widespread recognition of the problem of sexual harassment on college and university campuses, and the responsibility of educational institutions for the safety of students on campus, surprisingly few actual studies have been conducted by individual institutions to determine the severity of sexual harassment on their campuses (Beauvais, 1986). The study presented in this report is designed to explore the extent, nature, and sources of sexual harassment at a northeastern university, using the definition of sexual harassment adopted by the Council of Graduate Departments in Psychology.

The Study Setting

The University is a publicly supported institution comprising five undergraduate colleges, with a faculty in excess of 500 and a student body of more than 14,000.

Research Design

Methodology

This exploratory study of the sexual harassment of students on campus was carried out by twenty-two students enrolled in the Sociology Department's Social Research Course, under the direction of the class instructor.

The sample includes 176 female undergraduate students who entered the university in September 1986 and who were still continuing their studies in September 1989. The sample was selected by way of proportional quota sampling; that is, by determining the percentage of the undergraduate female students fitting the afore-mentioned description in each of the undergraduate colleges in the university.

Prior to the summer of 1989, the university had six undergraduate colleges. That number was reduced to five with the merger of the College of Liberal Arts and the College of Pure and Applied Sciences. Few students who were members of the new College were aware of the merger at the time of data collection. Thus, to alleviate confusion during data collection, sampling was based on the former six undergraduate colleges.

According to university statistics provided by the Office of Admissions, there were 384 female undergraduates who entered the university in September 1986, and who were registered in September 1989. To increase the representativeness of the study sample, a large sample size of 176 students (46 percent) was chosen. Proportional quotas were then determined by the number of students in each college (see Table 7-1).

Table 7-1
STUDY SAMPLE QUOTAS

Female Undergraduates Entering In September 1989 (n=384)	Percent of Undergraduates	Sample Proportion (n=176)
Liberal Arts (*n*=113)	29%	51
Pure & Applied (*n*=36)	9	16
Engineering (*n*=48)	12	21
Health (*n*=83)	22	39
Music (*n*=20)	5	9
Management Science (*n*=84)	23	40

Measurement

Data were gathered using a self administered anonymous survey. The questionnaire was designed to elicit information about student demographic characteristics and experiences of sexual harassment on campus. Demographic information includes the student's college residence status, age, and current grade point average. Sexual harassment data include student experiences with such incidents, the nature of the incidents, and the sources of the incidents (see Appendix 7-A).

Nonresponse Rate

A total of 188 students who fit the study sample description were approached to take part in the study. Of those, 12 refused to participate (nonresponse rate= 6 percent). No systematic bias could be attributed to nonresponse.

Analysis

Data were analyzed via the university VAX VMS Operations System using the Statistical Package for Social Scientists (SPSSX) (SPSS, Inc., 1988). Frequency distributions were used to assess the extent, nature and source of sexual harassment on campus. Cross-tabular analysis and tests of mean difference were used to determine the relationships between experiences of sexual harassment and student demographic characteristics.

Limitations of the Study

Probability sampling was impossible due to the time constraints of this one semester seminar. Even thought large sample size and the technique of proportional quota sampling greatly increase the representativeness of samples, some caution should still be exercised in generalizations to the larger population.

The list provided by the Office of Admissions was one that excluded students who transferred into the college after September, 1986. However, a few discrepancies were found on the list; a screening question therefore was added to the study instrument to eliminate such transfer students from the study (see Appendix 7-1).

Table 7-2

Demographic Characteristics of the Study Sample

Characteristics	Number of Students In the Study	Percent Distribution
Age (X=22.4 yrs.)		
19 to 24 years	151	86%
25 to 29 years	16	09
30 to 44 years	9	05
College residence		
Commuter	84	48
Off-campus	50	28
On campus	42	24
Grade-point average (X=2.92)		
2.92 or less	85	49
Greater than 2.92	90	51

Results

Characteristics of the Study Sample

Of the 176 students in the sample, ages ranged from 19 to 44 (X=22.4; $Md.$=21.0; $s.d$=3.84). Most, 48 percent were commuters, 28 percent lived off campus, and the remaining 24 percent lived on campus. Grade point averages ranged from a low of 1.90 to a high of 3.98 (X=2.92; $Md.$=2.95; $s.d$=.46) (see Table 7-2).

Sexual Harassment at the University

Of the 176 students, 44 (25 percent) reported at least one personal experience of sexual harassment, and 70 (40 percent) were aware of another student's personal experience.

Students who experienced a personal incident were asked to indicate the sources of their experiences from a list of university community personnel. Students who experienced multiple incidents were allowed to indicate multiple sources. The sources were considered in the analysis only if a student had contact with that source. Of the 44 students who cited personal experiences, 41 indicated sources.

Sixty-eight percent of the students named other students at the University as the source of their sexual harassment, and 36 percent named faculty members. Of those students who had contact with other university personnel, 10 percent named athletic personnel, 9 percent named teaching assistants, 7 percent named residence advisors and directors, 4 percent named placement personnel, 3 percent named deans, 3 percent named health personnel, and 3 percent named the campus police.

It is interesting to note that only 15 percent of students knew the University procedure for reporting a personal incident of sexual harassment. According to the university's Affirmative Action Officer, this may have resulted because the University policy on sexual harassment does not specifically address students, and there is no specific procedure for reporting an incident other than the general Affirmative Action procedure (see Table 7-3).

The Nature of Sexual Harassment

Fifty-one students provided written descriptions of the incident (personal or other) that they considered most serious. Most (43 percent) protested treatment by male students on campus:

> . . . the men at U-Lowell are very forceful and expect too much.

Table 7-3
CHARACTERISTICS OF SEXUAL HARASSMENT FOR STUDY SAMPLE

Characteristic	Number of Students Reporting Sexual Harassment	Percent Distribution
Personal experience		
Yes	44	25%
No	133	75
Aware of experience		
Yes	70	40
No	106	60
Know reporting procedure		
Yes	26	15
No	150	85
Source of harassment (percent yes only)		
Student	27	68
Faculty member	14	36
Athletic personnel	3	10
Teaching assistant	3	9
Resident advisor/director	2	7
Placement personnel	1	4
Dean	1	3
Health personnel	1	3
Campus police	1	3

Several students mentioned repeated obscene and suggestive comments made by their male colleagues, or complained about "peeping" toms' in dorm showers, and a disturbing number (thirteen) of students described incidents of sexual assault and rape. A few of these incidents took place in the university dormitories:

> . . . two strange (students) coming into my dorm room while sleeping, and trying to get in bed with me and my roomate.

> . . . sleeping in dorm room with door unlocked—male student entered room—woke up with him on top of me trying to assault me sexually.

> . . . a freshmen was raped in her dorm room.

Student parties provide another scene for sexual assault and rape. In several of the descriptions, students mention the use of alcohol, and a few imply that their use of alcohol means that the assault was their own fault.

> . . . at a party, persuaded persistently by a male student. Alcohol was a factor on my part but also on his, I believe, and I was barely willing. And he was extremely persistent. Very unfair.

> It was at a party and everyone appeared to be drinking beer. I was also, but far from drunk. Guys would assume that because alcohol was being consumed they could get what they wanted and that girls would be willing.

> My roomate was forced into sexual activity by force. She had had too much to drink but still said 'no' to him. He forced her anyway.

> I was almost raped at a student party, but I was able to get away. I did not report the incident, because I had been drinking and did not want to be blamed.

The students also wrote about sexual assaults and rapes that occurred either on the campus grounds or in the vicinity of the campus:

. . . attempted rape outside library (North Campus).

. . . girl jogging attacked by five men.

. . . a student was walking across the bridge at North Campus and got raped.

. . . last year, late night outside of Eames and the library, held and not allowed to leave.

. . . someone was almost raped at North Campus parking lot.

Another seventeen written descriptions described experiences of harassment that students had with their teachers. Offensive comments made to them or to others about them was a popular complaint:

. . . department head makes offensive comments to women. It appears to be his "power trip." Most people think he's a nice guy but dealing with him as a female student is impossible.

. . . one teacher told his son I passed his course because: "She thought she was smart but I gave her an A because she had huge tits." I am a friend of the son and his girlfriend.

. . . harassed in class, me personally. I reported to chairman of department and received a public apology.

. . . had a prof. who didn't like women and women scientists and made it very difficult for me. I ended up reporting him and dropping the class.

Other students complained about teachers badgering them for dates and propositioning them for grades:

. . . student repeatedly asked to join a professor for dinner, movies and [was] offered gifts.

. . . said he would give me an "A" if I went out with him.

. . . a student I know was telling me how one of her professors was coming on to her, and stopping by her apartment.

. . . my grade would suffer if I didn't go out to dinner with a teacher.

Characteristics of Students
Who Experience Discrimination

In general, one in every four students experienced a personal incident of sexual harassment, regardless of academic performance or physical attractiveness. However, a comparison of students who reported harassment from peers only and those who reported harassment from faculty only indicated that certain students are more at risk from these sources. One difference is that women students likely to experience sexual harassment from other students (peers) are younger students and those who reside on campus. Women students most likely to experience sexual harassment from faculty members are older students and those who excel academically (see Table 7-4).

Discussion

This study of 176 undergraduate women who entered a northeastern university in September, 1986 indicates that one in every four women (25 percent) will have experienced an incident of sexual harassment by the time they have completed six semesters of study. Although harassment by faculty members accounted for a third of reports, and personnel in seven other areas of the university were named, most (68 percent) of the students reported other students as the source of harassment. Further, a disturbing number (25 percent) of written descriptions of sexual harassment by students mentioned sexual assaults and rapes.

Analysis of the written descriptions provided by the students showed that sexual harassment perpetrated by other students tended to describe more severe or violent forms of sexual harassment including sexual assault and rape. Sexual harassment perpetrated by faculty members and others in positions of authority tended to involve flirting, verbal comments, and propositioning for dates. This difference in the interpretation of sexual harassment is explained by Pryor (1985). According to Pryor, women judge the behavior as sexually harassing because they believe that these actions reflect hostility or insensitivity to their feelings. Only when the behavior is more severe does the student consider sexual harassment from another student. Flirting, verbal comments of a sexual nature, and pressure for dates is more unexpected and intimidating from faculty members and others in positions of authority and thus the student interprets this behavior as harassment.

Faculty-To-Student Harassment

The results indicated that "non traditional" or older students are more likely than younger students to experience sexual harassment from faculty members. This vulnerability may stem from the fact that these students tend to be closer in age to faculty members or perhaps that older students tend to excel academically when compared to younger students (given that faculty harassers also tend to be drawn to students who do well academically).

Although many accused faculty may excuse their actions as romantic intentions that were misperceived, one wonders if they are really oblivious to the intimidation that is involved in a teacher–student power relationship. If not grounded in romantic intention, perhaps it may be that certain male faculty members feel threatened by older women students who are challenging traditional societal gender roles and who are less likely to idolize them.

For nontraditional students, these negative experiences may discourage them from continuing their education, especially if they did not receive adequate support for returning to school from other sources such as family and friends. However, the study shows that younger students are by no means exempt from faculty harassment.

Table 7-4

COMPARISON OF STUDENTS HARASSED BY OTHER STUDENTS AND THOSE HARASSED BY FACULTY MEMBERS

Characteristic	Percent of Students Harassed by Students	Percent of Students Harassed by Faculty Members
Age		
Under 30 years	68%	32
30 years or over	0	100
Grade-point average		
Less than 2.92	74	26
Greater than 2.92	44	56
College residence		
Commuter	27	73
Off-campus	67	33
On campus	89	11

The younger group's vulnerability is enhanced by the fact that its members are often inexperienced, view faculty members with awe, and are likely to be flattered by an offender's initial attention.

To offset the attrition rate of female students, particularly from male-dominated fields of study such as science and engineering, faculty members must be made to understand that sexual harassment is a form of sex discrimination. If women cannot obtain their education in a friendly and nonintimidating environment, they will not enjoy equal freedom to pursue their educational interests. Women cannot legally be denied access to educational opportunities, but they can be discouraged from pursuing their goals through sexual harassment by members of college and university faculties.

Peer-to-Peer Harassment

The major finding of this study is that a disturbing number of female undergraduates reported severe sexual harassment from their fellow students. The written descriptions appear to indicate that many male students consider sexual aggression to be "normal" and acceptable behavior. Indeed, recent studies of violence on U.S. campuses demonstrate an increasing frequency of sexual assaults (Adams & Abarbanel, 1988). A recent survey of over 6,000 female students in thirty-two colleges across the country show that one in every six students reported being a victim of rape or attempted rape during the preceding year and that the majority of perpetrators were fellow students (Koss, Gidycz, & Wisniewski, 1987).

This study also suggests that few of the students reported their experiences of sexual harassment. This lack of reporting has been noted in numerous studies, particularly when the experience is one of sexual assault. As Sweet (1985) points out, 90 percent of students who are sexually assaulted fail to come forward with that information. Further, for the relatively few who do report these incidents, colleges and universities often have not equipped themselves to deal with this campus problem.

The written descriptions in this study indicate that female students' participation in student parties and the drinking behavior that accompanies these events may be a crucial factor in their not reporting incidents of sexual assault and rape. A few descriptions point to the confusion among women students in their understanding that regardless of this participation, forced sexual activity by a stranger or an acquaintance is never justified. Knowing the aggressive person or engaging in drinking behavior with this person does not make indecent assault and battery, or rape, anything more than indecent assault and battery, or rape. However, the confusion that these women express is a reflection of the stereotype that we hold in this society toward drinking behavior. The stereotype that drinking is acceptable male, but not female, behavior is still prevalent in our society. Men in our society, as well as many women, are still likely to interpret women's drinking as an "invitation for sex." Indeed, alcohol is still advertised by the media as an accompaniment to sexual activity and as something that increases sexual attractiveness. Thus, women friends, as well as men friends, are hesitant to defend a victim of harassment should that incident have occurred at a student party or any setting in which alcohol was consumed.

According to Roark (1987), young college students are particularly vulnerable to campus violence because they are under peer pressure and live in new settings away from parental supervision and among those who are experiencing new freedoms. For these students, invitations to student parties are often interpreted as pathways to popularity. This is particularly true today. While other drugs such as marijuana and cocaine have lost some popularity and appeal among college students, consuming alcohol is still considered to be "cool behavior."

And it is among these young and vulnerable women that the social and psychological effects of sexual assault are most pronounced. Such effects include anxiety about sexuality, guilt, suicidal feeling, sexual dysfunction, confusion, and fear. Further, mistrust that results from these experiences often serves as a barrier to the forming of subsequent relationships (McCormack, Janus, & Burgess, 1986).

Strategies to deal with peer-to-peer sexual harassment should parallel those instituted to deal with faculty (and others in authority)-to-student sexual harassment. Suggested strategies include a clear institutional definition and policy prohibiting sexual harassment, multiple routes for receiving complaints, a clearly defined grievance procedure, a sexual harassment committee with representation from every sector of the community, and a disciplinary board. Also included are the suggestions that access to therapy be instituted to help victims deal with their guilt and other symptomatology, that resident hall staff participate in training programs on sexual harassment, and that escort services be available to students for evening events and library study.

However, underlying the effectiveness of any strategy to combat sexual harassment on campus is administrator recognition that they are responsible for the safety of students while those students are engaging in study at their institutions. Indeed, there is increasing societal recognition of the responsibility of colleges and universities to provide a non-violent learning environment. In a review of legal cases, Adams and Abarbanel (1988) explain that courts generally have been considering the following questions in determining whether a university is liable for a sexual assault committed against a student on campus:

1. Was the assault foreseeable?
2. Are the security measures utilized by the campus reasonable under the circumstances?
3. Did the campus warn students of known dangers?
4. Did the campus meet the standards required of landlords if the student was attacked in campus housing?

It is by addressing these questions that campus personnel can ensure that they have safeguarded the student environment. Perhaps the growing pressure on administrators of colleges and universities will help those officers recognize that an unsafe environment does not lend itself to education. Without this recognition, the problem of sexual harassment of students will never go beyond the 'boys will be boys' mentality that has reigned for so many years.

References

Adams, Aileen, and Gail Abarbanel. 1988. *Sexual assault on campus: What colleges can do.* Rape Treatment Center, Santa Monica Hospital Medical Center.

Beauvais, Kathleen. 1986. Work shops to combat sexual harassment: A case study of changing attitudes. *Signs: Journal of Women in Culture and Society* 12(1):130–44.

Betz, N.E., and L.F. Fitzgerald. 1987. *The Career Psychology of Women.* New York: Academic Press.

Carmody, Deirdre. 1988. Sexual harassment on campus: A growing issue." *The New York Times* (July 5, 1988):B6.

Council of Graduate Education. 1980. Annual meeting of American Psychological Association, Toronto, Canada.

Decker, Robert H. 1989. Can schools eliminate sexual harassment? *The Education Digest* (January):59–60.

Dziech, Billie W., and Linda Weiner. 1984. *The Lecherous Professor: Sexual Harassment on Campus.* Boston: Beacon Press.

Hornig, Lilli S. 1984. Women in science & engineering: Why so few? *Technology Review* (Nov/Dec):29–34.

Kauffman, L.A. 1988. How political is the personal? *The Nation* (March 26, 1988):419–20.

Koss, Mary P., Christine A. Gidycz, and N. Wisniewski. 1987. The scope of rape: incidence and prevalence of sexual aggression in dating situations: incidence and risk factors. *Journal of Consulting and Clinical Psychology* 55(2):135–43.

Marhoff, Nancy, and Linda Forrest. 1983. Sexual harassment in higher education: An assessment study. *Journal of NAWDAC* 46 (2):3–8.

McCormack, Arlene. 1988. Sexual harassment of students by teachers: The case of students in science. In A. Burgess (ed.) *Rape and Sexual Assault II.* New York: Garland Publishing.

McCormack, Arlene, Mark-David Janus, and Ann W. Burgess. 1986. Runaway youths and sexual victimization: gender differences in an adolescent runaway population. *Child Abuse and Neglect* (10):387–95.

Pryor, John B. 1985. The lay person's understanding of sexual harassment. *Sex Roles* 13:273–78.

Reilly, Mary Ellen, Bernice Lott, and Sheila M. Gallogly. 1986. Sexual harassment of university students. *Sex Roles* 15(7/8):333–57.

Roark, Mary L. 1987. Caring enough to respond: A report from the American College Personnel Association Commission I Task Force on Victimization and Violence on Campus. *Proceedings: University Symposium on Personal Safety.* State University of New York, Albany:22–27.

SPSS, Inc. 1988. *SPSS-X User's Guide* (3d. ed.).

Sweet, Ellen. 1985. Date rape: The story of an epidemic and those who deny it. *MS/Campus Times* (October):44.

Appendix 7-1

UNDERGRADUATE STUDENT HARASSMENT SURVEY—FALL, 1989

Please, *DO NOT PUT YOUR NAME ON THE SURVEY*
I.D. # (_____)

IF YOU ARE A STUDENT WHO HAS TRANSFERRED INTO THE UNIVERSITY, PLEASE DO NOT COMPLETE THE SURVEY

The following survey is being done to assess the 'climate' of The University for undergraduate students. To ensure anonymity, after completing your survey *put it in the plain white envelope provided, seal it, and drop it into the larger manilla envelope containing other surveys.*

We appreciate your responding honestly to all questions. Thank you for your time.

PLEASE CIRCLE THE NUMBER OF THE APPROPRIATE RESPONSE TO THE FOLLOWING QUESTIONS:

1. What is your college residence status? (circle one)

    Live on campus _____ 1

Noncommuter (off-campus) _____ 2
Commuter _____ 3

2. What is your age?

_____ years old

3. What is your grade-point average?   _____

How do you see yourself compared to other students? (circle one in each row)

	YES	SOMEWHAT	NOT AT ALL
4. I am an important member of the University community.	1	2	3
5. I am physically attractive.	1	2	3
6. I am a worthwhile individual.	1	2	3

Sexual harassment is defined as the use of one's authority to coerce another individual into sexual relations or to punish the other person for his or her refusal. Sexual harassment also includes any deliberate, repeated, unsolicited oral or written comment, statement, anecdote, gesture, or physical contact of a sexual nature that is offensive and unwelcomed.

7. Do you know the University procedure for reporting a personal incident of sexual harassment? (circle one)

yes _____ 1
no _____ 2

8. Have you personally experienced an incident(s) of sexual harassment? (circle one)

yes _____ 1
no _____ 2

9. Are you aware of any incident of sexual harassment involving an undergraduate student at the University? (circle one)

yes _____ 1
no _____ 2

IF YOU HAVE NOT PERSONALLY EXPERIENCED SEXUAL HARASS-MENT, PLEASE GO TO QUESTION 25. If you have personally experienced harassment, please circle the numbers below to indicate which members of the U-Lowell community harassed you. (CIRCLE 1 IF A MEMBER OF THIS GROUP HARASSED YOU. CIRCLE 2 IF A MEMBER OF THIS GROUP DID NOT HARASS YOU. CIRCLE 3 IF YOU HAVE NOT HAD ANY INTERACTION WITH THIS GROUP.

	YES	NO	NO CONTACT
10. Faculty members	1	2	3
11. Admissions Office personnel	1	2	3

12. Residential advisors (RAs and RDs)	1	2	3
13. Financial Aid personnel	1	2	3
14. Campus police	1	2	3
15. Teaching assistants	1	2	3
16. Library personnel .	1	2	3
17. President and Vice Presidents	1	2	3
18. Athletic personnel	1	2	3
19. Deans	1	2	3
20. Counselling personnel	1	2	3
21. Media personnel	1	2	3
22. Health Services personnel	1	2	3
23. Placement personnel	1	2	3
24. Students	1	2	3
Other (please specify)	1	2	3

25. If you have personally experienced sexual harassment, please *briefly describe the most serious incident below.* If you were *not* harassed, but are aware of such incidents, please *briefly describe the most serious incident below.*

_____

_____

_____

Chapter 8

Prostitution: Buying the Right to Rape

Evelina Giobbe
WHISPER
Minneapolis, MN

■

*I would like to thank my co-worker, Denise Gamache, for contributing her
ideas and considerable editing skills to this article.*

■

Rape, or sexual assault, is commonly understood to mean the forced
compliance or submission of an individual to unwanted or coerced
sexual activity. Prostitution conversely is commonly believed to be an
equal exchange of sex for money based on mutual consent. This paper
presents a theory that the experience of being bought for sexual use is
most like marital rape—even when women give mitigated consent.
The framework of this analysis is an examination of the individual,
institutional, and cultural factors that facilitate a woman's decision to
engage in prostitution. Support for this view is drawn from existing
studies and also from the unpublished preliminary results of a research
project conducted by WHISPER in Minnesota.

Contrary to cultural mythology, the institution of prostitution most
resembles the institution of marriage rather than a form of employment. In the marketplace the relationship of worker to proprietor (or
the collective) is a legally binding contract that explicitly outlines the
exchange of labor for compensation (cash and benefits). Unlike a
labor contract, traditional marriage and prostitution are both predicated on ownership and unconditional sexual access to a woman's
body. In fact, sexual harassment laws protect laborers from this
presumption of sexual access.

Traditional marriage is premised on the long-term private owner-ship of a woman by an individual man, whereas the institution of prostitution is built upon the short-term public ownership of women by many men. Women are kept socially, sexually, and economically subordinate to individual men in marriage and to men as a class in prostitution. These systems allow males to exercise their prerogative to own and control women in both the private and public spheres. Based on the parallels between these two institutions, I argue that if the sexual act is predicated on ownership, as it was in traditional marriage, can be in modern marriage, and is vis-a-vis "rental" in prostitution, the act itself and its subsequent effects are that of rape.

Prostitution as Rape

Prostitution is like rape. It's like when I was 15 years old and I was raped. I used to experience leaving my body. I mean that's what I did when that man raped me. I looked up at the ceiling and I went to the ceiling and I numbed myself . . . because I didn't want to feel what I was feeling. I was very frightened. And while I was a prostitute I used to do that all the time. I would numb my feelings. I wouldn't even feel like I was in my body. I would actually leave my body and go somewhere else with my thoughts and with my feelings until he got off and it was over with. I don't know how else to explain it except that it felt like rape. It was rape to me.

A hypothesis that equates prostitution with rape must provide a working definition of free choice and examine a woman's "choice" to engage in prostitution within the social context in which it occurs. Choice implies the chance, right, or power to choose, usually by the free exercise of one's judgment (Webster's New World Dictionary, p. 247). To choose is to pick out by preference from what is available, to take as a choice, to select (Webster's, p. 248). In order for a choice to be made freely there must be an absence of coercion or violence. One must recognize that she has a choice, have a full range of comparable options to choose from, and have full mental capacities with which to make this choice. A freely made choice is an informed choice; one must know what she is choosing and realize the implications or consequences of the choice. Bribes, manipulation, or trickery are persuasive tactics that mitigate choice. Ideally, one would have personal or community support to actualize her choice. Minimally, one should have the right to change her mind should she realize that she has made a poor choice.

Social and Cultural Factors that Shape a Woman's "Choice" to Engage in Prostitution

The function of the institution of prostitution is to allow males unconditional sexual access to females, limited solely by their ability to pay. Culturally supported tactics of power and control facilitate the recruitment or coercion of women and children into prostitution and effectively impede their escape. The tactics are educational deprivation, job discrimination, and poverty; child sexual abuse, rape, and battery; and racism, classism, and heterosexism.

Economic necessity is one factor that facilitates the recruitment of women and girls into prostitution. In 1983, half of all poor families in the United States had a female head of household, and women comprised two-thirds of adults living below the poverty line (Sivard, 1985). Although poor women may be eligible for welfare, this system maintains women at subsistence levels and punishes them if they secure employment by proportionately reducing subsidies. Eighty percent of American women work in sex-segregated, low paying jobs, most often without the benefit of health insurance or pension plans, and notwithstanding the rare exceptions, without subsidized child care. (Morgan, 1984). Discriminatory hiring practices have systematically barred women from jobs that have been traditionally defined as "men's work" and which are well-paid, secure, and include comprehensive benefit packages. In all of these ways women are kept economically subordinate to men. By maintaining a society in which women are kept economically marginalized, the system of male supremacy ensures that a pool of women will be vulnerable to recruitment and entrapment in prostitution. But this is only one factor.

Approximately 25 percent of women in the United States are sexually assaulted before the age of 13. One in three women are raped during their lifetime, and a rape occurs every three minutes (Morgan, 1984). Additionally, it is estimated that some woman is battered by her husband or male partner every fifteen seconds (Ms, 1990). Although child sexual abuse, rape, and battery are crimes committed by individual men, an argument can be made that they are institutionalized forms of social control because of their prevalence, the fact that they differentially target females, and the failure of male-controlled social institutions to prevent or redress the victims' injuries.

Prostitution creates an environment whereby crimes against women and children become a commercial enterprise. When a "john" uses a juvenile prostitute for his own sexual gratification he is committing the crime of child sexual abuse. When he demands that a prostitute allow him to use her in sadomasochistic sex scenes, he is battering her. When a john compels a woman to submit to his sexual demands as a condition of "employment," he is guilty of both sexual harassment and rape. He is committing rape by a feminist (if not legal) definition, which differentiates between compliance and consent. The fact that a john gives money to a woman or a child for submitting to these acts does not alter the fact that he is committing child sexual abuse, rape, and battery; it merely redefines these crimes as prostitution.

Racism and classism maximize oppressive conditions that make poor women, women of color, and white ethnic women particularly vulnerable to to prostitution. Limited educational and career opportunities foster dependence on an inadequate and punitive welfare system, creating economic vulnerability. Pornographic stereotypes of poor, black, and ethnic women as well as ordinances that zone sex oriented businesses and prostitution into poor and minority neighborhoods make the women who live there especially vulnerable to harassment from both pimps and johns. Additionally, the lack of community-based services in these areas leaves women with limited resources, increasing the probability that they will not receive effective advocacy to escape abuse.

Heterosexism defines heterosexuality as the only normal form of intimacy. This view supports the male sexual imperative: the belief that men have uncontrollable sexual urges that must be fulfilled or they will be driven to rape "innocent" females. Herein lies the ultimate justification for prostitution.

All of these factors are compounded by unequal application of laws prohibiting prostitution. Only a token number of johns and even fewer pimps are arrested or convicted. By allowing men to traffic in women and children with impunity while simultaneously prosecuting prostitutes, the legal system tacitly supports sexual exploitation and, through the collection of fines, profits from it. Over all, sexism, the values and beliefs used to justify the oppression of all women in a male supremacist system, overtly and covertly supports tactics of control and, by so doing, maintains systems of prostitution in the culture.

Socially Supported Tactics of Power and Control Used by Individual Men to Compel the Acquiescence of Women Used In Prostitution

In his book *Anatomy of Power*, Galbraith identifies three forms of power that allow groups or individuals to force the submission of others to their will: coercive power, compensatory or economic power, and conditioned power. Within the institution of prostitution johns use all three forms of power to compel prostitutes to engage in unwanted sex.

The most overt form of power used by men to ensure a prostitute's compliance is compensatory or economic power. Because an exchange of money occurs between the prostitute and the john, the john is given permission to use the woman's body in any manner that he chooses. Any refusal on the woman's part can result in the withdrawal of compensation, or the john may use another form of power to enforce his wishes. His ability to do so is enforced directly and indirectly by pimps and owners of prostitution businesses to maximize their profits. Jayme Ryan (1989), a woman who had been used in the legal brothel system of Nevada, explained the house rules for prostitute/client interactions:

> When you got a customer in your room you had to perform any sex act that he wanted . . . S&M, "water sports," . . . Sometimes the men demanded that we wear costumes, other times we were filmed or photographed chained up, being whipped or being penetrated with various objects. . . . We were strictly forbidden to use condoms unless the customer asked for one as it took away from the customer's maximum pleasure. (pp. 3–4)

"House rules" were enforced by a system of fines levied against the women by the brothel. Reports of misconduct were directly relayed to pimps for disciplinary action (Ryan, 1989). The compensatory power that johns use against prostitutes must also be viewed within the broader context of women's economic subordination to men generally and the specific educational and economic limitations that shape the lives of the majority of women used in prostitution.

A john can and often does use coercive power against a prostitute by threatening, battering, or raping a woman who refuses to meet his sexual demands. It is not unusual for police to find weapons (usually guns) in the possession of men arrested for soliciting undercover agents posing as prostitutes. Customer violence against prostitutes is quickly hidden by brothel owners whose primary concerns are happy customers and maximum profits. Ryan (1989) reported:

> Once you were alone in your room with a customer you had no protection from him. There were many different occasions where a woman was brutally beaten or raped by a john, but as long as he paid the house it was kept quiet. (p. 3)

Johns benefit indirectly from the coercive power that pimps wield over women under their control. A woman whose pimp uses violence or threats to force her to earn a certain amount of money daily (a quota) is unlikely to refuse to cooperate with the sexual demands placed on her by a customer. Furthermore, because of her stigmatized status, a prostitute is most often unable successfully to obtain legal redress for a crime of violence committed against her (Levine, 1988; The New York Times, 1990). In this way, society reinforces the ability of men to use violence against prostitutes. A survivor of prostitution (WHISPER, 1988) told of her unsuccessful attempt to bring charges against a john who had raped and stabbed her:

> The police came the next day and told me that since I was a prostitute and I had records to show that I was, that they could never convict this man. I said that I gave [his] description to a "T." They sounded like they knew him, that he was a known rapist, but since I was a prostitute . . . they would just laugh at me [in court] and so instead of embarrassing me they were doing me a favor.

In spite of the relative advances of the second wave of feminism, women in western society are socialized to cultivate attractiveness, to be passive and nurturant, and to seek approval from and defer to men. Traditionally a woman's success has been measured by her relationships as opposed to her achievements. In a technological society, the media is one of the foremost transmitters of cultural norms. As such, television, films, and advertising have been especially pernicious in emphasizing women's primary value as sex objects.

The sexual objectification of women was exacerbated by Hugh Hefner's creation of the Playboy Bunny: half Barbie Doll, half geisha, with silicone-filled breasts and airbrushed waistlines, flatteringly photographed through greased lenses. Typically in their late teens and early twenties, these young women were used to set an impossible standard of attractiveness for adult women to emulate. With the explosion of "hard core" pornography onto the open market in the 1970s the definition of a woman's value as sex object expanded to include her willingness to engage in myriad "sexual acts," to which women were subjected in X-rated videos and magazines. Although pornographers claim to be sexual radicals, pornography presents the narrowest picture of the traditional female sex role. Women in pornography are passive; they are "nurturing" in their sexual ministrations to men; they appear to be seeking approval from the men for whom they are posed; they are depicted in a variety of stereotypical male fantasies; and because of pornography's implied promise of unconditional sexual availability, they are always in postures of deference to male consumers.

In a gender-stratified culture men exert conditional power over women when they use or manipulate sex role expectations in order to obtain their desires. This may happen overtly, as in the case of a husband who refuses to share child-care responsibilities because "that's a wife's job," or more subtly, as the man who shows disapproval or withholds affection from his partner because her career interferes with her attention to his self-defined needs. In both examples, female socialization that reinforces male expectations may constrain a woman from acting in her own best interest and contribute to her capitulation to his demands.

Women used in prostitution have not only been socialized in the traditional sense but may be further socialized in "hyperfeminine" roles after initial entry into prostitution. Sociologists describe this as an apprenticeship period during which the woman learns an occupational ideology that provides her with positive or neutralizing definitions that glorify prostitution and justify her participation. Positive definitions include the promise of financial success, the allegation that prostitutes contribute to the stability of marriage by performing sexual acts in which wives refuse to engage, and the myth that prostitution prevents rape. Neutralizing definitions include the justification that prostitutes are like other working women, that everyone is immoral or dishonest in some way but prostitutes are less hypocritical about it than "squares," and the idea that all male/female relationships (husband/wife, boyfriend/girlfriend) are a form of covert prostitution, that is, housewives and girlfriends get "paid" with dinners and gifts, prostitutes get their money "up-front." (Hirschi; 1962; Jackman, 1963; Bryan, 1966; Winick & Kinsie, 1971).

Sociologists explain that a prostitute learns these rationales within the "deviant subculture" of prostitution, from a pimp or john, and to a lesser extent, from other prostitutes who have learned and accepted this vocabulary of motivation. Their focus, however, is on how she internalizes these messages rather than the beneficiaries of her socialization—the men who receive economic gain or sexual gratification from the sale of her body. When the teacher of an idea also benefits through its actualization, the lesson learned is suspect.

Johns exert conditioned power over prostitutes by using and manipulating traditional sex role expectations of women as well as the particular occupational ideology of prostitution. They rigidly define and control the conditions under which prostitution occurs and strictly proscribe prostitute/customer interactions. The role of prostitute is consistent with the traditional female sex role in that it requires that the woman make herself attractive to males, that she behave passively (prostitutes stand on street corners or line-up in brothels for men to "pick"), and that she nurture and defer to men's needs and desires by complying with their sexual demands. Johns also exert conditioned power over prostitutes by reinforcing positive and neutralizing definitions of prostitution. Last, johns indirectly benefit from positive and neutralizing definitions of prostitution that are instilled in women by pimps and perpetuated in the mainstream media and pornography.

In all of these ways a woman's "choice" to engage in unwanted sexual acts for financial consideration is shaped by individual men within a social context that promotes women's social, sexual, and economic subordination to males. From this perspective then, a woman's "choice" to engage in prostitution is mitigated to the point of meaninglessness.

Long- and Short-Term Effects of Prostitution

Legally, rape is recognized as a crime with physical aspects only; namely the penetration of the vagina by the penis against the will of the victim. In effect however, the real crime is the annihilation by the man of the woman as a human being. (Statement of French woman at the International Tribunal on Crimes Against Women, in Griffin, 1979).

Studies of marital rape have revealed that women who are raped by their partners suffer many of the same physical and emotional effects as other rape victims: physical trauma, humiliation, guilt, and self-blame. In addition, they experience feelings of betrayal, isolation, and entrapment. Women describe feeling dirty and degraded, physically defiled, and used following such assaults (Finkelhor & Yllo, 1987). Furthermore, wives who are frequently sexually assaulted by their husbands suffer greater damage to their self-esteem, and are more likely to have psychosomatic symptoms and to attempt suicide (Finkelhor & Yllo, 1987).

Common long-term effects of marital rape include lingering fears, emotional pain, flashbacks and nightmares, and an aversion to intimacy and sex. Women who have been raped by their husbands have subsequent difficulty establishing intimate relationships with men; display extreme mistrust or caution; and may desire no contact with men. Their feelings about men range from disdain to hatred. In some cases it centers on "certain kinds of men," in others it generalizes to all men. These problems can keep women from having a social life or interfere with subsequent marriages (Finkelhor & Yllo, 1987).

Anecdotal information provided by women used in prostitution who have contacted WHISPER for assistance, who have attended our weekly education groups, and who participated in the WHISPER Oral History Project, have revealed a pattern of responses to the sex demanded of them in prostitution that is shockingly similar to those expressed by women who have been sexually abused and raped by their husbands.

Interestingly, marital rape victims who also suffered verbal abuse typically were called "no-good tramp" and "whore" by their husbands. Recognizing on some level that that society set aside a certain group of women for that kind of verbal and sexual abuse, one woman said, "I felt like a prostitute afterwards," and another reported, "I felt like a two-bit French whore. What I was engaged in was nothing but prostitution (Finkelhor & Yllo, 1987).

Like victims of marital rape, women typically report feeling humiliated by the acts in which they were repeatedly required to engage with multiple customers daily. Most reported feelings of degradation, defilement, and dirtiness, sometimes for years after leaving prostitution:

> *Sometimes I still feel dirty—you know that feeling*
> *when you turn a lot of tricks, and you feel like*

you've got to scrub, and no matter how much you scrub your body, it's still going to be dirty? Sometimes I still feel that way. (WHISPER, 1987)

DT: *I've felt like shit for years. Like I was dirty, nasty, not worth anything, no self-esteem, no confidence. I lost everything.* (1989)

Not unlike women who have been raped by their husbands, women escaping prostitution had subsequent difficulty establishing intimate relationships with men. These difficulties resulted in wishes to have no contact with men and expressions of extreme mistrust or caution:

MC: *I don't like them [men] as a whole. I don't want one of my very own. I'm kind of heterosexual, and I don't want a relationship right now. I don't think, I know, I will ever marry again. I doubt sincerely if I will ever live with another man again, and I have strong reservations about having a relationship with a man—a love relationship with a man. One, because I don't think much of them; two, I think it's gonna be hard to find a man that doesn't engage on some level, in trafficking in women, either through pornography, prostitution, something like that. And I just, for companionship, I like women. I like to be with women. So, it would be an extraordinary man, for me to want to have a love relationship with him. And I don't know if that exists, and to tell you the truth, at this point in my life, everything is so good, I don't want to make any compromises, just to be with some fucking guy.* (1988)

DT: *I don't trust a man as far as I could throw him. I think men are just, they're low lifes. . . . I mean, even in relationships now, you can't let your feelings get involved because all they're gonna do is use you and hurt you. That's exactly the way I feel about men.* (1989)

RP: *Having been treated so poorly for so long . . . keeps me from interacting with men, because I expect them to abuse me, I expect them to disrespect me, I expect them to come on sexually. And that is what they continue to do, even though I set boundaries. (1989)*

Like victims of marital rape, survivors of prostitution typically express disdain for men and sometimes outright hatred. In some cases their anger focuses on specific groups of men, in others it generalizes to all men:

KD: *I hate white men. . . . Because to me, you know, they're tricks, I don't think I could go with a white man. And that's because I would feel like I was turning a trick. (1989)*

RP: *[I think] that they're perpetrators, that they're abusers, that they don't understand women, that they think women are just for their purposes and that, that's about it. . . . I think they're liars, I think they're cheats, I think they don't have morals, I don't think they have values. I think 99 percent of them are fucked up, and I don't want anything to do with 99 percent of them. And the other 1 percent, I don't know much about. (1989)*

CB: *For a long time I hated all men. (1989)*

These feelings caused problems in forming new relationships:

KD: *I feel like my life is over when it comes to ever having a relationship . . . No one's ever going to want me anymore. (1989)*

EB: *I'm trying not to be involved emotionally, with anyone, so you know, there's a couple of people that I'm seeing but it's more like, it's so casual, well, they're friends, but at the same time the sex aspect of it is real casual. It's like, when they want*

> *to have sex, you know, and I don't want to push*
> *it because I feel like, if I go ask them, "Well, let's*
> *get together" and you know, I'm afraid of getting*
> *emotionally involved. So I don't want to like them*
> *too much and I don't want to get things going,*
> *push things.* (1986)

MD: *I'm afraid that the men are thinking of me as a*
sexual object. Whether they love me or not, you
know, it's a question, you know. There's lack of
trust with men now. (1987)

As in the case of marital rape, prostitution has a profound impact on a woman's sexuality:

RP: *Well, I think it's [prostitution] caused gross*
amounts of confusion, with my own sexuality—
who am I, what am I, and what do I do with it.
(1989)

Some women have fears about the physical aspects of sexual intimacy:

AD: *I am most definitely afraid to have sex. Most*
definitely. I have problems with my hips now
because I had arthritis when I was a child . . . but
I think it's gotten worse since being a prostitute,
from all the positions, and this and that. (1987)

Other women report that after years of sexual abuse and training themselves to disassociate their minds from their bodies during the sex act, it becomes difficult to reintegrate:

MD: *Well, sexually, I'm having a hard time. It's just*
something I'm going through, you know. It's hard
for me to enjoy sex anymore. (1987)

KJ: *Sex isn't something that I particularly enjoy. I*
think [prostitution] kind of like made me numb
towards sex. (1989)

MC: *I was pretty ruined. I don't think my sex life will*
ever be what it might have been, if I hadn't been

> *totally sexually assaulted every fucking conceivable way possible in my life. For a long time after I got out of prostitution, it was very difficult for me, you know, intimacy. To turn myself back on, 'cause you turn yourself off when you turn tricks.* (1988)

Women describe coping with the trauma to their sexual selves in different ways. Some women sadly accept the loss and go through the motions of sexual intimacy in order to maintain the façade of a full relationship:

> RJ: *I'll have sex with somebody if I'm like having a relationship with 'em, just because it's more expected, but. . . . As far as like orgasm, I mean, I, it's easier for me to have an orgasm by myself than it is having sex with somebody. . . . I don't have orgasms when I have sex.* (1989)

Other women engage in sex avoidance:

> KD: *I haven't had sex since I left prostitution [six and one half years ago] . . . I just feel like no one wants me. I gained a lot of weight, to protect myself, 'cause no man's going to want that woman.* (1989)

And still other women remain celibate for a period of time in order to heal from the abuse:

> AK: *I was celibate for a whole year. And I, it actually kind of helped me kind of balance.* (1987)

> CB: *I'm not celibate anymore. I've had sexual relations with my ex-husband, after nine years of nothing at all, because I couldn't see myself having sex without a bottle around . . . or without something to numb the experience.* (1989)

As in the case of marital rape, long term effects of prostitution include flashbacks (sometimes exacerbated by prolonged drug use) and nightmares. It's not unusual for adult women who have survived this kind of abuse to sleep with the lights on, or to take a small stuffed doll, a pet, or their infant children to bed with them at night:

> MC: *I had acid flashbacks for more than a year. I had to take thorazine. . . . It was bad. I'd keep having flashbacks of guys, I would hallucinate full grown human beings that weren't there, trying to rape me. It was horrible. I'd be in my apartment and I would hallucinate them banging on the window, hundreds of them, trying to get in my apartment to rape me and kill me. And it really scared me.* (1988)

Survivors also typically suffer lingering fears—

> MD: *I'm afraid of men, really, . . . afraid of being abused, of being hurt, again.* (1987)

—and deep emotional pain that often resembles grieving:

> MD: *I feel like I imagine people who were in concentration camps feel when they get out. It will never go away. It's a real deep pain, an assault to my mind, my body, my dignity as a human being. I feel like what was taken away from me in prostitution is irretrievable. There's part of me that's dead, that's never gonna come back, that will never, ever be fixed, that can't be fixed, . . . like somebody cut off your arm, it can't grow back, like a hurt on this incredible deep, deep level. It's the pain that's not like any other pain that I can imagine. And the only way that I live is not to be in contact with that pain. Otherwise, I couldn't live.* (1988)

Women who have survived prostitution may also suffer from a unique, and quite irrational, fear that could be coined "the scarlet letter syndrome." They believe that people, especially men, can "tell" that they were prostitutes by merely looking at them.

LV: *I feel like I can walk in a store and a man will look at me like . . . "I know I can give you some money and we can have sex." Like they just know.* (1987)

This can cause great emotional stress and in extreme cases cause a woman to hurt herself:

RM: *I have to go see a psychiatrist once a week. . . . To find out why I'm doing things to myself. . . . Like trying to commit suicide.*

SW: *Do you still feel like you want to commit suicide?*

RM: *At least once a month.*

SW: *Why?*

RM: *I'm tired.*

SW: *Tired of what?*

RM: *The life that I've lived. The life that—the way people look at me.*

SW: *How do people look at you?*

RM: *Like I'm dirty. . . . just a funny look they give you, when they know you've been on the streets.* (1987)

In fact, public hospitals report 15 percent of all suicide victims are prostitutes. One survey of call girls revealed that 75 percent had attempted suicide (Geis, 1974).

The sexual abuse inherent in prostitution results in numerous health complications and lasting physical damage: trauma from beatings and rapes; complications from persistent bladder infections; and repeated exposure to venereal disease that often results in chronic pelvic inflammatory disease and infertility. However, it is the devastating emotional damage of prostitution that women label as the most profound impact on their lives.

DT: *I did have [a] broken nose, broken neck, stitches in my head. Those are health costs, those things*

> *healed, and they healed pretty fast. The mental,*
> *emotional part is still healing. Probably will for*
> *years, and years, and years, if ever. I don't know*
> *if that would ever be something that could be*
> *healed.* (1989)

When women's experiences in prostitution are incongruent with the culturally supported idea that prostitution is a victimless crime, women tend to blame themselves "for not doing it right" rather than acknowledging the abusive nature of the institution. This is not unlike the battered woman who believes that if she were more sexually forthcoming or inventive her husband wouldn't be reduced to forcing her to have sex. Both the prostitute and the sexually abused wife's realities are denied in the larger culture. Both are isolated within a closed system whose rules they have not designed, cannot control, and only minimally benefit them, if at all.

Finally, much has been hypothesized about the connection between a woman's "lack of self-esteem" and her victimization by her partner. Similar hypotheses have been advanced about "low self-esteem" as an antecedent to prostitution. Women used in prostitution have repeatedly expressed ideas and opinions of themselves that would lead an observer to comment on their poor self-image. However, like the woman who has been repeatedly sexually abused and/or battered by her partner, she has merely incorporated his definition of her valuelessness in an attempt to make sense of the abuse that she suffers. For a woman in prostitution, her valuelessness is reinforced on a daily basis by the numerous men who use her for their own sexual gratification without any regard for the physical, psychological, or emotional impact on her. Many women reported that during their first experiences in prostitution they openly cried while turning tricks, only to be shocked by the realization that their obvious emotional or physical distress did not affect nor diminish the customer's pleasure.

The parallel trauma responses that are found in victims of marital rape or prostitution are only replicated in victims of massive sexual abuse, rape, and battery. There is no other interpersonal, social, or work related type of situation or interaction that elicits these massive traumatic effects on its "participants," nor would we, as a society, condone or permit such an interaction to continue without intervention.

Conclusion

In determining the existence of prostitution as a manifestation of psycho-social and socio-economic coercion . . . it would not be mere indulgence in rhetoric to castigate prostitution as a form of collective rape, actually and symbolically. (Levine, 1988)

In spite of the abusive conditions in their lives prostitutes are afforded neither the status of victim nor survivor, but are defined as fully consenting participants in an industry that, if viewed objectively, would be understood to be the commerce of sexual abuse and inequality. Prostitution is sexual abuse because prostitutes are subjected to any number of sexual acts that in any other context, acted against any other woman, would be labeled assaultive or, at the very least, unwanted and coerced. Yet because an exchange of money occurs, irrespective of whether the woman herself maintains control of or benefits from this exchange, the client is given permission to use the woman in a manner that would not be tolerated in any other business or social arrangement (including marriage in some states); and the woman's acceptance of the money is construed as her willingness to engage in such commerce.

If this construction were applied to other victims of sexual assault then one logically would have to assume that women raped by their husbands or teenagers molested by their fathers, for example, also choose abusive relationships because they accept monetary considerations from their assailants in the form of food, lodging, and sometimes actual cash. This analogy sounds strained only because we have learned to recognize the violence to which these particular women and youths are subjected. We have learned to distinguish the victim from the perpetrator. We do not assert that, because a victim is powerless at a particular moment in time to change the objective circumstances of her life, she has chosen those very circumstances, and in fact, is compensated handsomely for her acquiescence. On the contrary, we create alternatives for those so victimized.

As other victims of sexual assault and battering, women and girls used in prostitution need and deserve tangible assistance to escape and overcome the trauma of commercial sexual exploitation.

Less than a decade ago, marital rape was permitted by both church and state. The assumption of a male's ownership of his wife's body was so culturally entrenched that it was unthinkable for a woman to deny a husband sexual access. It was only by listening to women who had survived this ongoing sexual abuse in their homes that we, as a society, were willing to strike down the marital rape exemption in most states, thus sending a message to males that a $25 marriage license is not a license to rape their wives. We must send a similar message to males, through education and public policy, that that same $25 cannot buy them the right to rape any other woman.

References

Bryan, J.H. 1966., Occupational ideologies and individual attitudes of call girls. *Social Problems* 13:443.

Finkelhor, David, and Kersti Yllo. 1987. *License to Rape: Sexual Abuse of Wives*. New York: The Free Press, 120.

Galbraith, John Kenneth. 1983. *Anatomy of Power*. Boston: Houghton Mifflin Company.

Geis, Gilbert. 1974. *One-Eyed Justice: An Examination of Homosexuality, Abortion, Prostitution, Narcotics and Gambling in the United States*. New York: Drake, 174.

Griffin, Susan. 1979. *Rape: The Power of Consciousness*. San Francisco: Harper and Row, 39.

Hirschi, Travis. 1962. The professional prostitutes. *Berkeley Journal of Sociology* 7:37–48

Jackman, N.R., O'Toole, R., and G. Geis. 1963. The self-image of the prostitute. *Sociology Quarterly* 4:157–58.

Levine, Philippa. 1988. Prostitution in Florida: A Report Presented to the Gender Bias Study Commission of the Supreme Court of Florida.

Morgan, Roin (ed.). 1984. *Sisterhood Is Global*. New York: Anchor Press/ Doubleday.

On the legislative front. *Ms. Magazine* (September/October 1990):45.

Ryan, Jayme. 1989. Legalized prostitution in Nevada. *WHISPER* (Vol 3; No. 2 Winter/Spring 1989):3–4.

Sivard, Ruth Leger. 1985. *Women . . . A World Survey*. Washington, DC: World Priorities, 16.

Webster's New World Dictionary, Third College Edition, 247, 248.

WHISPER Oral History Project, A.D., 1987.

WHISPER. 1988. Prostitution: A matter of violence against women. New York: Perone Productions. video.

Winick, C., and P. Kinsie. 1971. *The Lively Commerce: Prostitution in the United States*. New York: Signet, 50.

Chapter 9

Adult Male Sexual Assault in the Community:

A Literature Review and Group Treatment Model

Paul J. Isely
Boston University
Doctoral Candidate
Boston, MA

■

Men are vulnerable to sexual assault regardless of age, race, class, or sexual preference, yet, sexual assault against adult males in the community is one of the most hidden and unaddressed forms of sexual abuse (Kaufman, 1984; Miller, 1983).

For the purpose of this article, an adult male will be considered 16 years or older, since most state laws place the age of sexual consent at 16 years of age. Sexual assault is considered any nonconsensual sexual act perpetrated against an individual by either a man or a woman. Reported male offences usually involve forced fellatio and sodomy as primary abuses perpetrated against the victim. Although most authors would agree that sodomy constitutes a "rape" definition, it has only been within the past few years that state laws have begun to include sodomy against a male under their rape statutes.

The exact amount of male rape occurring is difficult to assess since the majority of these adult males never report their assault. Colderwood (1987) reports the estimate that only one in ten men report their sexual victimization. Victimization often occurs in a "community setting," as opposed to institutional (e.g., prison) ones, where the majority of men never receive medical or psychological help after their assault. Clinical data on this phenomena indicate that the majority of both victims and perpetrators are heterosexual (Groth & Burgess,

1980). Male rape, therefore, is not a violent outgrowth of the homosexual community, nor is it isolated to prison settings (Kaufman, 1984).

Research on the prevalence of male rape is virtually nonexistent, receiving little attention in professional literature (Masters, 1986; Myers, 1989). This is not surprising given that it has been only since the early 1970s that the women's movement succeeded in bringing the issue of rape of women to the nation's attention (Temkin, 1986). Moreover, social myths surrounding male and female gender roles and attitudes, has aided in keeping this particular type of male victimization from attracting the professional and public attention it deserves. This article reviews the existing literature on the subject and presents a group model drawn from a psychoeducational therapy group for adult male rape victims conducted at the New York City Gay and Lesbian Antiviolence Project. Although the model is limited both by its sample size and population, it nonetheless represents the only known group facilitated for such men. The significance of this group is represented by its unique contribution to sexual assault survivors and its therapeutic implications for clinicians in the field of sexual victimization. The degree of sexual assault occurring against adult males has been vastly underestimated and therefore should be more closely addressed by treatment professionals and our society.

Sexual Assault of Adult Males

While society was beginning to focus its attention upon the sexual abuse of women and children, a small group of professionals were investigating and treating adult males experiencing similar types of victimization. Stories of male-on-male rape, surfacing among prison populations began to receive recognition in professional literature in the mid-1970s and early '80s (Weiss & Friar, 1974; Scacco, 1975; Lockwood, 1980; Groth & Birnbaum, 1979; and Cotton & Groth, 1982). Yet, in spite of these early efforts, sexual assault of men remains virtually unrecognized. Although the subject arises occasionally in the popular media, it nevertheless remains marginally addressed in professional journals. However, Groth and Burgess (1980), Mezy & King (1989), and Kaufman (1984), believe that their limited samples represent only a fraction of the actual abuse occurring to adult males in our communities. Although these articles rarely cite significant supporting references regarding the amount of abuse occurring, an accurate computation of figures presented in the existing literature surprisingly reveals 281 reported adult male victims. This figure is significantly greater than the handful normally reported (see Table 9-1). The most significant of these studies is the 1987 Los Angeles Catchment Study in which 107 men reported having been sexually assaulted (Sorenson, Stein, Siegel, Golding, & Burnam, 1987). This work represents the only reported research on adult males sexually assaulted in the community having been setting—107 men reported being sexually assaulted.

Table 9-1
ADULT MALE VICTIMS OF MALE-ON-MALE RAPE

Author, Date of Study	Number of Men Reported Assaulted	Range of Victims' Ages	Number of Victims and Assailants	Victims' Sexual Orientation
Meyers (1989)	9	17–32	2 = 3 7 = 1	1 = heterosexual 6 = homosexual 1 = bisexual 1 = asexual
Mezy and King (1989)	22	16–82	18 = 1 4 = 4–8	8 = heterosexual 0 = homosexual 4 = bisexual
Sorenson et al. (1987)	107	N/R*	N/R	N/R
Kreuger (1985)	100	N/R*	N/R	N/R
Goyer and Eddleman (1984)	13	18–31	2 = 1 3 = 2 4 = 3 4 = 4	11 = heterosexual 1 = homosexual 1 = bisexual
Kaufman (1984)	14	16–49	5 = 1 3 = 2 3 = 3 3 = 4	N/R (most victims not affiliated with homosexual community)
Forman (1983)	3	16–43	3 = 1	N/R
Sarrel and Masters (1982)	7	17–40 1 = 3	5 = 1 3 = N/R	4 = heterosexual
Groth and Burgess (1980)	6	16–28	5 = 1 1 = 3 1 = N/R	3 = heterosexual 1 = homosexual 1 = bisexual
TOTAL	281	16–82	N/A 231 = N/R	23 = heterosexual 19 = homosexual 7 = bisexual 1 = asexual

* Not reported

Recently, Muehlenhard and Cook (1988) conducted a study of 503 undergraduate men regarding experiences of unwanted sex in their adulthood. Ninety-three percent reported incidents of reluctant involvement in sexual behavior. Likewise, Struckman-Johnson (1988) conducted similar ground breaking research into men experiencing unwanted sexual activity while dating. She reports that out of 268 men surveyed on a college campus, 43 or 16 percent had been victim to one forced episode in their lifetime. Twenty-three men ranging in age from 18 to 27 had experienced a forced incident in the last twelve months. Contrary to the myth that men can be sexually assaulted only by other men, Masters (1986) and Struckman-Johnson (1988) report of men being physically forced, coerced, and threatened into unwanted sexual encounters by women. Research in the homosexual community has also yielded instances of date rape among gay and lesbian couples (Waterman, Dawson, & Bologna, 1989). Although these studies represent significant research into this field, many were not included in Table 9-1 because it is difficult to ascertain the exact number of men who fall into a sexual assault category. This research debunks the notion that men do not experience undesired sex and, like women, may be compelled to engage in sex for complex reasons.

Survivors are vulnerable to being revictimized by the police, community agencies, and bewildered friends (Kreuger, 1985). Only 10 to 20 percent of women report and seek professional help after being raped (Kaufman et al., 1980). Even fewer men seek such services. Talking about their rape can be humiliating. Many feel their "manhood" has been robbed, and they fear being misunderstood, ridiculed, or labeled as homosexual. They often feel safer suffering in silence and are reluctant to be revictimized by an unsympathetic legal system or disbelieving treatment professionals. Few survivors ever tell family members, friends, or significant others about their assault. Those who do report a sexual attack often experience hostile and isolating reactions from the very service providers that are available to provide help. Too often, seeking assistance in dealing with the trauma that can follow a rape too often becomes a humiliating experience in which feelings of depression, anger, guilt, sexual confusion, and anxiety are reinforced in survivors as they become revictimized by the police, community agencies, and bewildered friends (Krueger 1985).

Although men tend to reorganize their lives quickly after a rape, their "controlled" response style (stoical, withdrawn, controlled emotional expression, sullen, etc.) is often disguising major hidden psychological trauma that can last for years (Kaufman 1984). Masters (1986) claims that men are often abused more violently, sustain more serious injuries, and are more likely to be gang raped. "Male Rape Trauma" (Cotton & Groth 1982) is a common reaction in which depression, anger, guilt, fear of being homosexual, sexual malfunctioning, flashbacks, and suicidal feelings are experienced from weeks to years after an assault (see Table 9-2). The small body of professional literature confirms the fact that, like women, male rape survivors experience a disruption in their biopsychosocial functioning. Mezy and King (1987) suggest that male victims may become more stigmatized than female victims, that they often experience greater subsequent anger and guilt, and are less likely to report their assault. Masters (1986) states that men often experience greater shock after a rape (adult males are not "supposed" to be sexually assaulted), and even greater depression.

Existing clinical literature stresses that much is unknown about the sexual assault of men. Reports based on clinical experience (Kaufman, 1984; Groth & Burgess, 1980; Forman, 1983) clearly indicate the need for comprehensive research. These men are reluctant to report their assaults because of the many negative attitudes that surround the sexual identity and victimization of adult males. Instead, they feel

---

Table 9-2

MALE RAPE TRAUMA

1. PHYSICAL
   Injury and disease infection
2. EMOTIONAL
   Increased anxiety, fear, depression, shame, anger, mood swings, phobic reactions
3. COGNITIVE
   Flashbacks to or preoccupation with memories of the assault, impairments in ability to concentrate, difficulty in attending to tasks at hand and so forth
4. PSYCHOLOGICALLY
   Discomfort in feelings of safety and adequacy
   Devaluation in regard to his identity and self-esteem
   Disruption in social relations, with increased distrust, withdrawal and isolation, intensified aggressiveness
5. SEXUAL/SOCIAL ISSUES
   Concerns pertaining to "manhood" or sexual identity, impaired sexual functioning, negative sexual attitudes, and so forth

compelled to keep their assault a secret, and along with that secret is the devastating aftermath of psychological trauma, which therefore remains untreated.

Male Rape Group

In 1987, the Gay and Lesbian Antiviolence Project ran an eight week male rape survivors group consisting of four men who had been raped in their adulthood or late adolescence. Since 1980, the Project had received numerous calls from male survivors, and consultation requests from other service providers who turned to the Project for assistance with male rape cases in their practice. A large number of these clients were heterosexual and were unable to find treatment for themselves. Although the Project provided individual peer and professional counseling for these men, the staff became convinced that since group therapy was a common treatment modality with female survivors, a therapeutic group would be helpful in the treatment of these men. Unable to locate the existence of such a group for men, I was asked to design a psychoeducational model based upon current literature on the subject and on my professional experience in counseling male heterosexual victims of sexual assault. (Interestingly, this model has since been used successfully at St. Luke's-Roosevelt Rape Intervention Program/Crime Victims Assessment Project Rape Intervention Program in New York City for the treatment of adult men sexually abused as children.) Four men participated in the group, which was led by David M. Wertheimer (executive director of the Project) and myself. Three of these men were gay and one was a bisexual who had chosen to live a heterosexual lifestyle. When the possibility of an article was discussed with group members, participants were understandably resistant to any disclosures regarding their assault histories. Many perceived the article as a violation of their confidentiality—even though their names would remain anonymous. The publishing of these "secrets" that they had concealed from others seemed to symbolically represent another revictimization. However, after much discussion, they decided to allow vague descriptions of their assaults in order to help other male victims. This decision represented a courageous act of trusting in the therapists with their previously unpublicized abuse histories.

Most sexual abuse groups require that members talk about their assaults. This appears to be helpful in these groups, but we decided against it considering the adult males' difficulty with intimate sharing between each other. This is true for gay men as well as heterosexual men. The group discovered and admitted that talking about such a powerfully intimate subject as an assault with another man was extremely difficult and seemed to transcend alternative socialization of males roles even in the gay community. The Design assumed that if a safe therapeutic atmosphere could be created, these men would share their assault histories.

Group Outline and Process Summary

In the aftermath of a sexual assault, male survivors experience a complex psycho/social crisis. A survivor typically experiences a diverse sequelae of posttraumatic symptomatology that can last for years. This syndrome may include intense feelings of sadness, depression, anger, rage, isolation, shame, guilt, fear, confusion, and suicidal ideation. Many survivors experience frequent concerns about autonomy, control, male identity, sexuality, and related difficulty in interpersonal relations. Prior conflicts around these issues may be exacerbated by their assaults, and a survivor's pretrauma level of social, vocational, and interpersonal functioning may be significantly impaired. It is often difficult for men to seek help in coping with their sexual victimization. The overwhelming majority never receive professional assistance. The group modality attempts to respond to these acute needs by providing a supportive atmosphere in which men can share experiences, feelings, and concerns.

The intention of this group is to provide a safe environment in which consensual validation and mutual understanding of survivors' reactions to their assaults can take place. This experience would provide an opportunity to explore and share affective, cognitive, and behavioral posttrauma reactions and then impact on interpersonal relating in an attempt to return to pretrauma levels of functioning. The group consisted of four men who had requested group therapy in conjunction with their individual treatment. Private therapy was required by all members due to the short-term nature of the group and the possible feelings it would evoke in the participants. Two men were in their early forties and had been raped in their early twenties. One man had been held at gunpoint, forced into his apartment, tied up, and held hostage while he was sodomized throughout the night. The other man had been recently sodomized by several male assailants who claimed to be heterosexual. This occurred in a bathroom of a nightclub that was frequented by both gay and heterosexual patrons. Shortly after the assault, he called a rape-crisis hotline for assistance and was told that men could not be raped. The phone counselor terminated their conversation three times, assuming they were prank calls. The third group member was a man in his mid-fifties who experienced sexual abuse by a priest while a teenager and forced sodomy as an adult perpetrated by a live-in lover. The fourth group member was a bisexual man in his late twenties who had been seduced and sodomized as a teenager on a camping trip by an adult male counselor in his early forties.

The following is a brief summary and skeletal outline of the group experience. It is hopeful that this model will encourage treatment professionals to utilize group therapy with male survivors and provide a useful example of treatment with male victims. As mentioned earlier, descriptions of the group experience remain vague at the participants request. The summary of group sessions focuses upon the overall process versus the specific content of their interactions. This should provide sufficient instructional material for the group therapist conducting a male rape group.

SESSION I

(A) Introduction

(B) Establish goals (personal and group), norms, and expectations

(C) Establish ground rules

- ■ No one has to talk about what happened if he doesn't want to.
- ■ No physical or verbal violence in the group.
- ■ What is said is private unless it affects the group's safety.

(D) Establish rapport and cohesion among members.
   Group exercise/ice breaker (Silverberg, 1986)

Group members are divided into pairs (counselors as well, in order to demonstrate that a man can be in a position of leadership or authority and still self-disclose and express feelings). Members are asked to interview each other in order to find out as much about the other as possible in a ten- or fifteen-minute framework. Everyone knows in advance that this is a group-level activity, and disclosed information will be shared with the group. Counselors ask one pair to interview the other for this period of time, then give a signal for the pair to reverse procedures for another ten or fifteen minutes. At the end of this time, the group is asked to form a circle and each person then shares with the group what he has found out about the person he has interviewed. Topics include: name, occupation, where he grew up, schools attended, siblings, interests, hobbies, favorite foods/movies, and so on.

(E) Closure: How does it feel to be in the group?

Process Summary

The counselors sensed a great amount of anxiety in the group and attributed this to the many negative interpersonal encounters these individuals experienced in past disclosures of their rape. Therefore, the counselors introduced general ground rules that seemed to relax group members. A few members expressed comfort in knowing the limits or "boundaries" on confidentiality and the explicit goal to confront destructive behavior.

Silverberg's (1986) "rapport exercise" helped members begin to feel comfortable with each other. The facilitators' involvement seemed to create a greater cohesiveness. The men discussed feelings about participating in the group, and some members expressed their fear of being vulnerable in the group. Often, the word *incident* was substituted for the words *rape* or *sexual assault*.

SESSION II

THE MALE MYTH

(A) Rapport building: Feelings about being back in the
   group

(B) Group exercise

   Wertheimer's group exercise on male stereotypes (see process summary), designed to look at stereotypes that become problematic when accepting males as sexual assault victims. Participation is voluntary.

(C) Reflection on the exercise

(D) Psychosexual education

   Men as victims/survivors of sexual abuse
   Discuss topics of prevalence, sexual orientation, and so on.

(E) **Facilitative discussion**

(F) **Closure**

Process Summary

The session began with members reflecting on how they felt about the first group meeting. Generally, people felt good about returning to the group, but they were also very anxious and scared. Talk began to center around group membership based on their sexual victimization. Therapeutic interventions were focused on an increasing sense of "consensual validation" of each person's rape experience. A statement by one of the facilitators about the group symbolically forming a "community of the abused" freed group members to establish a sense of ownership in their right to be participating in the group.

The counselors presented Wertheimer's Gender/Abuse exercise and encouraged active participation by all the group members. Collectively, the men are asked to create two lists of male attributes generally assumed by society. The first column consists of attributes associated with "being a man." The second column consists of attributes associated with being a male rape victim. The group quickly discovered that these attributes were complete opposites. For example, "men" are strong, and male victims are weak and vulnerable. This exercise seemed to create a renewed cohesiveness between individuals and many intense emotional reactions were expressed regarding the attributes. Group members shared a common experience of being labeled negatively by society, friends, lovers, and themselves when they had shared their rape experience. They began to express feelings of anger, guilt, and loneliness—thus validating these feelings as normal reactions of men being raped as adults. The trust created by the shared reactions in the exercise allowed members to begin briefly talking about their assaults. The men decided to extend the group another half-hour because of the need for more time to deal with issues surfacing in the group. The counselors supported this decision in an attempt to facilitate a sense of control by the members in the group process.

SESSION III

(A) **Feelings about returning to the group**

(B) **Termination preparation: Review time-limited nature of group**

(C) Psychosexual education: Silverberg's Male Myths (see process summary)

(D) Open group discussion

(E) Closure

Process Summary

The group began with members sharing positive feelings about returning for this session. In the previous session membership work had been strong, and it was clear that the group had worked through a "forming" stage.

Issues of power and authority began to surface in the group as members subtly questioned the material presented by the counselors and challenged the structure of the sessions. Process interventions were based on the power issues in the group as they related to the counselors. A sense of rebelling against the existing structure became evident in the members' interactions, but they were still unable to confront the counselors directly and work their authority issues.

The counselors presented Silverberg's (1985, p. 10) Male Myths, which were quickly challenged by the group. For example, the men became very angry about the following values held in our society:

> Masculine power, dominance, and control are essential to proving one's masculinity.
>
> Vulnerabilities, feelings, and emotions in men are signs of femininity and are to be avoided.
>
> Masculine control of self, others, and environment are essential for men to feel safe, secure, and comfortable.
>
> Men seeking help and support from others show signs of weakness, vulnerability, and potential incompetence.
>
> Interpersonal communications that emphasize human emotions, feelings, intuitions, and physical contact are considered feminine and are to be avoided.

The group worked on how many of these male myths were a part of their own belief system even though they intellectually rejected them. This freed members to talk about how many in their own gay community have difficulty accepting men as rape victims. Members shared personal stories about the negative responses of significant others when the rape was disclosed. Frequently, the men had encountered reactions such as hysterical laughter and assumptions about how "gay men would want to be raped." The counselors facilitated discussion on the male myths and how they relate to male victims. One member disclosed his bisexuality to the group and process interventions focused upon group differences.

SESSION IV

(A) Debriefing feelings about last session

(B) Psychosexual Education: Male rape trauma

■ Definition of sexual assault
■ Rape as violence expressed sexually
■ Post-Traumatic Stress Syndrome

(C) Open group discussion

(D) Closure: Termination reminder

Process Summary

One group member did not attend because of a summer vacation. One counselor was also unable to attend Session IV and V (his planned absence was discussed in the initial meeting). The remaining counselor became the focus of conversation during the first half-hour. The members questioned the structure of the group, the absent counselor's role/leadership style, and each others' participation as members. The counselor used process interventions that contained references to power/intimacy, and to the group's movement from a stage of "adolescence" to "adulthood." Members' feedback skills were practiced, and the group began to focus on how they could begin to trust each other with their stories and feelings. One member was able to ask the others to (1) take care of him if he was in pain, and (2) to let him take care of them if they were in pain. This barometric event in the group's life allowed members to contract between each other about how they would begin talking about their assaults. One man decided to share his rape experience.

Interventions based on proper feedback helped members to communicate more freely and look at how they use self-blame to defeat an honest expression of their power and control issues in the group. The session ended very powerfully with a more resistant member realizing that he too dismissed his own feelings of self blame.

The members seemed to take control over the group by dismissing the counselor's scheduled talk on rape trauma. This shift was made explicit by the therapists. The members felt very happy about their assertiveness. Rape trauma, nonetheless, became a focus in the group when a rape story was shared. Members occasionally asked the counselor for clarification on a particular aspect of the trauma.

SESSION V: REVICTIMIZATION OF THE RAPE SURVIVOR

(A) Debriefing feelings about previous session

(B) Revictimization from: service providers, friends, lovers, and family

(C) Men as legitimate rape survivors and the rapist as stranger, friend, lover, relative, and community leader

(D) Group discussion

(E) Closure

Process Summary

Again, one client and one counselor were unable to attend the session. The men continued to work on issues of group membership as it related to sharing their rape experiences in the group. This new level of "forming" seemed united with two different emerging themes in the group:

1. *Interpersonal.* Members worked on creating supportive interpersonal relationships. They offered and gave feedback on fellow members' leadership skills in the group, and recognized how important they were to each other. In addition, they talked about difficulties in interpersonal relationships due to the rape experience .

2. *Power.* Members discussed their feelings of anger at the absent therapist. Many felt his clinical skills and leadership abilities were questionable. Interventions focused on members being able to talk to him and upon power issues related to being raped.

The group seemed to reached a new level of intimacy, and expressed the need to talk with the other counselor. The members left with positive feelings about their interpersonal work. However, questions remained about whether they could maintain this level of intimacy with the other counselor present.

SESSION VI: EXPRESSION OF FEELINGS

(A) **Open group**

(B) **Closure: Termination discussion**

Process Summary

The group started with a brief summation of last week's session for the missing group member and counselor. Work quickly began on the issue of the returning counselor's inadequate group leadership skills. The group pointed out shortcomings in his counseling style and suggested how he could be a more productive group leader. Process interventions surrounding power issues with male authority helped the group deal with the conflict about the counselor. A theme of power and intimacy emerged as members acknowledged their need to be liked by the counselor and to be "perfect clients" for him. Power issues related to rape were discussed, and members were able to accept the counselors as powerful males who would not abuse them. The group worked on the paradox between the fear of powerful males and the need to be cared for by such men.

The group's ability to accept the counselors as powerful, but not intrusive, seemed to help the men in their work on power issues among themselves. They were able to share feelings of powerlessness and victimization regarding their assaults. Upon leaving the session, some men expressed the feeling that a terrible burden had been lifted from their shoulders.

SESSION VII

(A) **Discussion of last week's group and requested feedback**

(B) **Focused termination talk**

(C) **Closure**

Process Summary

Upon their return, members of the group immediately shared the effects of last week's session. When termination issues were introduced, members began a more explicit discussion of the remaining power issues between themselves and the counselors. In addition, individuals talked about their sense of powerlessness in relation to their victimization. Members were able to acknowledge their own powerfulness in surviving their rape and how they often do not acknowledge the control they exhibit in their careers and personal life. For the first time since their assaults, they received positive feedback on what a powerful influence they have in interpersonal interactions. Their realization that the rape did not make them powerless in every aspect of their lives was an extremely important insight. The majority of the remaining time was spent on issues of power and control in male rape victims.

SESSION VIII: TERMINATION

(A) Objectives:

1. To summarize group experience
2. To share perceptions, insights gained, and review group/personal goals
3. To provide an intimate closing experience for group members

(B) Open discussion on group termination

Members conduct a final processing of interactions.

Process Summary

This last group proved to be a very difficult challenge for the group members. Only one man came on time for the session, and although some members had earlier been excited by the possibility of successfully completing the group, their feelings had now changed. Interventions around termination issues were angrily acknowledged or dismissed. The members desired more sessions and even wished to start another group. Some men attempted to share previously secretive aspects of their assault experience. The counselors self-disclosed their own feelings of guilt and fears of abandoning the group members. These disclosures allowed the men to share abandonment feelings about the therapists and eventually to each other. The group requested an extra half-hour, and this was allowed by the counselors, considering the volatile nature of the experiences members felt compelled to share.

The group ended with a contract among members to meet again. For the first time in the group's life, the counselors and the group participants spontaneously embraced each other. The men expressed sincere appreciation for the group experience and urged us to lead another one. The men stayed another half hour and casually chatted with each other. Obviously, it was very difficult for them to say goodbye.

Discussion

The Antiviolence Project phoned a number of rape crisis centers around the country in order to ascertain whether such a therapy group had ever been conducted. Frequently, we were told such a group would be impossible—male survivors would not tolerate this type of interaction with other men because of their unwillingness to discuss their rape and because of men's inability, in general, to communicate intimately with other men. We believed, however, that, like women survivors, emotional healing could be facilitated through male rape survivors' experiencing the support of fellow victims in a safe therapeutic environment. We were proven correct. The men overwhelmingly felt that the experience was successful and greatly desired to continue working as a group. To our surprise, the members continued to meet monthly for dinner and found this rewarding and supporting.

The original expectations for this pilot group was for its membership to reach six to eight men. In retrospect, it was agreed, by all involved, that this would have been too large. The model size seemed to facilitate a safe environment for the men who struggled to take the risk of sharing their abuse stories. Likewise, our explicit permission not to share their stories enabled these men to empower themselves vocatively. Their rapes and consequent scares of powerlessness and intimidation were kept as sacred stories that belonged to them. They expressed appreciation for our lack of authoritarianism regarding our request for disclosure. In retrospect, it might be helpful to extend this group four more sessions in order to permit the men more time to express their feelings and share the traumatic aftermath of their assaults. This model was originally created for short term rape crisis centers and therefore is constrained in its length. Ideally, a long term group consisting of larger membership should be considered.

Conclusion

Male sexual assault, perhaps the most hidden of all sexual abuse, remains virtually unrecognized by service providers and our society.

Thirty years ago, very few women or children sought help for their sexual victimization. Today, it is the adult male who needs acknowledgment and support. The male rape group conducted at the Antiviolence Project is an attempt at such an acknowledgement. We quickly discovered, however, that resistance to a male group is great among treatment professions. Many therapists expressed fears about the male victim's rage and anger. Yet, it is rare that victims turn their anger outward and hurt another person. More common, they turn it toward themselves. These men, isolated and alone, must rely on the same disabilitating social myths that kept them from seeking help after their assaults. Even when they do tell, the subsequent rejection from close friends and service providers drives them into the very isolation they sought to escape. Society remains unwilling to hear their stories.

Comprehensive research on adult male sexual assault will be an essential vehicle for bending the professional ears of service providers in our communities. It is hoped that this chapter will both inspire therapists to lead similar groups for male victims and conduct comprehensive research on adult male sexual assault.

References

Burgess, A., and L.L. Holmstrom. 1974. *Rape: Victims of Crisis*. Bowie, MD: Brady Co.

Calderwood, D. 1987. The male rape victim. *Medical Aspects of Human Sexuality* 7: 53–55.

Cotton, D.J., and A.N. Groth. 1982. Inmate rape: Prevention and intervention. *Journal of Prison and Jail Health* 2(1):47–57.

Forman, B.D. 1983. Reported male rape. *Victimology: An International Journal* 7(1–4):235–36.

Goyer, P.F., and H.C. Eddleman. 1984. Same sex rape of nonincarcerated men. *American Journal of Psychiatry* 141:576–79.

Groth, A.N. and B.A. Birnbaum. 1979. *Men Who Rape: The Psychology of the Offender*. New York: Plenum.

Groth, A.N., and A. Burgess. 1980. Male rape: offender and victims. *American Journal of Psychiatry* 137:806–10.

Kaufman, A. 1984. Rape of men in the community. In I.R. Stuart and G.J. Greer (eds.) *Victims of Sexual Aggression: Treatment of Children, Women, and Men*, pp. 157–77. New York: Van Nostrand Reinhold.

Kaufman, A., P. DiVasto, R. Jackson, D. Voorhess, and J. Christy. 1980. Male rape victims: Noninstitutionalized assault. *American Journal of Psychiatry* 137:221–23.

Kruegar, F. (1985, May). Violated. *Boston Magazine*, pp. 138, 140–42.

Lockwood, D. 1980. *Prison Sexual Violence*. New York: Elsevier.

Masters, W.H. 1986. Sexual dysfunction as an aftermath of sexual assault of men by women. *Journal of Sex and Marital Therapy* 12(1):35–45.

Mezy, G., and M. King. 1987. Male victims of sexual assault. *Medicine, Science, and the Law* 27:122–24.

Mezy, G., and M. King. 1989. The effects of sexual assault on men: A survey of 22 victims. *Psychological Medicine* 19:205–09.

Miller, N. 1983, November. Male rape. *Boston Phoenix*, pp. 12–14.

Muehlenhard, C.L., and S.W. Cook. 1988. Men's self-reports of unwanted sexual activity. *The Journal of Sex Research* 24:58–72.

Myers, M.F. 1989. Men sexually assaulted as adults and sexually abused as boys. *Archives of Sexual Behavior* 18(3):203–15.

Sarrel, P., and W.H. Masters. 1982. Sexual molestation of men by women. *Archives of Sexual Behavior* 11(2):117–31.

Scacco, A. 1975. *Rape in Prison*. Springfield, IL: C.C. Thomas.

Silverberg, R.A. 1986. *Psychotherapy for Men*. Springfield, IL: C.C. Thomas.

Sorenson, S.B., J.A. Stein, J.M. Siegel, J.M. Golding, and M.A. Burnam. 1987. The prevalence of adult sexual assault. *American Journal of Epidemiology* 126(6):1155–64.

Struckman-Johnson, C. 1988. Forced sex on dates: It happens to men, too. *The Journal of Sex Research* 24:234–41.

Temkin, J. 1986. Women, rape, and law reform. Rape. In S. Tomaselli and R. Porter (eds.) *RAPE* (pp. 16–40). New York: Basil Blackwell.

Waterman, C.K., M.A. Dawson, and M.J. Bologna, 1989. Sexual coercion in gay male and lesbian relationships: Predictors and implications for support services. *Journal of Sex Research* 26(1):118–24.

Weiss, C., and D. Friar, 1974. *Terror in the Prisons*. New York: Bobbs-Merrill.

Part 3

Care
Providers

■

Chapter 10

Sexual Assault and Sexually Transmitted Disease: The Issues and Concerns

Linda E. Ledray
Sexual Assault Resource Service
Minneapolis, MN

∎

Whenever a sexual assault victim presents for care, five areas of concern must be addressed by the health care provider to ensure that treatment is complete. These five areas include: (1) care of injuries; (2) collection of evidence; (3) crisis intervention and advocacy; (4) pregnancy risk evaluation and prevention; and (5) evaluation of sexually transmitted diseases. This chapter addresses the issues and concerns of the adult and adolescent rape survivor and the health care provider in dealing with the issue of sexually transmitted diseases (STD) directly after a sexual assault.

The Extent of the Problem

According to the latest FBI crime report (1989), there were 94,504 reported rapes in the United States in 1988. This represents a 1.5 percent increase over the previous year. Since it is generally accepted that for every reported rape there are at least five additional unreported rapes, we can estimate that close to 500,000 additional women were raped but did not report. These women, too, are in need of medical care and may go to a hospital, clinic, or their private physician. Those who do come for care are often concerned about having contracted a sexually transmitted disease from the assailant.

In a study of ninety-seven adult sexual assault survivors, the Sexual Assault Resource Service (SARS) in Minneapolis found that concerns about sexually transmitted diseases (STDs) were their second most important concern. The number one reason rape victims stated they had come to the emergency room was to have evidence collected that could be used to convict their assailant. The third most important reason was prevention of pregnancy. STD concerns brought 36 percent of a sample of ninety-seven adult women to the emergency room after a sexual assault. Care of injuries was the fourth reason they gave for coming to the emergency room. (Ledray, 1980). Because this study was completed prior to the outbreak of AIDS in the United States, it is likely that concerns about contracting an STD from a rape would be greater today.

Sexually Transmitted Disease Infection Rates

Although many victims report concern about contracting sexually transmitted diseases, the actual risk rate is difficult to determine, and reported rates vary widely from study to study and from area and area. The risk of a sexual assault victim contracting a sexually transmitted disease is affected by many variables. One of these is the regional prevalence rates for sexually transmitted diseases. One might assume that the more sexually transmitted disease in the area, the more likely the assailant will be infected and pass the infection to the victim. However, even though sex offenders often report engaging in high risk sexual behaviors that may increase their likelihood of infection, the high rate of sexual dysfunction in other sex offenders (Groth and Burgess: 1977) may actually reduce their infection rate.

Other factors that may affect the risk to the victim include the orifices involved, the number of assailants, and the presence or absence of ejaculate. Although studies are available that address this issue, there are a number of inherent problems in interpreting the data. Often studies that report STD statistics do not indicate if the percentage of positive STD cases is taken only from those at risk, (e.g., only those cases of sexual assault that include contact of the sexual organs), or if the statistics reflect the percentage of victims who contracted a STD from the total population including sexual assault victims without sexual organ contact. (Blackmore, Keegan, & Cates, 1982).

Until recently, most studies in the literature reported on infection rates for gonorrhea and syphilis. More recent studies include additional STDs; however, the STDs tested for vary from study to study.

It is also unclear if positive gonorrhea cultures obtained at the initial exam are actually preexisting or are positive from the assailant. Whereas an initial positive emergency room gonorrhea culture was at one time considered a preexisting infection (Hayman and Lanza, 1971), there more recently has been evidence that a positive emergency room gonorrhea culture could indeed be positive as a result of the rape (Blackmore et al., 1982). In a report by DeJong (1985), *N. gonorrhea* was isolated from the vagina of a 12-year-old girl hours after the rape. She had had no prior sexual contact.

SARS had three similar cases in which after careful consideration and much skepticism we, too, were certain the *N. gonorrhea* cultured in the emergency room after the assault was not preexisting. One of these involved an elderly woman who had not been sexually active in nearly twenty years. The second was a sexually inactive nun. The third was a married woman whose husband tested negative. The initial cultures in these cases were taken seven to twenty-four hours after the rape. Although it may be more likely to obtain the positive culture on follow-up, it is important to recognize that the cultured gonorrhea may have been from seminal fluid deposited in the vagina by the assailant at the time of the rape.

Another problem in interpreting the STD data provided is the typically low follow-up rate for reculture. It is difficult to know if the follow-up group is overrepresented by victims with symptoms that precipitated their return for care, and thus more STDs, or if it is a representative group.

In many cases there is no initial data. Only follow-up data is available, so it is impossible to differentiate preexisting STD from those contracted as a result of the rape. For example, Forster and others (1986) reported on STD exams completed on forty-six women who had come to a London hospital after a rape. Evidence of STD was found in fourteen (30 percent). It is, of course, impossible to relate these infections directly to the assault because there is no baseline data available.

A recent Seattle study found 43 percent of 204 rape victims they tested positive for at least one STD in the emergency room. These positives were considered to be preexisting prior to the rape. Rather extensive testing was done to include: gonorrhea, chlamydia, cytomegalovirus, herpes simplex, trichomonas, bacterial vaginitis, syphilis, HIV virus. Of the initial 204 victims, 109, (53 percent) returned for follow-up. Of those who returned, 37.5 percent were found to have new STD infections not diagnosed at the time of the rape (Jenny et al., 1990). Unfortunately, this study did not provide an STD rate for the general population in the Seattle area. It has since been criticized for disparaging the rape victim by concluding that rape victims have a high rate of preexisting STDs, despite its lack of a comparison group, small sample size, and low follow-up rate (Baxter, 1990; Gray & Whitehouse, 1990).

A similar, though less extensive, study of rape victims completed in the Midwest found a much lower rate of preexisting STD infections. In this later study 11 percent of 232 rape victims tested positive for gonorrhea or chlamydia at the time of the rape. These rates were not significantly different from a comparison group of 399 randomly selected patients reporting to the emergency department with complaints of gynecological problems. Only 73 victims, 31 percent of the initial sample, returned for follow-up. Of these, there was only one new infection, a positive vaginal chlamydia (Sturm et. al., 1990). Though the rates in this study are much lower than those reported in the Seattle study, fewer STDs were tested. If only the positive gonorrhea and chlamydia cultures are included from the Seattle study, the initial positive rate is 16 percent and the positive follow-up rate for these two STDs was 6 percent (Jenny, et al., 1990).

SARS STD Data

The Sexual Assault Resource Service in Minneapolis recently reviewed the records of 1,007 adult sexual assault victims seen in the emergency department by the SARS nurse within seventy-two hours of a sexual assault. Of these, 919 involved vaginal penetration, 369 oral sexual assault, and 210 anal penetration. In 111 cases all three orifices were involved. Vaginal and oral involvement occurred in 184 cases, and vaginal and anal penetration was reported in 68 cases. Of the cases in which there was sexual penetration, 16 percent had an STD on initial examination: 7 percent were positive for vaginal chlamydia; 5 percent for vaginal gonorrhea; 2 percent for anal gonorrhea; and 1 percent for oral gonorrhea. Syphilis was found in 1 percent of those tested. Because prophylactic antibiotics are used with adult victims in the emergency department, follow-up STD testing is not routinely done. These findings are quite similar to the Sturm et al. study data reported earlier.

In a separate records review of 110 adolescent sexual assault victims age 12 through 16, initial testing identified sixteen positive cultures in

14 adolescents: seven vaginal gonorrhea; one oral gonorrhea; seven vaginal chlamydia; and one rectal chlamydia. All initial tests were negative for syphilis, yeast, and *Trichomonas*. Just over half, 59 (51 percent), of the initial sample returned for follow-up testing and treatment. Of tests on those, there were eight (13 percent) additional positive findings: one vaginal gonorrhea; two vaginal chlamydia; three rectal chlamydia, and two *Trichomoas*.

SARS AIDS Study Results

Minnesota passed a law in the summer of 1990 requiring that all hospitals and clinics treating sexual assault victims provide them with information on sexually transmitted diseases including AIDS. The initial impetus for this bill came from the growing concern of rape victims and rape crisis centers throughout the state about the possibility of a victim becoming HIV positive as the result of a rape. In an attempt to deal with their concerns in a more comprehensive way, the legislators decided to broaden the requirement to include information on risk, testing, treatment, and prevention of all sexually transmitted diseases.

The initial request to the Minnesota legislature was to require HIV testing of convicted sex offenders. The legislators, however, recognized that the testing of the convicted sex offender for HIV falls short of providing for the victim's needs. Unfortunately, few rapists are ever convicted of rape. Even when they are convicted, considerable time has elapsed since the rape—in most cases more than three months, and in many cases more than six months. With this extensive time delay, even if the assailant is convicted, the victim is better off being tested herself.

The threat of giving the victim a deadly sexually transmitted disease has become a new form of torture used by some rapists to further torment their victims long after their departure. In the past year, SARS has had two rapists tell their victims they were HIV positive, "so now you're going to die from AIDS." One of the two assailants was never apprehended, but the victim was tested at three and six months postrape. She did not seroconvert. The other rapist was apprehended. He was found to be HIV negative.

For the past two years SARS has also been testing adult rape victims in the emergency room, and again at three and six months post rape for hepatitis B and the HIV virus responsible for AIDS. Initial testing was completed on 412 sexual assault victims who were raped anally, vaginally or both. Of those 31 percent returned for the three month testing and 12 percent for the six-month testing. One percent tested positive for hepatitis B at the initial testing, and 1.5 percent on follow-up at three months. There was thus a 0.5 percent conversion rate for hepatitis B. Fortunately, there were no initial HIV positive tests, nor were there any positive follow-up HIV tests. We thus concluded that at the present time the risk of a rape victim contracting the HIV virus as the result of a sexual assault in Minneapolis is extremely low.

STD Protocol Options and Considerations

When a rape victim comes into a clinic or hospital emergency room after a sexual assault, there are two primary options for dealing with her concerns about sexually transmitted diseases. The health care provider can test for STDs, or prophylactic treatment can be provided.

STD Testing

There are three primary reasons a sexual assault treatment protocol might call for STD cultures/testing rather than prophylactic treatment. First, the health care provider may want to avoid unnecessary use of antibiotics in uninfected individuals. Second, the care provider may want to collect STD information for use as evidence, and third, the health care provider may see his or her job as providing routine medical care to someone who might otherwise not come in for routine medical care.

Deciding Which Orifices to Culture

The first decision when cultures are taken is which orifices to culture. The protocol must specify if cultures are to be taken from all orifices or only from the orifices the client indicates were involved in the assault. In the conscious adult victim the latter is the more likely choice. There are differences of opinion when the child and adolescent victim is being seen.

It had been the policy of the pediatric department of one of the hospitals that SARS is associated with to culture all orifices of children and adolescents regardless of the orifices the child or adolescent reports were involved in the assault. The rationale for this is that the child or adolescent might not admit to a rectal or oral assault because of embarrassment. The value of this practice was evaluated in 1990 when the SARS nurse began doing the adolescent evidentiary exam at that hospital.

SARS reviewed the records for 116 adolescents, 12 through 16 years of age, seen by the pediatric department. It is interesting to note that there was not one positive specimen of any kind (STD, sperm, or acid phosphatase) taken from an orifice the adolescent did not state was involved in the assault.

Rationale for STD Testing
Avoiding the Unnecessary Use of Antibiotics

We have all likely heard about the mounting numbers of antibiotic resistant strains of bacteria that have resulted from the extensive use of antibiotics. We have all likely witnessed the indiscriminate prescribing of antibiotics for general flu-like symptoms. If we could be assured that all rape victims who have been exposed to a treatable STD such as gonorrhea or syphilis would return for further testing, and then return again for treatment if the tests are positive, that would indeed be the preferred method of care *if we are concerned only with the medical issues.*

The literature, however, indicates that although as many as 43 percent of the rape victims tested are positive for at least one STD on the initial exam and 37.5 percent had new STDs on follow-up (Jenny et al, 1990), as few as 8 percent of rape victims may return for even one follow-up visit (Kaufman et al, 1976). This means that potentially thousands of women go untreated.

Even though there are times to be conservative in our use of antibiotics, unless we can ensure better follow-up, the risk of the rape victims not being treated appear to far outweigh the risk of giving prophylactic antibiotics in this particular population.

STD Test Results as Evidence

When cultures are taken to be used as evidence, they must be taken in the emergency room to be used as baseline data to identify preexisting disease, or the absence of disease, and then again on follow-up to identify STDs contracted as a result of the assault. These follow-up cultures typically occur at three to five weeks and twelve weeks after the assault.

If the victim is negative at the time the initial cultures are taken and positive on follow-up, the later cultures are then assumed to identify diseases contracted from the assailant as a result of the sexual assault. In theory, these results may be useful evidence that may be used in court as further proof that the rape occurred. In theory, if the assailant, too, has the same STD, that could be used to identify him as the assailant and prove sexual contact.

Unfortunately, since SARS began seeing rape victims in 1977, there is only one known case in which a positive STD culture was useful in convicting an assailant. In this particular case the assailant claimed he had never been involved with the woman sexually. She tested negative in the emergency and positive on the follow-up. While the assailant denied having any STD, the county attorney was able to locate clinic records showing he had indeed been treated for the same STD the victim had acquired. He was convicted.

There have, however, been a number of occasions in which positive STD cultures were used against the victim in court. These include positive STD cultures obtained on initial exam as well as on follow-up. Positive STD cultures on initial exam have been used to discredit the victim as sexually promiscuous.

Positive STD cultures on follow-up either have not been helpful to a case or they have actually harmed an otherwise good case. In most instances the positive STD follow-up results just have not been helpful in convicting an assailant. Defense attorneys have argued successfully that a rape victim could not prove beyond a reasonable doubt that positive culture on follow-up only could have been the result of the rape rather than of consenting sex that occurred after the time of the "alleged" rape but prior to the second testing.

In addition, in one otherwise good case a positive follow-up gonorrhea culture appeared to be a primary piece of evidence that allowed one woman's assailant to go free. This particular woman was negative for gonorrhea in the emergency room and positive on follow-up. She had not been sexually active between tests. When the assailant was finally tested for gonorrhea long after the rape, he was negative. While he would not, of course, admit to having been treated, there are many locations in the Twin Cities area where anonymous testing and treatment can be obtained. In all likelihood, he was treated soon after the rape when he developed symptoms. His attorney used his negative gonorrhea status to get the charges dropped.

STD Testing as Routine Health Care

Some health care professionals believe strongly that rape victims should be given a complete physical exam, including a complete medical history (Glaser, Hammerschlag, and McCormack, 1989). It may indeed be true that the rape exam is an opportunity to provide health care and health teaching to an individual the system may not otherwise reach. The question is whether this is the appropriate time to do so. The answer to that question likely will vary from institution to institution, or even case to case.

Prophylactic Antibiotic Treatment

Wide spectrum antibiotics given to rape victims in the emergency room provide treatment for many existing asymptomatic STDs as well as preventing the contraction of an STD as a result of the rape. There are a number of advantages to the use of antibiotics prophylactically after a sexual assault. First, if the victim is being treated prophylactically, there is no need to take cultures in the emergency room and there is no need for the victim to return to clinic for the follow-up visits for additional cultures. Not only does this significantly reduce the cost of the initial exam by hundreds of dollars, but even more important, it saves the victim from at least two clinic visits requiring another pelvic exam. Since most victims do not return for follow-up anyway, it also ensures that more victims are being treated for acquired STDs.

Equally as important as the medical advantages of prophylactic treatment is the psychological benefit of avoiding the fear of acquiring an STD. This fear can greatly add to the victim's distress and feeling of being "soiled."

Avoiding the Fear of Contracting an STD

Contracting a sexually transmitted disease at any time, but especially as the result of a rape, is much more than a medical problem. It carries grave psychological impact with it for the rape victim. Especially if the rape victim is involved in an ongoing sexual relationship, the time she must wait for testing to be complete puts an additional burden on an already stressed relationship.

As health care providers it is all too easy for us to become hardened to the psychological impact of disease, especially sexually transmitted diseases. It may be that we are not doing our jobs as well as we give ourselves credit for, even if we take the extra time to contact the rape survivor to get her in for follow-up cultures. It may be that we owe rape victims more than that. If we can prevent them from contracting an STD, perhaps we have a responsibility at least to let them know that prophylactic treatment/prevention is an option.

Allowing the Rape Survivor to Decide

When SARS first began to offer prophylactic treatment as an option to rape victims, we were surprised by the high percentage, 98 percent, of clients that requested the antibiotics in lieu of follow-up cultures. We were even more surprised by the reason they gave us for preferring treatment. Although not having to return to clinic was certainly a factor, the primary reason they told us they wanted to be treated was that it made them feel cleansed. Rape victims often report repeated bathing to try to wash away the filth they feel after being raped. Feeling "unclean" is expressed weeks after the assault. The antibiotics, however, have the psychological effect of making the victims feel cleansed from the inside out.

Although antibiotics will not provide 100 percent treatment, nor will they prevent 100 percent of the STDs, they do lessen the likelihood that a rape victim will have to deal with the added psychological turmoil, depression, humiliation, and anger that can result if she contracts a sexually transmitted disease.

A disadvantage of providing prophylactic care, in addition to treating unaffected patients, as discussed earlier, is that we lose information on the rates of infection following a sexual assault. It is also possible that some victims may be falsely reassured that they are disease free, could overlook symptoms of diseases not covered by the antibiotics, and might not return for additional testing when they should do so. Unfortunately, even stressing that the treatment is not 100 percent effective and providing the client with literature may not prevent these outcomes.

The SARS Solution with STDs

SARS has been providing services to sexual assault victims in the Twin Cities area since September, 1977. Our Sexual Assault Nurse Clinicians are on call to six community hospitals, seven days a week, twenty-four hours a day. Whenever a sexual assault victim comes to any of these emergency departments, the hospital staff pages the SARS nurse. She then comes into the emergency room and provides for all of the initial needs of the rape victims, including dealing with their concerns about STDs.

At the Sexual Assault Resource Service we are very clear with our clients that we are not providing routine care. We do not do routine pap smears as a part of the pelvic exam, and we do not do a routine physical exam. We do, however, note obvious pathology, or symptomology. We work closely with the emergency room physician to ensure that the victim's medical needs are met if there is any obvious or questionable pathology.

We do not routinely do STD cultures in the emergency room. We offer the rape survivor prophylactic antibiotics. While the drug of choice may, of course, vary, the Sexual Assault Resource Service protocol is based on the recommendations of the local health department and local communicable disease experts to minimize the contraction of chlamydia, syphilis, and gonorrhea.

If the victim chooses prophylactic treatment and is not pregnant, she is treated with ampicillin 3.5 gm P.O. with 1 gm. probenecid P.O., plus Doxycycline 100 mg P.O. b.i.d. x 7. A pregnancy test is done in the emergency room for all clients. If the victim is pregnant (or at risk of becoming pregnant from the rape and did not choose to take Ovral), and not allergic to penicillin, she is given erythromycin 500 mg P.O. q.i.d. x 7 instead of the doxycycline. In addition, if the woman has a history of yeast infections, is using birth control pills, or is diabetic or pregnant, she is also given Monistat-3. She is instructed to begin using the Monistat on the fourth day of antibiotic use. (See Table 10-1.)

For those adult and adolescent victims who choose not to take the prophylactic antibiotics, we make an appointment for them to return to the Ob-Gyn clinic, or their primary physician, for STD testing. Because we do cultures for medical purposes only and not for use as evidence in court, no cultures are taken in the emergency room for the asymptomatic adolescent or adult rape victim. If the victim is symptomatic, cultures are, of course, done in the emergency room, and a follow-up appointment is made as well.

Dealing with the concerns of the rape victim in relation to sexually transmitted disease is a much more complex issue than one might at first realize. There are important medical and psychological issues to consider. Unless we consider all of these aspects of our care we are not meeting the victim's needs to the best of our ability. SARS is continuing to evaluate our care of the rape victim in all of its aspects, including how we deal with the issues of sexually transmitted disease.

Table 10-1

PROPHYLACTIC TREATMENT FOR SEXUALLY TRANSMITTED DISEASES

The goal of prophylaxis is to minimize acquisition of Gonorrhea, chlamydia, and syphilis infections in sexually abused victims. Regimens A, B, C and D should all be effective in achieving this goal. Other alternatives that *might* be effective are listed below.

Pregnant or at Risk for Pregnancy?

NO				YES	
Allergic to Penicillin?				Allergic to Penicillin?	
No		Yes		No	Yes
Allergic to Doxycycline?		Allergic to Doxycycline?		B	D
No	Yes	No	Yes		
A	B	C	D		

A Ampicillin 3.5 gm + probenecid 1gm p.o. × 1 *plus* doxycycline 100 mg p.o. bi.d. × 7d[6].

B Ampicillin 3.5 gm + probenecid 1 gm p.o. × 1 *plus* erythromycin base 500 mg p.o. q.i.d.. × 7d[6].

C Consult with ED staff [2, 3, 4, 5] regarding giving ceftriaxone 250 mg IM *plus* doxycycline 100 mg p.o. b.i.d. × 7d[6].

D Consult with ED staff [2, 3, 4, 5] regarding giving ceftriaxone 250 mg IM *plus* erythromycin base 500 mg p.o. q.i.d. × 7d[6].

---

*Notes

1. For the purposes of this algorithm, if a patient at risk is prescribed Ovral, she will no longer be considered at risk.

2. Some patients who are allergic to penicillin will also be allergic to ceftriaxone.

3. Alternatives that will prevent gonorrhea include:Spectinomycin 2 gm IM (O.K. in pregnancy; does *not* cover syphilis); Ciprofloxacin 500 mg p.o. × 1 (contraindicated in pregnancy; does *not* cover syphilis); Norfloxacin 800 mg p.o. × 1 (contraindicated in pregnancy; does *not* cover syphilis).

4. Alternatives that *might* be effective against incubating syphilis include: Doxycycline 100 mg p.o. b.i.d. × 14d; Erythromycin base 500 mg p.o. q.i.d. × 14d.

5. If any alternative other than A, B, C, and D is used, the patient should be scheduled for repeat cultures at 3 months.

6. Any patient given antibiotics who is also is pregnant, is using birth control pills, is diabetic, or has history of yeast infections will also be given Monistat-3.

References

Baxter, R.A. 1990. Letter to the editor. *New England Journal of Medicine*, 323(16):1141.

Blackmore, C.A., R.A. Keegan, and W. Cates. 1982. Diagnosis and treatment of sexually transmitted diseases in rape victims. *Reviews of Infectious Diseases* 4:877–82.

DeJong, A.R. 1985. Vaginitis due to *Gardnerella vaginalis* and to *Candida albicans* in sexual abuse. *Child Abuse Neglect* 9:27–29.

Forster, G.E., J. Pritchard, P.E. Munday, and D. Goldmeier. 1986. Incidence of sexually transmitted diseases in rape victims during 1984. *Genitourin Med.*, 62:267–69.

Glaser, J.B., M.R. Hammerschlag, and W.M. McCormack. 1989. Epidemiology of sexually transmitted diseases in rape victims. *Reviews of Infectious Diseases* 11(2):246–54.

Gray, M.L., and S. Whitehouse. 1990. Letter to the editor. *New England Journal of Medicine* 323(16):1141.

Groth, A.N., and A. Burgess. 1977. Sexual dysfunction during rape. *The New England Journal of Medicine* 297:764–66.

Hayman, C., and C. Lanza. 1971. Sexual assault on women and girls. *American Journal of Obstetrics and Gynecology* 109:480–86.

Jenny, C., Hooton, T.M. Bowers, M.K. Copass, J.N. Krieger, S.L. Hillier, N. Kiviat, L. Corey, W.E. Stamm, and K.K. Holmes. 1990. Sexually transmitted diseases in victims of rape. *New England Journal of Medicine* 322(11):713–16.

Kaufman, A., J. Vandermeer, P. DiVasto, S. Hilaski, and W. Odegard. 1976. Follow-up of rape victims in a family practice setting. *Southern Medical Journal* 69(12):1569–71.

Ledray, L.E. 1980. Unpublished data.

Sturm, J.T., Carr, M.E., Luxenberg, M.G., Swoyer, J.K., and Cicero, J. The prevalence of neisseria gonorrhoeae and chlamydia trachomatis in victims of sexual assault. *Annals of Emergency Medicine* 19(5):587–90.

U.S. Department of Justice. 1989. *Uniform Crime Report*. Washington, DC.

Chapter 11

Coping with Interpersonal Violence and Sexual Victimization:
Perspectives for Victims and Care Providers

Pamela Brede Minden
Charles River Hospital
Wellesley, MA

■

Sections of "The Victim Care Service: A Program for Victims of Sexual Assault" are reprinted with permission from Archives of Psychiatric Nursing, *W.B. Saunders.*

■

In February, 1989, "The Victim Care Service: A Program for Victims of Sexual Assault," appeared in *Archives of Psychiatric Nursing*. The article described a program at Boston City Hospital (BCH) that was designed to meet the various needs of individuals seeking care following sexual victimization. It seemed ironic that the article was published the very month that the hospital reorganized its management structure and did away with my position as the assistant director for psychiatric nursing. A major part of my role as the assistant director had been to coordinate the Victim Care Service (VCS).

The reorganization came about as the result of the increasing fiscal constraints being placed on all aspects of health care. Initially it seemed quite threatening. After all, it meant the elimination of my middle management job. In reality, it presented me with an opportunity to critically evaluate the program and my role in it. The administration said it recognized the value of the VCS and would welcome my continued involvement with it. They agreed with my assessment that not only did the VCS need to continue, but in fact it needed to be expanded to provide care for victims of all kinds of violence. In the process of making recommendations for restructuring the service, though, I began to feel overwhelmed by the enormity of the problem of interpersonal violence.

It wasn't that I didn't feel a sense of accomplishment. I had participated in the recovery process of a number of victims of violence and derived great satisfaction from seeing the VCS become an integral part of BCH. But I also felt emotionally depleted. While my interest in interpersonal violence remained strong, I had lost my direction in terms of how to approach it in a meaningful and effective way. At the end of February I decided to leave Boston City Hospital.

In less than a month of respite from the stresses of BCH and the VCS I began to feel more hopeful about having an impact on the problem of interpersonal violence. I wanted to approach it from a more global perspective this time. I entered a program of doctoral study that would allow me eventually to address the issue at the societal level, through research and policy development.

In December of 1989, as I was finishing my first semester of course work, a second irony occurred. Ann Burgess invited me to update my *Archives of Psychiatric Nursing* article to be included as a chapter in *Rape and Sexual Assault III*. I was presented with another opportunity to describe the VCS for a wide audience. But I was no longer coordinating the service, and my parting recommendations had yet to be implemented.

Publicly the message was that the VCS was still operating in pretty much the same manner but, at the time of Dr. Burgess's invitation, there was still no one identified to oversee the VCS. It was also public knowledge that continued budget cuts had resulted in more positions being lost, and existing staff were reshuffled to provide necessary services.

Although the actual number of sexual assault victims seeking assistance had not increased, the brutality involved in the cases being treated had. During my tenure at BCH almost all sexual assault victims were discharged directly from the Emergency Department. In 1989 two victims had to be hospitalized for injuries incurred during the assault. From January to August, 1990, this number had increased to eight victims requiring hospitalization. (J. Meunier-Sham, personal communication, August 23, 1990.) A study done by the VCS in conjunction with Dan Bibel from the Statistical Analysis Center of the Massachusetts Committee on Criminal Justice identified that 80 percent of the sexual victimization cases seen in 1984 and 1985 involved only one perpetrator (Bibel, Minden, Dimatio, 1988). In 1990 the number of adult cases involving multiple assailants had increased to 33 percent (J. Meunier-Sham, personal communication, August 23, 1990).

Knowing well the dedication of the clinicians still involved in the VCS I could assume sexual assault victims would still receive quality care. And yet, with ever-decreasing resources and the increasing incidence of violence in Boston, I wondered how the care providers were faring.

I have remained in contact with my colleagues at BCH and the VCS. I can readily identify the urgent and obligatory tone in their voices when they talk about their work with victims. They acknowledge that they may be a bit stressed but assure me that they can handle it. I can remember myself saying something similar, and adding that I really felt there were many rewards in working with victims. Now that I have some distance from the situation I recognize that my involvement in the VCS had taken quite a toll. Even while still at BCH I knew this, at some level. Then I was so caught up in the demands of providing care for victims, though, that I believed I was indispensable. I knew I was tired but I didn't see how I could quit. Had it not been for the reorganization, I might not have been able to see what a martyr I had become and allow myself to move on.

I do not mean to imply that all people who work with victims at BCH, or anywhere, are necessarily doomed to martyrdom. When I left the hospital it was clear to me that there were many energetic and committed clinicians there who would continue to provide superb care to victims. A year after my departure an assistant deputy commissioner position was created to coordinate all victim-related programs within the hospital and the greater Department of Health and Hospitals, of which it is a part. Although slow to materialize, the position has been filled by an astute and experienced Master's-prepared nurse, who had been a prominent member of the Victim Care Committee responsible for the development of the VCS. Her appointment, and the administration's support of her vision for expansion of services to address all kinds of interpersonal violence, is evidence of the hope and enthusiasm that miraculously survives in a system besieged by the aftermath of incredible violence.

It is partly my admiration for the devotion of the clinicians who stayed to solve the problem of interpersonal violence in the face of great odds that motivates me to again present the VCS and the assumptions upon which it was based. I also hope that by reading about the VCS others who have grown weary of caring for victims can gain some perspective. Although not a perfect program, a review of the experiences of the VCS brings to light many salient points that are useful to consider when developing or revising services to sexual assault and abuse victims. The Service's five phases of care may also serve as a model from which ideas for dealing with victims of all kinds of violence can be drawn. The description that follows delineates how the VCS operated from the beginning of 1986 until February 1989.

The Victim Care Service

Boston City Hospital is a large public hospital that serves a population diverse in its ethnicity and socioeconomic characteristics. The BCH Emergency Department (ED) is a major trauma center that treats over 50,000 adult patients and 25,000 pediatric patients annually. Each year between 200 and 250 of these patients come to the ED reporting sexual victimization. The Victim Care Service is an integral part of the ED that addresses the medical, medical-legal, and emotional needs of these patients.

The development of the VCS dates back to the early 1970s when Burgess and Holmstrom first established their victim counselling program at BCH. Their book, *Rape: Victims of Crisis* (1974), outlines the counselling approach developed in the first year of that program. Their work not only laid the foundation for the current VCS, but also significantly influenced rape-counselling approaches and services throughout the world.

The VCS involves a multidisciplinary team approach to care. The program coordinator is a Psychiatric Nurse Clinical Specialist, and the other clinicians span the disciplines of medicine, nursing, and social work. The VCS has evolved into a five-phase program.

Phase I, program development, focuses on setting standards and training treatment providers in victim care. The program coordinator acts as a liaison with other programs at the city, state, national level in order to maintain a comprehensive network of victim services.

Another important aspect of phase I is community education. The VCS joins with other service agencies to present educational programs on violence and rape prevention.

Phase II, acute intervention, operates under the auspices of the Victim Care Committee. This multidisciplinary team of experts defines the process of care during this phase and delineates the roles and responsibilities of the clinicians involved. Phase II is activated whenever a BCH patient is identified as a victim of sexual assault. This usually occurs in the ED but the hospital's inpatient units and outpatient clinics are included in the VCS network.

Phase III, follow-up, is a direct extension of phase II. All patients seen in phase II are offered up to four supportive counselling sessions provided by a team of Masters-prepared psychiatric nurses and social workers. Individuals with a history of physical, psychological, or social difficulties prior to the sexual assault may need more than crisis counselling. The phase III clinicians act as advocates for these patients and make sure they are hooked up with the necessary other supports and services.

Phase IV, ongoing therapy, operates on a referral basis only because BCH does not have the capacity to provide outpatient mental health services. The VCS maintains a linkage system with other community programs that offer individual, family, and group therapy in order to provide continuity of care for its patients.

Phase V, evaluation and research, involves ongoing quality assurance monitors to ensure that the standards established in phase I are met. The VCS also initiates and participates in research relevant to sexual victimization.

The five phases of the VCS are organized around six fundamental assumptions. These assumptions are presented in some detail in an attempt to elaborate on the functioning of the five phases.

Assumption 1:
There is a continuum of sexual victimization

Any individual who has experienced unwanted sexual activity, regardless of the exact nature of the activity, meets the VCS's flexible criteria for having been sexually victimized. The service provides care for patients who present with complaints ranging from harassment to rape.

Within the VCS the phrase "sexual victimization" is used generically to mean a number of possible types of sexual assault or abuse.

Sexual assault is not defined as a sexual act, but rather as a form of aggression and violence in which sex is the weapon. It is an assault even if no physical injury was incurred. Sexual abuse is defined as the abuse of power by one individual over another. This term is used most frequently in the context of children.

Rape represents sexual assault or abuse in its most extreme form. Rape is a legal term that is defined at the state level. Many state laws define rape as sexual intercourse by force or threat of harm, and without consent (Estrich, 1986; Schwartz & Clear, 1980).

It is a basic premise of the VCS that a patient does not need to meet any stringent legal criteria for rape in order to be considered sexually victimized. The legal system bears the burden of determining the validity of a given charge of rape, whereas the primary responsibility of the VCS is to care for the patient reporting sexual victimization.

Assumption 2:
Sexual victimization occurs frequently

Determining the actual incidence and prevalence of sexual victimization is difficult. Sexual victimization is a rather fluid term than can be defined in many ways. In fact, it can occur, according to an observer's perspective, without the actual victim regarding it as such.

There is much in the literature and media to suggest that rape may be America's fastest growing violent crime (Bard & Sangrey, 1986). In 1986 the Federal Bureau of Investigation estimated that for every 100,000 females in the United States there were 73 reported rape victims. This number represents an increase of 2 percent since 1985 and an increase of 10 percent since 1982 (U.S. Department of Justice, 1986a).

Even though *rape* may be more specifically defined than the term *sexual victimization*, estimating its actual incidence and prevalence is hampered by the fact that many victims simply do not report the crime. Only one in three of all personal crimes are reported to the police (U.S. Department of Justice, 1986b).

The National Crime Survey (NCS) estimated that between 1973 and 1982 one and one-half million rapes and attempted rapes occurred in the United States. This means that there was approximately one rape for every 600 females age 12 years and older (U.S. Department of Justice, 1985). The NCS interviewed a representative national sample so that even rapes that are not reported to the police are reflected.

The NCS only addresses victimization rates for persons age 12 and older. Child sexual abuse represents a problem of great magnitude (Russell, 1983; Thomas & Rogers, 1984). Estimates of the number of cases of child sexual abuse range from 50,000 to over one million annually (Burgess & Grant, 1988). It is a widely accepted tenet that much of child sexual abuse goes undetected.

Each year the VCS sees over 100 adult and 100 pediatric patients who report sexual victimization. The service tends to see a fairly young population of patients. Nearly 25 percent of all the patients are under 10 years of age at the time of their ED visit. Over 66 percent of the patients are under the age of 25 years. The service sees very few patients who are over the age of 45 years (Bibel, Minden, & Dimattio, 1988).

Assumption 3:
Responses to sexual assault victims have frequently been based on myths and stereotypes

Many people believe that sexual assault victims are somehow responsible for their victimization. This myth is reflected in the still commonly held belief that all women have rape fantasies and that it is all right for men to fulfill such fantasies. The myth is also evidenced in the attitude that people who dress provocatively, stay out late, or frequent dangerous places get what they deserve. Although engaging in certain behaviors may increase the risk of sexual victimization, the VCS maintains that it is the perpetrator alone who is to blame for the victimization.

Another myth is that rape is a crime that is prone to false complaints. There is no sound basis for the belief that there are more women who make false rape reports than there are other crime victims making false reports. Recent analyses in fact suggest that victims of rape are disinclined to make complaints under current laws and that those who do so frequently later refuse to continue their testimony because they are treated badly (Schwartz & Clear, 1980).

Several other prevalent myths about sexual victimization are that it only happens to "other people" and that it most often occurs in a dark alley at the hands of a stranger. Contrary to popular belief, confidence rape, an assault by someone who is known to the victim, is a more frequent occurrence than is stranger rape, and it most often happens in the victim's home or another familiar place.

Sexual assault and abuse cross all boundaries of class and culture. Anyone, regardless of age or sex, can become a victim. Culturally accepted stereotypes of what it means to be male have contributed to a reluctance to recognize men as potential victims. The strength of the myth that men cannot be raped is reflected in the Uniform Crime Reporting definition of forcible rape as " . . . the carnal knowledge of a female. . . ." (U.S. Department of Justice, 1986a). In Boston there is concrete evidence of male sexual victimization. Of the 501 cases of sexual assault reported in 1987 to the Boston police, 64 were assaults on men (M. O'Malley, personal communication, April 6, 1988).

The fact that victims can be of either sex helps to negate the myth that women are naturally better equipped than men to care for sexual assault victims. The clinician, whether male or female, must be accepting of the patient. A female clinician caring for a female victim might defend against her own feelings of vulnerability by rejecting the patient. In contrast, that same patient might benefit from interaction with a male clinician who acts in a nurturing manner, especially if she was victimized by a male. At BCH it is attitude rather than gender that determines a clinician's ability to provide victim care.

Individuals who have been sexually victimized frequently describe it as the most traumatic experience of their lives. Whether or not an individual is able to cope with the trauma depends on a number of factors, including the nature of the assault, the presence of other stressors, the patient's precrisis functioning and coping skills, and the available support system. The clinician who can communicate a sense of optimism for recovery may help nullify the enduring negative effects of sexual victimization.

One final myth is that one must be an expert to care for sexual assault victims. These patients do have some particular needs, and the VCS inservices all the ED clinicians in principles of victim care. The working knowledge of crisis intervention techniques is more important for the ED clinician than a thorough understanding of sexual victimization. The VCS attempts to minimize the differences between sexually victimized patients and other patients seeking emergency services. The victim care inservice is designed to reinforce the basic skills that doctors, nurses, and social workers have to intervene with traumatized individuals.

Assumption 4:
Sexual assault or attempted sexual assault represents a trauma or crisis that results in a disruption of the victim's physical, emotional, and social equilibrium

Many acts of sexual victimization do not leave bruises, cuts, or other evidence of physical harm. The potential for psychological harm, however, is great. Sexual victimization transcends time and situation. In other words, it leaves a lasting impression on the individual who survives the assault.

The state of disequilibrium that follows sexual victimization is marked by intense stress and anxiety (Janoff-Bulman, 1985). Victims experience a wide range of feelings and exhibit a variety of behaviors. The victim may act completely controlled or even be stoic. At the other extreme victims may appear overwhelmed or act very crazy. Viktor Frankl (1963) said that "an abnormal reaction to an abnormal situation is normal behavior." It is important to reassure victims of the normalcy of their responses.

To characterize the traumatic stress reactions of rape victims, Burgess and Holstrom (1974) coined the term *rape trauma syndrome*. They identified that rape victims pass through two phases in an attempt to recover:

> The victim experiences a period of acute disorganization following the assault. This is an immediate impact reaction that lasts from one to six weeks after the assault. It has behavioral, emotional, cognitive, and physical manifestations.
>
> The reorganization phase lasts anywhere from the sixth week to six months after the assault. The victim may experience a variety of symptoms over time. The severity and frequency of these can vary greatly. During this period the victim may make changes in lifestyle, experience numerous somatic complaints, have mood swings, and develop phobias. There are some individuals who never resolve the rape trauma and go on to develop actual clinical disorders (post-traumatic stress disorder).

Sexual victimization also makes a distinct impression on the victim's social sphere. Family and friends may experience some symptoms of rape trauma syndrome in response to the victimization of their loved one.

The VCS sees patients in both phases of rape trauma syndrome. Many of the patients openly admit their victimization and have sought help soon after the incident. They evidence symptoms indicative of the phase of acute disorganization. Other patients, with an undisclosed history of sexual assault or abuse, may make use of the ED for some other reason. The astute clinician may be able to identify symptoms of the reorganization phase and offer the patient appropriate assistance. The VCS advocates that history-taking in the ED include assessment of whether the patient has ever been a victim of any kind of violence. This is especially helpful with those patients (such as children or battered women) who may be victims of ongoing abuse but are afraid to disclose their circumstances.

Assumption 5:
Crisis intervention facilitates a positive resolution of the victimization experience

Patterns of coping with trauma can be adaptive or maladaptive. The purpose of crisis intervention is to steer the individual in the direction of adaptive coping and away from maladaptive behaviors.

The forte of the VCS is crisis intervention, and it is the essence of phases II and III of the program. The emphasis of these phases is on moving the patient from being a victim to being a survivor. The care of the sexually assaulted or abuse patient is considered a high priority in the ED.

A salient feature of victimization for the patient is a loss of control. Emergency department clinicians can easily mirror the patient's crisis and may also experience feelings of being overwhelmed by the trauma. Practically no one feels really comfortable with a victim. Witnessing the patient's tragedy makes the clinician feel vulnerable. The VCS has developed a very structured process for providing victim care. This has helped to reestablish a sense of control for the clinicians who can then put their energies into stabilizing the patient. A brief description of the process of care during phases II and III follows.

PHASE II

A triage nurse is the patient's first contact in the BCH ED. The triage nurse immediately escorts the patient to a private treatment room and assigns a victim care coordinator (VCC). The VCC is an ED registered nurse or social worker who oversees the provision of care throughout the patient's stay in the ED. There is a predetermined call system for identifying the VCC each shift.

There is a team approach to care. The specialty of the physician and nurse involved in the team varies according to the age and sex of the patient. For example, an ED pediatrician will see a child victim and an obstetrician/gynecologist sees all adult female victims. The actual number of clinicians involved with the patient is kept to a minimum and the VCC coordinates their efforts. The VCC also coordinates the activities of outside service providers such as the police and child protection authorities.

In order to simplify the process of care a victim care kit that contains all necessary supplies has been developed. The VCC obtains the kit when the patient arrives and is responsible for stocking it when the patient has left.

At BCH there is a standardized approach for diagnosing and treating patients who report sexual victimization. This is a generic approach that is applicable to both adults and children. It was developed in an attempt to enhance the likelihood of a positive resolution of the trauma for both the patient and the clinician. It is based on the sexual assault protocol and involves doing a sexual assault examination.

The sexual assault protocol is a five-page form that is used to organize and document the sexual assault exam. The sexual assault exam can be divided into three intertwined categories: emotional, medical, and medical-legal. The sequence in which they are addressed is made unique by the particular clinical presentation of each individual patient. Meeting the patient's emotional needs is a critical part of the exam. During the acute phase of intervention patients require constant reassurance about their safety and well-being. They are informed of their medical and legal options and the consequences of choosing each alternative. This includes being informed of the right to refuse any, or all, aspects of the sexual assault exam.

The medical component of the exam includes treating the patient for injuries. Tests for infection, especially sexually transmitted diseases, are performed and the patient may be treated prophylactically to prevent illness. Adult and pubescent females are offered pregnancy testing, prevention, and/or treatment.

The examination of the sexual assault victim in the ED is unique in that the clinician must not only address the emotional and medical needs of the victim, but must also obtain and document legal evidence. The chain of evidence must be maintained until transferred to the authorities. Many hospitals buy commercially prepared rape evidence collection kits (rape kits) for this purpose. In an effort to simplify and standardize evidence collection, Massachusetts has designed a rape kit and an associated sexual assault protocol. The VCS participated in the development of the kit and protocol. The BCH ED was the pilot site for their use before they were made available, free of charge, to all hospitals in the commonwealth.

Evidence collection is the essence of the medical-legal aspect of the sexual assault exam. Indications of sexual contact are sought and injuries that can corroborate the use of force are documented. Any physical evidence that can identify the assailant is also collected. Patients are encouraged to have evidence collected even if they are undecided about taking legal action. Failure to do so makes it more difficult to follow a legal course should the patient decide later to press charges. The VCS will notify the legal authorities only with the patient's permission, however.

Patients are discharged from the ED only when they feel safe and have a reasonable plan for follow-up care. All patients are given written discharge instructions that reiterate what tests and treatments they received and outline what medical follow-up is indicated. The instruction form also addresses the wide range of emotions and responses that victims can expect in the aftermath of the trauma. It prepares victims for physical symptoms that may result from the stress of the experience. It also prepares them for the responses of family, friends, and others they may interact with. Resources for continued care and support are listed as well.

PHASE III

The chart of every sexual assault victim seen in the ED is reviewed by one of the phase III clinicians. The phase II clinicians are given feedback about the completed protocol in an effort to enhance their skills and reward good work. The phase III clinicians take an active stance in initiating further therapeutic contact. The patient in crisis has difficulty following the traditional expectation of being the one to secure ongoing assistance. An attempt is made to call the patient in the next several days. If contact is not made within a week, a letter offering further service is sent. If after a month there is no response to this letter, a closing letter is sent. This is done as much for the clinicians as for the patients. The clinicians need to put closure on the involvement with the patient. The progress of the patients who do have ongoing contact with the VCS is reflected back to the phase II clinicians. This is an important step in validating the efforts of the phase II clinicians and helps them to maintain a sense of optimism in working with victims.

Assumption 6:
Sexual victimization is a complex, multifaceted problem that no one individual or group can resolve alone

The five phases of the VCS serve as a framework for conceptualizing the continuum of victim care at BCH. The VCS primarily focuses on the acute management of the patient who has been sexually victimized. No one clinician or discipline can possibly meet all the emotional, medical, and medical-legal needs of such a patient. This is not logistically feasible in the ED, and it places an unnecessary burden of responsibility on one individual or group. A multidisciplinary team approach helps to meet the diverse needs of the victim. It also provides the caregivers with a support system for dealing with a very difficult and emotionally laden problem.

The support system for both the clinician and the patient needs to extend beyond the limits of phases II and III. Dealing with sexual victimization requires the collaborative and cooperative efforts of a network of services. Phases I and IV connect the VCS to the outside world so that there is continuity of patient care beyond the scope of what BCH can provide. The crucial function of phase IV is to maintain a referral system for VCS patients requiring ongoing therapy or services. Phase I links the VCS to the community at large and serves as the program's political action component. The liaison work of the program's coordinator includes advocating for victim rights and services, not only at BCH, but at the city, state, and national level.

The continuum of victim care must include prevention as well as secondary intervention. The VCS provides continuous victim care training for hospital clinicians to preclude secondary traumatization of patients reporting sexual assault or abuse. The service also joins with other programs in offering workshops to enhance community awareness of sexual victimization.

Summary

Reflecting on my experience with the VCS leads me to make explicit a further assumption that was, at least covertly, fundamental to its operation.

Assumption 7:
Working with victims takes a toll
on the providers of care

My own experience has lead me to conclude that working with victims of violence has some inherent risks for the clinician. Working in any aspect of health care these days is stressful. Ever escalating economic constraints and patient acuity present care providers with increasing challenges that are physically, intellectually, and emotionally draining. Superimpose on this the fact that working with victims is just inherently stressful.

Burnout, a syndrome of emotional and physical exhaustion that includes the development of a negative concept of one's self and job and a loss of concern for those with whom one is working, is frequently identified as a problem among nurses and other helping professionals (Lavandero, 1981).

In a recent study, nurse researchers assisting in a case-record review of rape crisis center records to determine demographic predictors of sexual abuse were found to experience subjective responses closely parallel to those reported in the literature on rape victims. This occurred despite the fact that data collection did not involve any direct contact with victims or their assailants (Alexander et al., 1989).

Although not formally documented, clinicians at BCH who participated in a similar chart review of sexual assault victims seen there in 1984 and 1985, reported that merely reading the records temporarily evoked in them a variety of symptoms suggestive of Post-Traumatic Stress Disorder (Bibel, Minden, & Dimattio, 1988). If reading about sexual victimization in the lives of others can precipitate stress reactions, one should expect that actually witnessing trauma in the lives of others would also.

VCS clinicians, like many individuals working in emergency departments in large city hospitals, have very direct and frequent exposure to trauma. In witnessing trauma, one must, at some level, feel vulnerable. But the overt recognition of such vulnerability can be clouded by a need to appear competent and in control; both for the sake of the victim for whom one is caring, and for one's own sense of security. A common manifestation of this are comments such as, "I know it's stressful to work with victims, but I can handle it." Clearly many clinicians can, and do, handle the stress of working with victims; but for how long and at what cost to themselves?

Although there are many rewards inherent in working with individuals who are victims of interpersonal violence, there are also many pitfalls. Not the least among these is a syndrome I call "Running on Empty." The clinician gets so caught up in the demands of the work that he or she becomes driven by it. Unlike the phenomenon of burnout, where the clinician begins to dehumanize the client, when "Running on Empty" the clinician continues to treat clients in a competent and concerned manner but "superhumanizes" himself or herself. By this I mean that the clinician comes to have unrealistic expectations of what he or she can and must do to deal with the problem of interpersonal violence. Although intellectually able to recognize that work with victims is difficult, the "victims" of this syndrome charge ahead without providing emotional respite for themselves.

The aftereffects of sexual violence on the victim are clearly and frequently documented in the literature. Articles describing methods of providing care to such victims, without retraumatizing them, are also quite readily available. "The Victim Care Service: A Program for Victims of Sexual Assault" was one such article. It very briefly addressed the issue of how clinicians can easily mirror a victim's crisis. Having a very organized and structured way of dealing with victims was suggested as a means of helping the care provider to regain control. A multidisciplinary team approach to victim care was identified as providing caregivers with a support system. Both of these tactics can help prevent clinicians from becoming overwhelmed by their work with victims, but they are not by themselves enough.

Research is now needed to further explore the short- and long-term effects on the care provider of working with victims and to identify strategies for providing care in a humane way without depleting the clinician's energies. Such strategies should address what can be done at the institutional level to promote caregivers' abilities to respond to the needs of victims, as well as what the individual clinician can do to facilitate his or her own coping skills.

References

Alexander, J.G., M. deChesnay, E. Marshall, A.R. Campbell, S. Johnson, and R. Wright. 1989. Research note: Parallel reactions in rape victims and rape researchers. *Violence and Victims* 4(1), 57–62.

Bard, M. and D. Sangrey 1986. *The Crime Victim's Handbook* (2d ed.). New York: Brunner/Mazel, Inc.

Bibel, D., P. Minden, and N. Dimattio. 1988. Rape victims at an inner-city hospital. Unpublished study.

Burgess, A., and C.A. Grant, 1988. *Children Traumatized in Sex Rings.* Washington, DC: National Center for Missing and Exploited Children.

Burgess, A., and L.L. Holmstrom, 1974. *Rape: Victims of crisis.* Bowie, MD: Robert J. Brady Company.

Estrich, S. 1986. Rape. *The Yale Law Journal* 95(6):1087–84.

Frankl, V.E. 1963. *Man's Search for Meaning.* New York: Washington Square Press.

Janoff-Bulman, R. 1985. The aftermath of victimization: Rebuilding shattered assumptions. In C.R. Figley (ed.), *Trauma and its wake,* pp. 15–35. New York: Brunner/Mazel, Inc.

Lavandero, R. 1981. Nurse burnout: What can we learn? *The Journal of Nursing Administration.* November–December, 17–23.

Minden, P. 1989. The victim care service: A program for victims of sexual assault. *Archives of Psychiatric Nursing* 3(1):41–46.

Russell, D.E.H. 1983. The incidence and prevalence of intrafamilial and extrafamilial sexual abuse of female children. *Child Abuse and Neglect* (7):133–46.

Schwartz, M.D., and T.R. Clear. 1980. Toward a new law on rape. *Crime and Delinquency* (4): 129–51.

Thomas, J.N., and C.M. Rogers. 1984. Sexual victimization of children in the U.S.A.: Patterns and trends. In J.L. Chamberlain (ed.), *Clinical Proceedings Children's Hospital National Medical Center,* pp. 211–21. Baltimore, MD: Waverly Press, Inc.

U.S. Department of Justice. 1985. The crime of rape. *Bureau of Justice Statistics Bulletin* DHHS Publication No. NCJ-96777. Washington, DC: U.S. Government Printing Office.

U.S. Department of Justice. 1986. *Uniform Crime Reports* Washington, DC: U.S. Government Printing Office.

U.S. Department of Justice. 1986. Criminal victimization 1985. *Bureau of Justice Statistics Bulletin* DHHS Publication No. NCJ-102534. Washington, DC: U.S. Government Printing Office.

Chapter 12

Confidentiality in the Sexual Assault Victim/Counselor Relationship

Mary Ann Largen
National Network for Victims of Sexual Assault
Arlington, VA

∎

Sexual assault is an invasion of bodily privacy in an intensely personal and traumatic manner that triggers strong emotional and psychological reactions in the victim. Successful recovery requires that counseling be provided in a setting where confidential communications can occur without fear of disclosure. This chapter briefly describes the nature of the sexual assault victim and counselor relationship, the need to protect confidential communications between victims and counselors from criminal proceedings, and the results of a nationwide survey of state laws concerning sexual assault victim/counselor confidentiality.

The Nature of the Sexual Assault Victim/Counselor Relationship

Communications common to the sexual assault victim/counselor relationship are of an extremely confidential nature. Under any circumstance, it can be embarrassing to reveal one's deepest intimate feelings, fears, and frustrations to another. A sexual assault victim is usually compelled to see a counselor because the nature of those feelings are such that she cannot reveal them to anyone else, especially not to her intimates. The victim/counselor relationship is therefore one in which the victim must feel free to discuss those matters that usually would not be discussed with others. Thus, the sexual assault victim/counselor relationship depends for its success upon the creation of an atmosphere in which embarrassing and painful information can be freed from conscious and unconscious censorship.

The Role of Rape Crisis Counselors in the Mental Health Field

Although communications between attorneys and clients, or doctors and patients, have long been exempt from disclosure in criminal, and some civil, proceedings, the legal privilege conferred on psychotherapist/client communications is of more recent origin. The laws of privilege (i.e., their exemption from criminal or civil proceedings) are still uncertain, and are often subject to judicial interpretation, but with the growth of new behavioral science "professions" over the past forty years, policy makers are beginning to rethink the social policy underlying professional privileges.

The mental health profession, once limited to psychologists and psychiatrists, now encompasses psychiatric nurses, social workers, and a variety of trained, but unlicensed, counselors (e.g., hotline counselors, group home counselors, crime victim counselors, etc.). Rape crisis centers, largely staffed by trained but unlicensed counselors, are a part of this growing mental health services system. The usefulness of these new helping professions is becoming recognized as an adjunct to psychiatry and psychology, enabling psychotherapy to reach beyond the traditional office or clinic. And, over the past decade, there has been a growing trend among legislatures and the courts to confer a legal privilege on communications between many of these service providers and their clients.

The Need to Protect Sexual Assault Victim/Counselor Communications from Disclosure in Criminal Proceedings

The need for privileged communications arises when the effectiveness of a confidential relationship deemed important to society is dependent on full mutual disclosure between the parties. The case for conferring a privilege on communications between sexual assault victims and counselors is a strong one.

Because information communicated to sexual assault counselors is generally far more confidential in nature than that which arises in some of the relationships presently considered privileged by law, the fear of disclosure would deter most sexual assault victims from seeking counseling. Further, when counseling is sought it may not benefit—may indeed harm—the victim by adding to her trauma if confidential communications with a counselor are utilized in criminal proceedings. Feelings of dismay or even betrayal may occur when counsellors are compelled to disclose the victim's confidences in an open court. Therefore, victims who are aware that their communications might be subject to public disclosure may avoid counseling altogether. For these reasons, rape crisis centers have traditionally honored victim confidentiality and resisted legal subpoenas of counseling records. However, as rape crisis centers have become more institutionalized, a general increase in subpoenas of records has led to recent legislative and judicial efforts to examine the sexual assault victim/counselor relationship in light of the social policy and legal criteria used to confer other statutory and case law privileges.

Social Policy and Legal Criteria for Privileged Communications

The social policy underlying a privilege assigned to protect some societal interest is that the privilege is justified by the relationship of trust and the necessity for complete mutual disclosure of information between the parties. Unlike other recognized legal privileges, a professional privilege is designed to protect the therapeutic function rather than a group of individuals.

The legal criteria for conferring a privilege is subject to constitutional safeguards. The general rule in American jurisprudence is that anyone called on by either party in a case must testify as to any knowledge that may bear upon the case. However, there are certain narrowly defined exceptions that exempt some information from this general rule. These exceptions arise when the social utility of a particular relationship is so great that it outweighs society's interest in having all possible evidence disclosed. Thus, although the policy for requiring testimony is strong, it is not absolute.

In conferring a privilege, lawmakers must assess whether the relationship meets the established criteria for privileged communications. That is, the communication originates in confidence, confidentiality is essential to the maintenance of the relationship, and the relationship is one that society deems worthy of protecting (see §J. Wigmore, Evidence, 02201 at 509-533, McNaughton Rev. 1961.)

A Survey of the Laws of Sexual Assault Victim/Counselor Privileges

A survey of nationwide laws conducted in 1989 showed that twenty states had assigned privilege to sexual assault victim/counselor communications. In eighteen of the twenty states the privilege is a statutory one conferred by legislative action. In two of the states, the privilege is a case law privilege conferred by court ruling. The scope of the privacy protections rendered varies from state to state. Tables 12-1–12-4 identify the states discussed in this section and give a brief synopsis of the variances in their laws of privilege.

A review of the legislative and case law histories of the sexual assault victim/counselor privileges in these twenty states indicate that in every instance lawmakers recognized public interest in helping the assault victims recover and the psychotheraputic function of sexual assault counseling. In a few instances, lawmakers asserted a primary public interest in criminal prosecutions (i.e., privacy protections afforded sexual assault victims might result in increased reporting of the crime) as a justification for the privilege.

Of the eighteen states enacting statutory privileges, eleven enacted statutes specific to communications between sexual assault victims and counselors, whereas seven enacted the privilege in conjunction with a privilege assigned to communications between other crime victims and counselors, most often involving the crime of domestic violence. The one state that statutorily assigned a privilege to communications between all crime victims and counselors exempted communications with counselors employed by city or county agencies (e.g., police, prosecutors) in order to avoid constitutionality problems. Because the relationship between such crime victim populations as burglary, theft, and so on, may not meet the legal criteria for privilege, the two generic victim/counselor privilege statutes are expected to be challenged in the courts.

By case law, one state conferred privilege by extending the statutory psychotherapist/patient privilege to sexual assault victim/counselor communications. And one state established a case law privilege only for communications between a sexual assault victim and a counselor employed by a federally funded agency.

Table 12-1

PRIVILEGED COMMUNICATIONS STATUTES/CASE LAW

States Having a Statutory Privilege

Alabama (AL) (1987): Code of Alabama, 1988 Cumulative Supplement, Volume 12A, Chapter 23, Article 2, § 15-23-40–§ 15-23-46.

California (CA) (1980; amend. 1983): West's Annotated California Codes, Evidence Code, Volume 29B, Article 8.5, § 1035–§ 1036.2.

Connecticut (CT) (1983): Connecticut General Statutes Annotated, 1989 Cumulative, Volume 24, Title 52: Civil Actions § 52-146k–§ 52-146l.

Florida (FL) (1983): Florida Statutes Annotated, 1988 Cumulative, Volume 8, § 90.5035–§ 90.801.

Illinois (IL) (1987: amend. 1984): Illinois Annotated Statutes, Chapter 110, § 8–802.1.

Indiana (IN) (1987: amend. 1989): Bums Indiana Studies Annotated—1989 Cumulative Supplement, Title 35, Chapter 6, § 35-37-6-1–§ 35-37-6-11.

Iowa (IA) (1985): Iowa Code Annotated, Volume 11A, Chapter 236A, § 236A.1.

Maine (ME) (1983): Maine Revised Statutes Annotated, Volume 9, Title 16, Chapter 1, Subchapter II, § 53-A.

Massachusetts (MA) (1987): Annotated Laws of Masachustees, Cumulative Supplement to chapters 233–236, *§ 20.*

Minnesota (MN) (1982): Minnesota Statutes Annotated, Chapter 596, § 595.02.

New Hampshire (NH) (1985): New Hampshire Revised Statutes Annotated, Volume 2-A, Chapters 146-A to 185, § 173-C:1.

New Jersey (NJ) (1987): New Jersey Statutes Annotated Title 2A § 2A:84A-22.13–§2A:84A–22.16.

New Mexico (NM) (1987): New Mexico Statutes Annotated 1987 Replacement Pamphlet 53, Chapter 31: Criminal Procedure, Article 25, § 31-25-1–§ 31-25-6.

Pennsylvania (PA) (1982): Purdon's Pennsylvania Consolidated Statutes Annotated, Title 42: Judiciary and Judicial Procedure, § 5945.1.

Utah (UT) (1983): Utah Code Annotated—1987 Replacement, Volume 9, Title 78, Chapter 3c, § 78-3c-1–§ 78-3c-4.

Washington (WA) (1984): West's Revised Code of Washington Annotated, Title 70, Chapters 70.90 to End, § 70.125.065.

Washington (WY) (1985): Wyoming Statutes, Title 1: Code of Civil Procedure, Chapter 12, § 1-12-16 and § 14-3-210.

States Having a Case Law Privilege

Arizona (AZ) (1989) [invocation of VOCA]:
State of Arizona v. Spano, *No. CR 809532 (A3 1989).*

Colorado (CO) (1986) [invocation of psychologist patient privilege]:
People v. District Court, City and County of Denver *(1986) 719 E2nd 722, 727.*

Table 12-2

Privileged Communications by State

AL	Bet. all victims of crime & counselors	(oral comm. & records)	criminal proceedings
AZ	Bet. sexual assault victims and counselors	(records)	criminal proceedings
CA	Bet. sexual assault victims and counselors	(oral comm. & records)	civil & criminal proceedings
CO	Bet. patients/psychologists (by extension sexual assault victims/counselors	(records)	criminal proceedings
CT	Bet. domestic violence & sexual assault victims & counselors)	(records)	criminal proceedings
FL	Bet. sexual assault victims & counselors	(oral comm. & records)	civil & criminal proceedings
IL	Bet. sexual assault victims & counselors	(oral comm. & records)	civil & criminal proccedings
IN	Bet. domestic violence & sexual assault victims & counselors	(oral comm. & records)	civil & criminal proceedings
IA	Bet. domestic violence & sexual assault victims & counselors	(oral comm. & records)	civil & criminal proceedings
ME	Bet. sexual assault victims & counselors	(oral comm. & records)	civil & criminal proceedings
MA	Bet. sexual assault victims & counselors	(oral comm. & records)	civil & criminal proceedings
MN	Bet. sexual assault victims & counselors	(oral comm. & records)	civil & criminal proceedings
NH	Bet. domestic violence & sexual assault victims & counselors	(oral comm. & records)	civil & criminal proceedings
NJ	Bet. all victims of violent crime & counselors	(oral comm. & records)	civil & criminal proceedings
NM	Bet. domestic violence & sexual assault victims & counselors	(oral comm. & records)	civil & criminal proceedings
PA	Bet. sexual assault victims & counselors	(oral comm. & records)	civil & criminal proceedings
UT	Bet. sexual assault victims & counselors	(oral comm. & records)	civil & criminal proceedings
WA	Bet. sexual assault victims & counselors	(records)	civil & criminal proceedings
WY	Bet. domestic violence & sexual assault victims & counselors	(oral comm. & records)	criminal proceedings

Most (85 percent) states designate both oral and written communications as privileged. Eleven of the states designate the sexual assault counselor as the primary holder of the privilege, and nine assign primary privilege to the victim. Those assigning primary privilege to the counselor treat victim/counselor communications the same as any other professional privilege. The counselor may not, in most cases, waive the privilege without victim consent. However, in a few states the counselor is permitted to waive the privilege in the event the victim brings suit against the counseling agency.

Those states assigning primary privilege to the victim generally adopt the position that the victim should be prevented from selectively testifying. That is, the victim may not testify regarding certain confidential communications and then assert the privilege as a basis for refusing to disclose additional confidential material.

States were evenly divided over the type of privilege to be assigned to sexual assault victim/counselor communications. Half (50 percent)

Table 12-3

NATURE AND HOLDER OF PRIVILEGE BY STATE

AL	Absolute	counselor
AZ	Absolute	counselor
CA	With exception (court order)	victim
CO	Absolute	victim
CT	With exception (matters of proof/prejury)	victim
FL	Absolute	victim
IL	Absolute	counselor
IN	Absolute	victim
IA	With exception (matters of proof/prejury)	victim
ME	With exception (court order)	counselor
MA	Absolute	counselor
MN	With exception (court order)	counselor
NH	With exception (prejury/court order)	victim
NJ	Absolute	counselor
NM	Absolute	counselor
PA	Absolute	counselor
UT	With exception (minor victim)	counselor
WA	With exception	rape crisis center
WY	With exception (minor victim, other)	counselor

of the states assigned an absolute privilege (i.e., there are no circumstances under which a counselor can be compelled to testify or to release counseling records to the court), and the other half (50 percent) assigned a privilege with exception (i.e., there are some circumstances under which counselors may be compelled to testify or release records). Some of these states adopted a victim/counselor privilege model that makes exceptions for instances in which the counselor has knowledge of a victim's intent to commit perjury, or in ambiguous "matters of proof." The other states make exception only when a court determines, based on in-camera review, that the probative value of the evidence outweighs the injury to the victim/counselor relationship.

Table 12-4

LEVEL OF STATE ADJUDICATION REACHED/RESULT

AL None

AZ Trial court//privilege extended

CA None

CO Supreme Court/upheld [constitutional]. *People v. District Court, City and County of Denver* (1986) 719E2d 722, 727.

CT Supreme Court/upheld [but refusal to waive can result in victim's testimony being stricken from trial record] In re Robert H. (1986) 509 A.2d 199 Conn. 693.

FL None

IL App. Ct./upheld [constitutional]. *People v. Foggy*, App. 3 Dist. 1986, 102 Ill. Dec. 925, 149 Ill. App. 3d 599, 500 N. E.2d 1026.

IN None

IA None

ME None

MA App. Ct./upheld. *Commonwealth v. Two Juveniles* (1986) 397 Mass 261 NE2d 234; *Commonwealth v. Giacolone* (1987) 24 Mass App 166, 5076 NE2d 769.

NH None

NJ None

NM None

PA Supreme Court/upheld. *Commonwealth of PA v. Anthony Johnson* No. 1441. Phila. (1983). *In re PAAr*, 494, 428A.2d 126 (1981).

UT None

WA App. Ct./overturned as violation of confrontation clause [invocation of VOCA now applied]. *State v. Espinosa* 47 Win. App. 85 733 P.2d 1010 (1987).

WY None

Because most disputes over confidential communications occur at pretrial level the matter is usually resolved at that level, with little significant case law by which to track judicial interpretation of the privilege statutes. However, in those states where rulings can be tracked, the privilege appears to be faring well.

Appeals in the appellate courts of two states, Illinois and Massachusetts (see *People v. Foggy*, App. 3 Dist. 1986, 102 Ill. Dec. 925, 149 Ill., App. 3d 599, 500 N.E. 2d 1026, and *Commonwealth v. Giacolone*, (1984) 24 Mass. App. 166, 507 NE 2d 769), and the Supreme Courts of three states, Colorado, Connecticut, and Pennsylvania (see *People v. District, Court, City and County of Denver* (1986) 719 E2d 722, 727; *In re Robert H.* (1986) 509 A.2d 475/199 Conn. 693; and *Commonwealth of Pennsylvania v. Anthony W. Johnson*, No. 1441, Phila. (1983)) have resulted in the upholding of the new laws, in two cases on Constitutional grounds. Significantly, four of these five cases involved in the rulings were appeals based on an absolute privilege, including two that dealt with the question of Constitutionality. In the Connecticut case, a privilege with exception was upheld by the State's Supreme Court as applied to that particular case, but in a rather punitive gesture, the court also ruled that a victim's refusal to waive the privilege could result in her testimony being stricken from the record. In only one state, Washington, has a privilege with exception been held unconstitutional by an appellate court.

References

———. 1957. The social worker-client relationship and privileged communications. *Washington University Law Quarterly* 362–65.

Largen, M.A. June 1989. *State-by-State Comparison of Sexual Assault/Victim Counselor Privileged Communications Statutes and Case Law*, Distributed by National Network for Victims of Sexual Assault.

LeGrand, C. 1980. *Legal Handbook for Rape Crisis Centers*, pp. 22–36. Distributed by the Institute for the Study of Sexual Assault.

McCormick, P. 1938. The scope of privilege in the law of evidence. 16 *Texas Law Review*.

Neuhauser, M.H. 1985. The privilege of confidentiality and rape crisis counselors. *Women's Rights Law Reporter* 8(3):185–96.

Purrington, S. 1986. An abused privilege. 6 *Columbia Law Review* 338.

Stovenko, R. 1960. Psychiatry and a second look at the medical privilege. 6 *Wayne Law Review*: 175, n. 46.

Chapter 13

HIV Counseling Issues and Victims of Sexual Assault

Anna T. Laszlo
The Circle
McLean, VA

Ann W. Burgess
University of Pennsylvania

Christine A. Grant
Widenor University

■

HIV, the virus that causes acquired immunodeficiency syndrome, is primarily transmitted through sexual contact with an infected person or through the sharing of contaminated IV drug needles. In the aftermath of sexual assault, victims and their families often have many concerns about possible risks for HIV infection. Therefore, these persons have specific counseling needs, and counselors should be aware of and adhere to the proper procedures for discussing with them all issues surrounding HIV testing and confidentiality of test results. The establishment of policies addressing these and other HIV-related topics will assist victim services agencies in providing necessary and appropriate services for their clients.

HIV Risk for Sexual Assault Victims

Perhaps the most difficult question for counselors to answer for victims of sexual assault is, "What are the chances that I may become infected with HIV as a result of the sexual assault?" Although researchers have noted that the risk of being infected with HIV from a single act of unprotected intercourse with an infected male is about 1 in 500 (Hearst & Hullen, 1988), there are currently no empirical data to unprotected intercourse with an infected male is about 1 in 500 (Hearst & Hullen, 1988), there are currently no empirical data to predict the transmission risk for victims of sexual assault. Not only are there are no published statistics on the number of persons who are assaulted by an infected offender or who seroconvert as a result of the assault, there have been no studies to identify the seroprevalency among sexual offenders. A few studies that examined the association of syphilis with HIV infection, concluding that there is a strong association between syphilis and HIV infection and underscored the need for comprehensive evaluation for sexually transmitted diseases among those at risk (Quinn et al., 1990). Murphy, Kitchen, Harris, & Forster (1989) were first to report that infection with HIV may be transmitted to a victim of sexual assault, noting one case from their hospital.

Additionally, some researchers have mistakenly commented that "in order to assess thoroughly the risk of HIV transmission for female rape survivors, empirical data regarding the number of females who are anally sodomized should be considered" (Blumberg, 1990). Such contentions fail to consider that *all* sexual contacts with an infected person, not merely anal intercourse, may transmit HIV and that both females and males may be victims of sexual assault. Furthermore, recent data indicates that the sexual behavior of heterosexual drug users is far more resistant to modification, even when that sexual behavior is consensual, than are drug-injection practices (Turner, Heather, & Moses, 1989). Finally, sex offenses may be committed by individuals who have been diagnosed as "sexually dangerous persons" and by individuals who rape opportunistically (e.g., as an afterthought to a planned burglary) or intermittently (e.g., between committing other types of crimes). Thus, offenders who are also IV drug users and commit sexual offenses, regardless of whether they are considered "sexually dangerous persons" may present an HIV risk for their victims.

In terms of the physical trauma of the assault, the forced sexual penetration itself can result in microscopic tears, thus increasing the risk of viral transmission. For both the young and the elderly, the chances of such tears or lacerations may be increased. Further, when abuse is ongoing, as in child sexual abuse, there is increased vulnerability to infection from a number of sexually transmitted diseases. In a Duke University study of 96 children who tested positive for HIV, 14 or 14.6 percent were confirmed to have been sexually abused. Of the

14 children, four acquired HIV from sexual abuse, and in six cases, it was a possible source (Gutman et al., 1991).

Children and adolescents who are sexually exploited through prostitution and child pornography may be at higher risk for infection than victims of single, isolated sexual assaults. Clearly, however, research addressing the incidence and prevalence of HIV infection in the sexual offender population is needed to understand risk levels for victims of sexual abuse of all ages. Until such data are available, victim counselors need to develop specific strategies to assist victims and their families. Such strategies must be based upon an understanding of current medical, psychosocial, and legal implications of HIV infection in the aftermath of sexual assault.

Guidelines for the Management of AIDS-Related Concerns in the Aftermath of Sexual Assault

Victims of sexual assault may seek information and/or counseling about the possibility and implications of HIV infection when they: (1) are in immediate crisis, (2) are undergoing counseling months after the assault, (3) are raising questions years after the assault, or (4) are concerned that they are HIV-infected as the result of an assault.

Sexual assault counselors are skilled in establishing rapport, providing guidance, and coordinating interactions with medical and criminal justice agencies for clients and their families. In the past, however, counselors may not always have been trained or prepared to deal with the psychosocial needs of victims who may be at risk for HIV infection or to advise victims regarding procedures for HIV antibody testing and the meaning of test results. Today, such training and preparation is essential for both counselors and their clients.

Because victims of sexual assault may seek services from a number of agencies, including hospital-based treatment services, community-based rape crisis centers, and private and public mental health agencies, each of these agencies should develop policies that address its specific roles and responsibilities. For example, hospital-based program administrators will have to decide whether to make HIV antibody testing a part of *routine* sexual assault examinations or whether to give victims the choice of having their blood drawn, stored, and tested at a later time. Likewise, directors of community-based programs will have to decide how best to provide pre- and posttest counseling as well as support services to the families of sexual assault victims.

Numerous states have formed interagency committees, consisting of AIDS educators, researchers, or counselors; victim service providers; hospital emergency department staff; legal counsels; and the state department of public health, to draft recommendations for the management of AIDS-related concerns in the aftermath of sexual assault.

Assessing the Client

The counselor may find it effective to assess the potential impact of the HIV-antibody test results on the client's lifestyle. Asking questions regarding clients' expectations about the test, what they believe the results (either positive or negative) will mean, and what changes they might implement following disclosure of the test results may elicit helpful information.

The counselor should determine the client's motivation for taking the test (e.g., sexual assault) and whether the client is being pressured by someone, such as a spouse or sexual partner, to take it. Clients can be asked directly: (1) why they want to consider taking the test; (2) when they believe they were exposed to someone who might be HIV-infected; (3) why they believe their assailant might be infected (e.g., observations, assailant's statements, sexual acts performed); (4) when and why they were last tested, if ever; and (5) the results of any previous tests.

The counselor should assess the level of rape trauma and concern with HIV transmission by reviewing the client's thoughts, feelings, and behavior since the rape.

Victims in Acute Crisis

In dealing with a victim in acute crisis, the counselor should use accepted counseling procedures, using a tri-level intervention for symptom monitoring and management (Burgess & Grant, 1988). The counselor should be aware that: (1) for the victim, dealing with the possible exposure to any STD, including HIV, compounds the rape trauma response and prolongs its resolution; and (2) the need for repeat testing for HIV may activate the victim's memory of the sexual assault and exacerbate symptoms of the acute phase. Therefore, it is important that the principles of crisis management for symptom reduction be followed (Burgess & Holmstrom, 1986).

HIV Testing for Victims of Sexual Assault
Pretest Counseling for Victims of Sexual Assault

Depending on individual state legislation or hospital protocol, HIV testing may be a part of the emergency department procedures *or* it may require the victim's special consent. In either case, it is critical that testing be preceded by thorough, effective counseling. The purposes of pretest counseling are to:

- Provide accurate, adequate information about the antibody test, including how it is performed, what it is able to detect, and what the results mean;
- Provide information about false-positive and false-negative test results;
- Explain the modes of HIV transmission;
- Discuss risks-reduction behaviors;
- Address possible implications of test result disclosure;
- Discuss the victim's follow-up medical and mental health needs.

Initial counseling should include information on the advisability of testing for *all* types of STDs, including HIV. The counselor should be aware that all negotiations related to testing and providing results should take into account the victim's *willingness* to be evaluated and to receive the results.

During initial client contact, the counselor should, after introductions and an explanation of his or her professional role, discuss the purpose of HIV antibody testing and the meaning of its results. The client should be made to understand that: (1) the test is to detect antibodies to HIV, not to tell whether a person will actually get AIDS; (2) negative test results do not necessarily mean a person is free of the virus; (3) positive results mean antibodies have been detected and a person has been infected; (4) follow-up testing is necessary at six months and twelve months if the initial test results are negative; and (4) risk reduction practices must be followed during the testing and retesting periods.

Explaining Testing Procedures

The testing procedure should be carefully explained to the client; that is, blood will be taken from the arm, there must be a follow-up appointment to discuss the results, and there are a certain number of days between the drawing of blood and disclosure of the results. The client should be assured of being assisted during the waiting period through rape crisis counseling and other support services, and he or she should be encouraged to use these resources.

Confidentiality of Test Results

Victims may have concerns about the confidentiality of their test results. Therefore, counselors should discuss: (1) the possible implications of test result disclosure, (2) the availability of anonymous testing sites, and (3) the confidentiality of medical and counseling records. Finally, counselors should support the victim's decision to either allow or defer testing.

Explaining Positive Test Implications

The Center for Disease Control (CDC) recommends that, even during the pretest counseling phase, all clients should be given information regarding the implications of a positive test. Clients should understand that since HIV antibody tests occasionally result in "false positives," a person testing positive is generally given a second HIV test, followed by a third, confirmatory, test.

The counselor should explain that a person who tests positive can transmit HIV to others through sexual contact and sharing of IV needles. The victim should be advised of the importance of notifying partners of any positive test results to give these partners the opportunity to be counseled and tested. The counselor can offer to help the client accomplish this if it becomes necessary by suggesting methods for sensitively discussing the subject or by actually assisting with notification. Because the virus can be transmitted from a mother to her unborn child during pregnancy and birth as well as possibly through breast milk, the client should be advised to seek counseling before becoming pregnant. Finally, the counselor should assist the victim with referrals to medical and mental health agencies specializing in services for HIV-infected individuals.

Explaining Negative Test Results

Clients should be cautioned that, because of the time period between exposure to HIV and the development of antibodies, a negative test result does not *necessarily* mean they are not infected. While most people seroconvert (develop antibodies) during a period of from six weeks to three months after exposure, some people may not develop antibodies for as long as one year. Therefore, if an assault occurred *within* the previous six weeks, for example, sufficient time for seroconversion may not have elapsed. Thus, it is important for victims to understand that, following a negative test result, further testing may be recommended at six weeks, twelve weeks, six months, and twelve months, depending on the existence and degree of risk factors. Further, counselors should explain and encourage risk-reduction practices during the testing and retesting periods.

Providing General Information

CDC recommends that prior to concluding the counseling session the client be given specific information on the means by which HIV is transmitted as well as prevented. CDC guidelines in this area have been designed for persons participating in consenting, high-risk behaviors (e.g., needle sharing, homosexual/bisexual practices). It is important for counselors to realize that the sexual assault victim has been forced into nonconsenting sex; thus, the general information provided to him or her should focus on this fact. The victim should be given information on how to stay as healthy as possible and to avoid activities that might result in exposure to the virus.

Concluding Counseling

Prior to concluding the counseling, the counselor should address any questions the client may have, provide educational handout material, and arrange for a return appointment. Where possible, the counselor should explain that he or she is the contact person for the test results. It is important that the client be given *specific directions* concerning *where*, *when* and *to whom* to return for the test results.

Posttest Counseling

As in pretest counseling, the posttest counseling should begin with the counselor offering an appropriate introduction or reintroduction of himself or herself, an explanation of the purpose of the meeting, and a brief review of confidentiality issues.

Procedures for Providing Negative Test Results

When the HIV-antibody test is negative, the client should be given the results immediately at the start of the counseling session. According to the AIDS Health Project of the University of California at San Francisco, the revelation of the test result is best "presented in a straightforward manner with direct eye contact and without undue expression of concern." The counselor should then caution the client that, despite the negative test result, risks still remain. HIV antibodies may not yet have developed at the time of the test and thus were not identified by the test.

Emphasizing Risk-Reducing Behavior

The client's return appointment to obtain test results is an opportunity for the counselor to reemphasize the importance of avoiding high-risk behavior and to advise against donating blood, plasma, tissue, or sperm if the client has used IV drugs since 1978.

Concluding Posttest Counseling for HIV-Negative Clients

The final segment of the posttest counseling for HIV-negative clients should be devoted to answering any questions, providing written handout material, and discussing retesting if the client has had a high-risk exposure within the past three months. The counselor should be prepared to offer additional sexual assault-related referrals, as needed.

Procedures for Providing Positive Test Results

The counselor who must inform a client of a positive test is presenting extremely stressful news. The counselor must pay specific attention to his or her own demeanor and skill in helping the client to process this devastating information. When informing the client of a positive test, the same procedure should be followed as when giving negative results: The counselor should introduce (or reintroduce) himself or herself, define the purpose of the session, and give the test result. Once the positive results are given, he or she should resist the urge to fill the silence. The counselor should assess the verbal and nonverbal cues the client offers and then judge when to discuss the results.

Victims will respond and react to the news of a positive HIV test in a variety of ways. Shock, disbelief, inability to speak, anger, sadness, fear, relief, or resignation are just some of the emotions the victim may express, and these responses will direct the remainder of the session. The counselor who can employ active listening may be most helpful. The client needs to be able to process the information, and the counselor's ability to convey understanding and to allow the client freedom to express himself or herself will facilitate this process.

The client will need help in understanding what the results mean. It should be emphasized that a seropositive test does not diagnose AIDS; rather, it detects the antibodies to HIV. It *does* mean the client is infected and *can transmit* the virus to a sex or needle-sharing partner; and if female can pass the virus to her child during pregnancy or birth and possibly through her breast milk.

Providing Resources and Referrals

A counselor who is preparing to tell a client of a positive test should have all the necessary resources available. Clients will need assistance in developing a health plan that focuses on staying as healthy as possible to reduce the possibility of developing AIDS. They should understand that AIDS occurs when the virus multiplies sufficiently to overwhelm the body's defense, or immune system. Clients also need strategies to cope with the interpersonal implications of the positive test result. They need to be able to talk with another person, preferably another rape victim, who has tested positive. The counselor should put the client in touch with support groups. Rape crisis centers or telephone contacts with other victims can be valuable resources for this information.

The client should be referred to a nurse practitioner or physician for evaluation and follow-up, particularly for the presence of tuberculosis, hepatitis B, and other infections. If this evaluation is not possible, the client should be given a description of symptoms that should signal a visit to a health clinic. Flu and pneumococcal vaccines may be advisable.

Addressing Risk Reduction for HIV-Positive Clients

The posttest counseling session for the HIV-positive client should focus on risk-reducing behavior. Depending on how much information the client can assimilate at this time, the counselor should stress the importance of avoiding IV drugs, needle sharing, and sex (unless a condom is used to avoid passing or receiving body fluids). The client should be strongly advised against donating blood, plasma, body organs, tissue, or sperm, and to avoid sharing toothbrushes, razors, or other items that could become contaminated with blood. Women should be cautioned against becoming pregnant, and men should be advised to avoid causing pregnancy. If appropriate, the client should be referred to a drug treatment program.

Table 13-1

SAMPLE HIV POLICY STATEMENT FOR VICTIM SERVICES AGENCIES IN THE MANAGEMENT OF SEXUAL ASSAULT POPULATIONS

Purpose:
The purpose of this policy is to provide guidelines for victim service agencies in the management of HIV infection among sexual assault populations.

General Policy Statement:
It is the policy of this agency to provide appropriate counseling and support services to victims of sexual assault and their families and to assist victims and their families in handling their medical, mental health, social, and educational/informational needs in the aftermath of sexual assault. This agency is committed to assisting victims and their families with specific needs as they relate to HIV infection and sexual assault.

Policy Statement Regarding Discrimination:
It is the policy of this agency not to discriminate against clients who are at risk for HIV infection or who are HIV-infected.

Rationale. Discrimination has serious repercussions on the infected person and his or her family as well as on efforts to control the epidemic. An infected person's fear of discrimination may impair his or her access to critical care and treatment as well as counseling to prevent transmission.

Federal and state anti-discrimination laws apply to clients with HIV disease—many extending to employment, housing and other public accommodations, public services, credit, education, and medical cware.

Implementation Strategy. Agency staff should be familiar with and adhere to all applicable anti-discrimination provisions. All efforts will be made to ensure that no client is discriminated against on the basis of his or her HIV status. All referrals to community medical, mental health, and social services; employment; housing; and education will follow established agency policy, without regard to the client's HIV status.

Informing Partners and Family of Positive Test Results

The client should be assisted in developing a plan for managing the test information and for determining who should be informed and how. The counselor should be aware of the profound impact a positive test result will have and should assess the client's ability to notify sex and needle-sharing partners as well as significant others. The counselor's role should be to focus solely on providing emotional support while discussing methods for informing these persons. Role-playing a potentially difficult situation may be effective.

Concluding Posttest Counseling of HIV-Positive Clients

The client who receives a positive test result needs both time and emotional support; the counselor should recognize that the test result

Table 13-1 (continued)

SAMPLE HIV POLICY STATEMENT FOR VICTIM SERVICES AGENCIES IN THE MANAGEMENT OF SEXUAL ASSAULT POPULATIONS

Policy Statement Regarding Testing and Counseling

It is the policy of this agency not to mandate client HIV testing. Voluntary testing will be discussed as a part of HIV education for clients. Agency staff should be familiar with and follow the guidelines addressing pre- and posttest counseling as described above.

Clients who wish to be tested for HIV antibodies will be referred to the appropriate medical services or testing site.

Rationale. It is important that clients be encouraged to take control of their own health care and that they have accurate medical and legal information to make informed decisions about HIV antibody testing. Clients should understand the reasons for HIV antibody testing, the implications of both positive and negative test results, and any potential need for behavior modification.

Implementation Strategy. Appropriate community-based medical resources should be established for client HIV testing and counseling referrals. Agency staff should be trained to assess the needs of clients for such counseling and testing and should be familiar with the appropriate referral agency that can best meet the client's needs.

Policy Statement Regarding Confidentiality of Client Records:

It is the policy of this agency to ensure that all client records remain confidential, accessible only to those individuals designated by the client. Further, it is the policy of this agency to disclose confidential information only with the written informed consent of the client.

Rationale. Federal Constitutional law and most state laws protect the confidenti-

---

is just a first step in a very long process. Life changes may be indicated, and the client needs a framework from which to facilitate these changes. Education, support, and access to resources are some of the basics a counselor can provide to the clients they serve.

Guidelines for Agencywide Policies Addressing HIV Inspection in Sexual Assault Populations

In addition to the specific counseling issues previously addressed, a number of other AIDS-related policies need to be developed by victim services agencies, including anti-discrimination and AIDS education.

Table 13-1 is a sample policy statement for victim services agencies in the management of HIV infection among sexual assault populations.

Table 13-1 (continued)

SAMPLE HIV POLICY STATEMENT FOR VICTIM SERVICES AGENCIES IN THE MANAGEMENT OF SEXUAL ASSAULT POPULATIONS

ality of HIV test results and other client records. Section 504 of the Federal Rehabilitation Act of 1973 provides protection against discrimination for persons with HIV infection; however, disclosure of HIV test results or of existing seropositive status still potentially can result in discrimination against the client.

Implementation Strategy. Staff will be educated regarding agency policy on confidentiality and are expected to adhere strictly to this policy. Appropriate sanctions will be placed against staff who knowingly reveal client record information to unauthorized persons.

Policy Statement Regarding Education

It is the policy of this agency to provide AIDS-related education and information to all clients.

Rationale. It is critical that all clients learn the causes, means of transmission, and means to prevent transmission of HIV. Education will decrease the potential for infection and/or the transmission of HIV and will help to allay unnecessary fears and misconceptions about the disease.

Implementation Strategy. All clients will be provided culturally sensitive and age- and language-appropriate educational materials addressing HIV disease. Agency staff will be trained to provide basic information to all clients about HIV, including means of prevention.

References

Blumberg, M. 1990. *AIDS: The Impact on the Criminal Justice System.* Columbus, OH: Merrill Publishing Company.

Burgess, A., and L.L. Holmstrom. 1984. *Rape: Crisis and Recovery.* Englewood Cliffs, NJ: Robert J. Brady Company.

Burgess, A., and C. Grant, 1988. *Children Traumatized in Sex Rings.* Arlington, VA: National Center for Missing and Exploited Children.

Gutman, L.T., K.K. St. Claire, C. Weedy, M.E. Herman-Giddens, B.A. Lane, J.G. Niemeyer, and R.E. McKinney, Jr. 1991. Human immunodeficiency virus transmission by child sexual abuse. *American Journal of Diseases of Children* 145(2):137–41.

Hearst, N., and S.B. Hulley, 1988. Preventing the heterosexual spread of AIDS: Are we giving our patients the best advice? *Journal of the American Medical Association* 259(16):2428–32: April 22–29.

Murphy, S., V. Kitchen, J.R.W. Harris, and S.M. Forster, 1989. Rape and subsequent seroconversion to HIV. *British Medical Journal* 299:218.

Quinn, T., et al. 1990. The association of syphilis with risk of human immunodeficiency virus infection in patients attending sexually transmitted disease clinics. *Archives of Internal Medicine* 150: June.

Turner, C.G., M. Heather, and L. Moses. 1989. *AIDS: Sexual Behavior and Intravenous Drug Use.* Washington, DC: National Academy Press, 1989.

Part 4

The Aggressors

■

Chapter 14

Hypothetical Biological Substrates of a Fantasy-Based Drive Mechanism for Repetitive Sexual Aggression

Robert Alan Prentky
Massachusetts Treatment Center

Ann W. Burgess
University of Pennsylvania

■

Preparation of this manuscript was supported by the National Institute of Justice (82-IJ-CX-0058), the Office of Juvenile Justice and Delinquency Prevention (84-JW-AX-K010), the National Institute of Mental Health (MH32309), and the Commonwealth of Massachusetts.

■

A Fantasy-Based Traumatogenic Model for Repetitive Sexual Aggression:
Biological Correlates

The role of fantasy in deviant, aggressive sexuality was proposed well over a decade ago by Abel and Blanchard (1974), and over the ensuing decade there has accumulated "abundant evidence" to support it (Marshall, Abel, & Quinsey, 1983). The commonly accepted explanatory model pairs fantasy with sexual arousal. The rehearsed fantasy is reinforced through masturbation. The deviant fantasy eventually becomes sufficiently reinforced, and inhibitions sufficiently eroded, to place the individual at high risk to act on the fantasy. Such a simple classical conditioning model may have some utility in explaining how markedly deviant fantasies become translated into behavior; however, the model stops short of suggesting what mechanisms may originate and drive the fantasy. Moreover, from an etiologic perspective, such a model fails to account for the virtual absence of paraphilic sexuality in females relative to the observed incidence in males (Gosselin & Wilson, 1984).

Advances in Model Development

Recently, Burgess, Hartman, Ressler, Douglas, and McCormack (1986) reported on a fantasy-based motivational model for sexual homicide. The model, which has five interactive components (impaired development of attachments in early life; formative traumatic events; patterned responses that serve to generate fantasies; a private, internal world that is consumed with violent thoughts and that leaves the person isolated and self-preoccupied; a feedback filter that sustains repetitive thinking patterns), was tested on a sample of thirty-six sexual murderers. In this initial study Burgess et al. (1986) found evidence for daydreaming and compulsive masturbation in over 80 percent of the sample in both childhood and adulthood. Using the same sample, Ressler and Burgess (1985) examined the role of the organized/disorganized dichotomy, which has proven to be a relatively powerful discriminator in two important areas (crime scene investigation and life history variables). Classification as organized or disorganized is made with the use of data present at the scene of a murder and is based upon the notion that highly repetitive, planned, well thought-out offenses will be distinguishable from spontaneous, random, sloppy offenses. According to prediction, the former, organized, case should be much more characterized by a fantasy life that drives the offenses than the latter, disorganized, case. Ressler, Burgess, Douglas, Hartman and D'Agostino (1986) found support for numerous differences between organized and disorganized offenders with respect to acts committed during the offense.

Repetitive Sexual Homicide

A recently completed study examined the role of fantasy as a drive mechanism for repetitive (i.e., serial) sexual homicide (Prentky, Burgess, Rokous, Lee, Hartman, Ressler & Douglas, 1989). The role of fantasy was examined by looking at putative differences between serial and solo sexual murderers. The working hypothesis was that serial sexual murderers were more likely to have an underlying internal mechanism that drives the assaultive behavior than solo sexual murderers. This internal drive mechanism was hypothesized to take the form of an intrusive fantasy life manifested in (1) a higher incidence of paraphilias, (2) a higher incidence of "organized" crime scenes, and (3) a higher incidence of fantasy.

The serial sexual murderer sample consisted of twenty-five of the thirty-six murderers drawn from an earlier study by the Federal Bureau of Investigation (Burgess et al., 1986; Ressler et al., 1986; Ressler, Burgess, & Douglas, 1988). Only those men with three or more sexual homicides were included in this study. The men were interviewed by special agents of the FBI in various U.S. prisons between 1979 and 1983. Data collection included information retrieved from official records (e.g., psychiatric and criminal records, pretrial records, court transcripts, interviews with correctional staff, and prison records). Information derived from these structured interviews and archival sources was coded using a questionnaire.

The solo sexual murderer sample consisted of seven offenders in the FBI sample who had murdered once and ten men residing at the Massachusetts Treatment Center who had murdered once. The data source for the Treatment Center subjects was archival. The clinical files were coded using a questionnaire similar to the one employed in the FBI study. (See Table 14-1.)

Table 14-1
DESCRIPTIVE CHARACTERISTICS

		SERIAL (N=17)	SOLO (N=25)
Race	Caucasian	96%	82%
	Black	4%	12%
Marital	Married	21%	20%
	Divorced/Separated	29%	27%
	Never married	50%	53%
IQ	Above average (> 110)	58%	29%
	Below average (< 90)	17%	29%
Age[1]	≤ 24	47%	52%
	25–30	36%	29%
	> 30	12%	24%

[1]At time of first murder ($x^2 = 1.02$, $p < .80$).

Because the age of the offender at the onset of violent criminal activity could be a critical factor, we compared the two samples on the mean age at the time of the first sexual homicide. The samples were remarkably similar (x^2 = 1.02, p < .80). The only noteworthy comparison concerned intelligence. As a group, the serial murderers had a higher IQ than the solo murderers, though the difference was not statistically significant (x^2 = 3. 14, p < . 21). Over half of the serial group (58 percent) was above average in IQ, compared with less than one-third of the solo group (29 percent). This apparent trend is entirely consistent with theoretical expectation and essentially parallels the difference between the groups with respect to organization of crime scene. That is, organized murderers are predicted to be higher in IQ than disorganized murderers (Ressler & Burgess, 1985). Although intelligence seems to have very little bearing on the quality or content of the fantasy, it may influence how well the fantasy is translated into behavior (i.e., "organized"), and how successfully the offender eludes apprehension.

Operational Considerations for Dependent Measures

Fantasy

Fantasy is a rather inclusive term that covers a wide range of cognitive processes. Our use of the term *fantasy* is based on an information-processing model that interprets thoughts as derivations of incoming stimuli that have been processed and organized (Gardner, 1985). Daydreaming has been defined as any cognitive activity representing a shift of attention away from a task (Singer, 1966). A fantasy, as it was defined in the study, is an elaborated set of cognitions (or thoughts), characterized by preoccupation (or rehearsal), anchored in emotion, and having origins in daydreams. A fantasy is generally experienced as a collection of thoughts, although the individual may be aware of images, feelings, and internal dialogue. For the purposes of the study, a crime fantasy (either rape, murder, or both) was positively coded if interview or archival data indicated daydreaming content that included intentional infliction of harm in a sadistic or otherwise sexually violent way.

Organized/Disorganized Crime Scenes

The homicide was classified as organized if the crime scene suggested that a semblance of order existed prior to, during, and after the offense and that this order was aimed at eluding detection (Ressler & Burgess, 1985). The homicide was classified as disorganized if the crime scene was characterized by great disarray, suggesting that the assault had been committed suddenly and with no apparent plan for avoiding detection. The crime scene classifications were made by two special agents from the FBI, using crime scene data only. Such data consist of physical evidence found at the crime scene that are hypothesized to reveal behavioral and personality traits of the murderer. The crime scene may include the point of abduction, locations where the victim was held, the murder scene, and the final body location. Examples of crime scene data include use of restraints, manner of death, presence of weapon, depersonalization of the victim (i.e., rendering the victim unidentifiable through disfigurement), evidence that the crime was staged, and physical evidence (e.g., personal artifacts of the victim or offender).

The degree of "organization" of the sexual assaults is hypothesized to be related to the elaborateness of the fantasy and the length of rehearsal prior to the assault. In other words, well-organized assaults reflect well-rehearsed fantasies. The critical mediating factors that are hypothesized to differentiate the organized from the more disorganized offender are social competence and impulsivity. That is, the organized offenders are predicted to be higher in intelligence, more socially skilled and interpersonally adept, more vocationally competent, and more stable in most aspects of lifestyle. In addition to being less accomplished in all of these domains, the disorganized offender is predicted to have a much more impressive track record of vehicular and criminal offenses beginning at an early age.

Paraphilias

The paraphilias may be understood as the behavioral expression of an underlying fantasy. Money (1980) noted in this regard, that the "paraphiliac's ideal is to be able to stage his/her erotic fantasy so as to perceive it as an actual experience"(p. 76). The paraphilias were coded as present if there was clear, unambiguous evidence in the archives or via self-report that the behavior was practiced and that it was not happenstance. The paraphilias were defined in concrete, behavioral terms with examples provided—for the subject in the case of self-report, and for the coders in the case of archival retrieval.

Results

Eight variables were identified in the FBI database and the Treatment Center database that were conceptually identical and theoretically meaningful for testing a series of hypotheses regarding these two samples. The two sets of variables were merged to create a new set of dichotomous variables. The dichotomous variables were analyzed using the chi-square statistic.

The *a priori* hypothesis regarding fantasy was strongly supported (X^2 = 14. 02, p < .001). Well over three-quarters of the serial group (86 percent), compared with less than one-quarter of the solo group (23 percent), evidenced sufficiently obtrusive fantasy to be noted in the records or through self-report.

To the extent that the paraphilias do indeed provide behavioral evidence of fantasy life, the difference between the two groups was again supported. There was a higher incidence of all five paraphilias in the serial group than in the solo group, with the last two— fetishism and cross-dressing—being statistically significant at the . 05 level (X^2 = 4.54 and 4.38, respectively).

Our *a priori* hypothesis regarding the organization or disorganization of the crime scene also was supported (X^2 = 8. 00, p < . 005). Over two-thirds of the serial murderers' first sexual homicides were organized, three-quarters of the solo sexual homicides were disorganized. (See Table 14-2.)

Assumptions of a Fantasy-Based Drive Model

Preliminary findings from these studies, based upon relatively small samples of offenders, provide tentative support for the hypothesis that fantasy life may be importantly related to repeated acts of sexual violence. Although the precise function of consummated fantasy is speculation, we concur with MacCulloch, Snowden, Wood and Mills (1983) that once the restraints inhibiting the acting out of the fantasy are no longer present the individual is likely to engage in a series of progressively more accurate "trial runs" in an attempt to "stage" the fantasy as it is imagined. Because the trial runs can never precisely match the fantasy, the need to restage the fantasy with a new victim is established.

We attempted to provide an operationalized drive mechanism for repetitive behavior that is characterized by polymorphous sexual fantasies in which aggression is a distinctive feature. Our work has

Table 14-2

	Solo (n=17)	Serial (n=25)	X2	p*
Fantasy	23%	86%	14.02	.001
Paraphilias				
Compulsive Masturbation	50%	70%	1.28	.23
Indecent Exposure	7%	25%	1.81	.19
Voyeurism	43%	75%	3.60	.06
Fetishism	33%	71%	4.54	.05
Cross-Dressing	0%	25%	4.38	.05
Organized/Disorganized				
Organized	23.5%	68%	8.00	.005
Planned 41%	42%	—	—	

* p value for X^2 derived from Fisher's exact test (1-tail).

been guided by a number of implicit assumptions. The first assumption is that the individual has created an inner world (a fantasy life) that is intended to satisfy, often in disguised or symbolic fashion, needs that cannot be satisfied in the real world (cf. Kardener, 1975). As such, this inner world can host a seemingly unlimited range of possible wishes and needs. Our present concern involves those inner worlds that are dominated by a maelstrom of sexual and aggressive feelings.

The second assumption is that the mechanisms that drive the fantasies and the factors that permit the enactment and reenactment of the fantasies are at least as important, if not more important, than understanding the specific content of the fantasies. This is a critical point, because it is commonly accepted that "normal" people often have sexually deviant fantasies (Crepault & Couture, 1980). Thus, merely having sadistic or homicidal fantasies does not mean that those fantasies will ever be acted out (Schlesinger & Revitch, 1983).

The third assumption is that the script or content of the sexual fantasy derives from explicit, protracted sexually deviant and pathological experiences first sustained at a young age. In this regard it was noted by Gosselin and Wilson (1984) that if "human males have certain broad 'innate releasing mechanisms' for sexual arousal, it would appear that these can be distorted or over-detailed by traumatic events in childhood" (p. 106). Kardener (1975) was even more explicit in his comments about children who are forced to "fill in the blanks with distortions, feelings of badness and primitive mythologies"

(p. 53). He remarked that "there is a horrible fascination for the grotesque distortions of what sex means contained in a vacuum of alternate expression that compels the murderer to master his distortions through acting out his forbidden fantasies" (p. 53).

The fourth assumption is that the parameters governing fantasy life in "normals" are different from the equivalent parameters in repetitive sexual offenders. The fantasies that are associated with sexually deviant or coercive behavior in "normals" are not typically rehearsed and are not typically preoccupying. The fantasies are usually associated with an exteroceptive stimulus and diminish in intensity, or extinguish entirely, after the withdrawal of the stimulus. Assuming that the fantasies are not acted on and assuming that the fantasies are not so disturbing that they interfere with daily living, they are of little concern other than to those who would speculate about why sexually aggressive fantasies appear to be so common among males.

We are concerned about those sexually aggressive fantasies that are intrusive (distracting and preoccupying), reiterative (persistent and recurrent), and interoceptive (internally generated). From an empirical standpoint, we hope to explore those factors that serve to disinhibit and facilitate the enactment of such fantasies and what factors promote the inexorable reoccurrence of such fantasies. The present review will explore one potentially fruitful area of inquiry that may shed some light on the three aforementioned parameters of fantasy life.

Putative Biological Mechanisms

In the second half of this chapter we address putative biological factors that may help to explain the repetitive component of repetitive sexual violence. Although these factors are strictly speculative, they have been incorporated into our cognitive motivational model, and we are preparing to put them to test. In discussing these hypotheses we will begin by reviewing the theoretical architecture that provides presumptive support.

Fantasy or imagery, at least as it exists in humans, is not a property of the visual system but is a cognitive process (Gazzaniga, 1985; Hebb, 1968; Lang, 1979, 1985). Fantasy has been conceptualized as an activated perceptual-motor memory (Kosslyn, 1988; Lang, 1985), and our own conceptualization of fantasy embraces these notions, as well as incorporating the elements of rehearsal and emotion. The imagery literature affords greater specificity, however.

Vividness of Fantasy

The vividness of a fantasy is a function of the amount of endogenous visual cortical activity (Farah, Steinhauer, Lewicki, Zubin & Peronnet, 1988). In the case of sexual fantasies, the more vivid or "real" the fantasy is, the greater the sexual arousal. Smith and Over (1987) reported that the extent to which men can induce erection through fantasy is a function not only of the sexual content of the fantasy but of the vividness of the fantasy as well. Consistent with this finding, it has also been reported that during a sexual fantasy the genital response and sexual arousal increase when subjects complement sexual scenes with imagined physical responses during sex acts (Dekker & Everaerd, 1988). In a related finding, visceral activity during emotional imagery varied positively with imagery ability (Miller, Levin, Kozak, Cook, McLean, & Lang, 1987). It thus appears that fantasies that incorporate more detailed visceral responses are more arousing. Although this is not a particularly startling conclusion, it does underscore the wide range of individual differences with respect to the "richness" or vividness of fantasies, ranging from drab, dull, poorly organized images to exciting, dynamic, three-dimensional images.

Location of Fantasy

Left Hemisphere

Speculations about the "location" of fantasy are relevant. It has been argued that the left hemisphere, not the right, appears to be responsible for generating fantasy (Gazzaniga, 1985). Although the orgasmic response seems to be localized in the nondominant hemisphere, the "script" for the orgasm (that is, the content of the fantasy accompanying sexual arousal) seems to be localized in the dominant hemisphere (Flor-Henry, 1980; Gosselin & Wilson, 1984). Flor-Henry noted that "pathologic neural organization of the dominant hemisphere provides the substrate for the abnormal ideational representations of the sexual deviations and leads to perturbed interhemispheric interactions so that only these abnormal ideas are capable of eliciting, or have a high probability of inducing, the orgasmic response" (p. 260). It has thus been concluded that left hemispheric dysfunction is more likely to affect the *content* of the fantasy, resulting in bizarre or deviant images, than right hemispheric dysfunction (Gosselin & Wilson, 1984). Although it is clear that the act of generating a fantasy is considerably more complicated than what is suggested here, there is reliable evidence to support at least two separate processes with hemispheric specialization for each process (Kosslyn, 1988).

Temporal Lobe

Another area of research suggests further specificity. Flor-Henry, in fact, referred to "The astonishing specificity of abnormal limbic mechanisms in the genesis of some of the sexual deviations..." (1980, p. 258). Two paraphilias in particular, fetishism and transvestism, have been associated with temporal lobe damage (cf. Langevin, 1983, for a discussion). It has thus been concluded that *dominant* temporal lobe dysfunction may be associated with fetishism, transvestism, and psychopathic sexual impulses (Flor-Henry, 1980). Although we certainly cannot conclude that temporal lobe dysfunction *causes* paraphilic behavior, Langevin has argued that very early onset paraphilias "may be organic in origin since most sexually anomalous behavior is only prominent about the time of puberty" (1983, p. 251). It is interesting to note in this regard that of the five paraphilias that we examined, the two with the largest group differences were fetishism and transvestism.

Limbic System

To go one further on our theoretical high wire, we have proposed that the coexistence of a dominant hemisphere dysfunction in the limbic system (particularly the hippocampus) increases the likelihood that abusive experiences in childhood will become encoded in memory and retrieved in the form of sexually pathological fantasy. Such a dysfunction is hypothesized to have occurred prenatally, at birth, or early in development.

There exists a sizable literature demonstrating that animals with hippocampal lesions act as if they lacked internal inhibition (e.g., Douglas, 1967; Kimble, 1968) and habituate more slowly than controls as a result of a deficit in response inhibition (e.g., Kimble, 1968; Jarrard & Korn, 1969; Leaton, 1965). It is noteworthy in this regard that one study found that humans who reported more vivid images responded with slower electrodermal habituation to imagined electric shock (Drummond, White, & Ashton, 1978). The logic of this finding, as presented by the authors, is simple and straightforward. Imagined stimuli produce similar physiological changes to real stimuli. Imagining a scene that provokes fear or anxiety produces autonomic responses that are more or less in proportion to the vividness of the image. Drummond, White, and Ashton argued that "if more vivid images do produce larger physiological responses, then individual differences in imagery vividness should affect rate of habituation to images, since it is well known that larger responses take longer to habituate" (1978, p. 193). The Drummond study may provide an important theoretical link between presumptive autonomic correlates of fantasy and autonomic correlates of hippocampal impairment. That is, hippocampal impairment may be associated with slow habituation due to a deficit in response inhibition. Slow habituation may also be associated with increased vividness of imagery.

In addition, Sano, Sekino, and Mayanagi (1972) related ergotropic (postero-medial hypothalamus near the lateral wall of the third ventricle) dominance to "violent, aggressive, restless behaviours or rage." Isaacson noted that "the hippocampal influence upon the hypothalamus could be the inhibition of the ergotropic systems in the posterior hypothalamus" (1972, p. 514). Thus, hippocampal impairment may also be associated with disinhibition of the ergotropic system.

There is also evidence that electrical stimulation of the hippocampus suppresses the release of adrenocortical steroids (Rubin, Mandell, & Crandall, 1966). As Venables (1974) pointed out, the relatively rapid recovery of the skin conductance response after hippocampal lesioning may result from chronic increases in ACTH, and hence elevated levels of adrenocortical hormones leading to faster sodium reabsorption. Although this pattern would suggest the presence of high levels of 17-OHCS, reflecting a constant undifferentiated arousal state, one might predict that the more important hormone is not a glucocorticoid (e.g., 17-OHCS) but the polypeptide ACTH, which directly affects PT level (Prentky, 1985). Interestingly, a chronic high level of ACTH may chronically suppress PT level, explaining why research on PT has failed to provide convincing evidence of markedly elevated levels among sex offenders. Even though there is predictably a high "arousal" state among serial offenders, the arousal may not be driven by PT. In the event of a limbic-related condition of chronic primary adrenocortical excess, it would not be surprising to see some Cushings-like side effects, such as elevated blood glucose, suppression of the inflammatory response with a resulting susceptibility to infections, and tangentially, a high cholesterol level (Prentky, 1985). The latter prediction (susceptibility to infections) is also consistent with the aforementioned hypothesis of Geschwind and Galaburda (1987) regarding an increased incidence of autoimmune disorders.

In a very interesting study in which sexual arousal to erotic movies was monitored using penile plethysmography, the reported fantasies were grouped according to those that were neutral, those that were avoided, and those that were common (Kling, Borowitz, & Cartwright, 1972). Common fantasies correlated positively with sexual arousal and negatively with plasma levels of 17-OHCS. Violent fantasies (the avoided ones) were negatively associated with sexual arousal and positively associated with 17-OHCS (i.e., levels increased). We would speculate that among serial sexual offenders violent fantasies would be positively associated with sexual arousal and 17-OHCS. In the case of 17-OHCS, the association would not be a stimulus-specific response to aversive images but a steady-state condition.

Brain pathology, such as we have discussed, is, of course, "quite subtle" (Langevin, 1990), and it clearly is premature to draw any conclusions. The studies discussed here represent preliminary excursions into a relatively uncharted terrain, beset by a variety of extraordinarily challenging problems, such as interpreting the influence of a target lesion on a specific behavior—or constellation of behaviors—and generalizing from that case to a larger subset of cases with common behavioral aberrations.

Neurochemical Considerations

Serontonin

Extreme cases of intrusive, recurrent fantasies may be associated with a state of chronic, undifferentiated arousal, defined as elevations in adrenocortical hormones and catecholamines (particularly norepinephrine—MHPG). If this arousal state is mediated by catecholamines, it is reasonable to conjecture that acetylcholine (ACh)—and perhaps serotonin—should suppress arousal by antagonizing the catecholamines (Mabry & Campbell, 1978). Thus, along with higher levels of MHPG we might also expect to find lower levels of serotonin (5-hydroxytryptamine, or 5-HT) and its metabolite 5-HIAA (5-hydroxyindoleacetic acid) and ACh. The most impressive effects of 5-HT depletion on male sexual behavior have been observed in the rat, where increased sexual excitement, increased mounting behavior and increased chasing/rolling have been noted (Prentky, 1985). For the most part, however, the results of studies employing monkeys and humans have generally been negative (Prentky, 1985). That is, the administration of 5-HT biosynthesis inhibitors (e.g., parachlorophenylalanine) did not affect sexual behavior. It is note-worthy, however, that until recently no human studies have used as subjects men with manifestly high levels of sexually deviant and/or aggressive behavior. Kafka (1990) examined the effects of fluoxetine, a 5-HT reuptake blocker, in ten men with diagnosed paraphilias (exhibitionists, fetishists, and transvestites), finding amelioration of deviant sexual behaviors and a reduction of sexual drive toward normative levels in nine of the ten subjects. This is, of course, a single study on a small group of volunteers; however, it does offer some support for future inquiry into the relation of serotonin to sexually compulsive and anomalous behavior in humans. Clearly, the relation, if indeed one exists, will be vastly more complex than what has thus far been observed in rats and rabbits.

Sex Hormones

The last important consideration concerns the relation between testosterone and sexual aggression. Although there is ample clinical evidence to suggest that gonadal hormones are involved in human aggression (Valzelli, 1981), the relatively few empirical studies have yielded conflictual and inconclusive results (Prentky, 1985). One finding that is of theoretical importance, as well as being reasonably reliable (Rose, 1978), suggests a relationship between markedly elevated levels of plasma testosterone (PT) and extreme violence and/or a long history of aggressive behavior beginning at a young age (Rose, 1978). Kreuz and Rose (1972) reported that prisoners with histories of more violent crimes in adolescence had significantly higher PT levels than prisoners without histories of adolescent violence. Bain, Langevin, Dickey, and Ben-Aron (1987) and Langevin, Ben-Aron, Wright, Marchese, and Handy (1988) have reported elevated PT levels in violent offenders.

Despite many clinical reports and some reliable empirical evidence, we are still unable to draw any firm conclusions regarding the role of circulating androgens and aggression in adult humans. This may be explained, in good measure, by the complex interaction of other variables, such as social learning, environmental factors, and disinhibiting agents.

There are two periods during development when testosterone may be influential with respect to aggressive behavior. The first period occurs in utero. The fact that male children are more aggressive than female children has been attributed to the presence of testosterone in males and its absence in females during a restricted period of in utero development (Simon, 1981). The second period when testosterone may be influential occurs during puberty, when there is a tenfold increase in testosterone production (Brown, 1981)

Within the last decade a related area of inquiry has provided a potentially important glimpse at the relationship between testosterone and aggression. This window is in utero, the first developmental epoch when testosterone may be influential with respect to aggressive behavior. In fact, one study found that the plasma-free testosterone level of male fetuses during mid-pregnancy may be more than twice as high as in adulthood (Stahl, Gotz, Poppe, Amendt, & Dorner,1978). As Kopera (1983) noted, "sex hormones exert regulatory influences on the central nervous system, particularly during limited 'critical' periods in the rapidly developing embryonic, foetal, postnatal brain" (p. 52). These influences "organize the sexually undifferentiated brain, with regard to neuroendocrine function and patterns of not only sexual but also non-sexual behavior" (Kopera, 1983, pp. 58–59).

The process of masculinization of the developing male brain is not, however, a simple, dualistic phenomenon. The amount of testosterone in utero, as well as the sensitivity of target tissues to testosterone and the metabolic inactivation of testosterone, may vary considerably. Thus, masculinization or feminization is, in reality, a matter of degree (Money, 1986), subject to a wide variety of factors such as the aforementioned "individual" differences, as well as endocrine abnormalities of the fetus, hormone-producing tumors in the mother, stress that alters the pregnant mother's own hormone levels, and substances—including steroid hormones—that enter the placenta after having been ingested or absorbed by the pregnant mother (Ehrhardt, 1978; Meyer-Bahlburg, 1978; Ward, 1984). Of the various congenital or drug-induced abnormalities (e.g., Turner's Syndrome (cf., Ehrhardt, Greenberg, & Money, 1970)), Androgen Insensitivity (Money, Ehrhardt & Masica, 1968) and Adrenogenital Syndrome (Ehrhardt, 1977), the latter case of congenital adrenal hyperplasia (adrenogenital syndrome, CAH) is of particular interest. CAH can be induced by androgenic progestins, such as provera, given to the pregnant mother to counteract toxemia. Studies of CAH and non-CAH female siblings found masculinized gender role behavior in the CAH sibs (Ehrhardt & Baker, 1974). The "feminizing" effects of estrogens in boys has also been noted. Yalom, Green and Fisk (1973) reported that the sons of diabetic mothers who had been prenatally exposed to elevated estrogen demonstrated feminized gender role behavior (i.e., fewer "masculine" interests and reduced assertiveness and aggressiveness). Reinisch and Sanders (1982) pointed out that medications containing barbiturates (e.g., sleeping pills), which may have a feminizing effect on the fetus, were taken by millions of pregnant women.

In order to draw any inferences about the prenatal influence of sex hormones on subsequent aggressive and/or sexually deviant behavior, it is necessary to follow "exposed" subjects into late adolescence when such behavior is expressed (Money, 1986). In one widely cited study, seventeen females and eight males who were exposed during gestation to synthetic progestins were compared to their sex-matched unexposed siblings on a paper-and-pencil inventory designed to assess potential for aggressive behavior (Reinisch, 1981). The mean physical aggression score for the progestin-exposed females and their unexposed sisters was 4.0 and 2.6, respectively. The mean physical aggression score for the progestin-exposed males and their unexposed brothers was 9.75 and 4.88, respectively. In both cases group differences were significant at the .01 confidence level. An excellent review by Meyer-Bahlburg and Ehrhardt (1982) concluded that research to date provides tentative support for the hypothesis that prenatal exposure to exogenous sex hormones may influence the development of human aggressive behavior. Another review of this research also concluded that "sexual deviations in the human may be based, at least in part, on discrepancies between the genetic sex and a sex-specific sex hormone level during brain differentiation" (Dorner, 1980, p. 192). Dorner (1980) further observed, based upon the examination of eighty-four human fetuses, that the critical period for sex-specific brain differentiation is between the fourth and seventh month of gestation. Lack of statistical power due to small samples and methodological problems (e.g., the unaccounted effect of the pregnancy abnormality for which the hormones were administered, and the period during gestation when exposure to the hormones occurred) again obviates any firm conclusions.

The influence of excess testosterone, or increased sensitivity to testosterone, in utero is the subject of Geschwind and Galaburda's (1984) remarkable and controversial cross-disciplinary, theoretical integration. They suggested that excess testosterone slows the development of the left hemisphere, resulting in an increased incidence of autoimmunity in left-handers by suppressing development of the thymus gland in the fetus (Geschwind & Galaburda, 1984).

Geschwind and Galaburda (1984) noted that the male fetal gonads, which owe their development to the H-Y antigen—a protein on the Y chromosome—produce testosterone at levels that may be comparable to that of adult males. It is interesting, in this regard, that Goodman, in a brief comment on the paraphilias, cited Federman (1981) as stating that "variations in the H-Y antigen complex . . . may well affect an individual's sexual profile" (1983, p. 219). This speculation is supported by at least one study of transexuals (Eicher, Spoljar, Cleve, Murken, Richter & Stangel-Rutkowski, 1979). Eicher and others (1979) examined the white blood cells of his subjects, looking for the presence or absence of H-Y antigen. Typically, H-Y antigen is present on the cell surface of males and absent in females. In some of their subjects Eicher and others (1979) found that the experienced or "felt" gender corresponded with the absence or presence of H-Y antigen rather than with the individual's body phenotype (external appearance).

In reality, the extent to which pre- or perinatal androgen excess potentiates aggressive and/or sexual behavior in humans is a vastly complex question, complicated by the inevitable influences of environment and rearing. It may well be, however, that such exposure does introduce a biological vulnerability, thereby increasing the risk for those individuals whose childhood and adolescent development is severely compromised by pathological experiences.

Following masculinization of the male brain in utero there is a surge of testosterone at about two weeks of age that ends at about three months of age (Money, 1986). Thereafter, there is a sex-hormone dormancy until the onset of puberty (Migeon & Forest, 1983), at which time there is, as noted, a tenfold increase in production of testosterone (Brown, 1981). When the sex hormone tap is turned on again at puberty testosterone and its metabolites activate a brain that has already been differentiated with respect to, as Money (1986) put it, "erotosexual programs." That is, the sex hormones activate the intricate developmental "software" that has been written over the preceding thirteen years.

This abrupt increase in release of testosterone provides an opportunity for "naturalistic" studies on developmentally related changes in testosterone level and a concomitant onset of aggressive behavior. Konner (1982) reported that, in one study of male prison inmates, the higher the testosterone level the earlier the age of first arrest. Kreuz and Rose (1972) also found a significant correlation between the age of first occurrence of more violent or aggressive crimes and PT levels ($r = -0.65$). If the age-related changes in criminal behavior can be tied to developmentally related changes in PT, it would provide important correlative support for the contribution of sex hormones.

Overview

As noted earlier, we have elsewhere proposed and begun to test a fantasy-based information processing model of repetitive sexually aggressive behavior (Burgess et al., 1986). In this chapter we have explored hypothetical biological correlates of the model. We began this chapter with the working assumption that fantasy is a cognitive process, essentially a retrieved memory. Moreover, we hypothesized that there are marked individual differences with regards to the strength or vividness of sexual fantasies and the intrusiveness and reiterativeness of sexual fantasies, and that the presence of these two factors will be pronounced in cases of repetitive sexual assault.

A fully integrated theoretical model will have to address three questions: (1) What coexisting "conditions" motivate the offense behavior? (2) What antecedent factors are associated with these conditions? and (3) What constitutional and situational factors serve to increase or decrease the likelihood of the occurrence of the behavior? We proposed in this chapter a highly speculative answer to question No. 1. It was argued that the presumptive "condition" motivating the offense behavior is an intrusive, sexually deviant fantasy life and that the parameters governing the salience of these fantasies (e.g., their vividness and intrusiveness) have a biological underpinning. The origin of the deviant fantasies (question No. 2) was hypothesized to be protracted experiences of abuse in childhood. Mediating or disinhibiting factors that increase or decrease the likelihood of acting on the fantasies (question No. 3) were not discussed in this chapter.

Concluding Caveat

Over all, it is not known what link, if any, in the causal chain of human sexual aggression is occupied by biology. Were it possible to identify the neural circuitry that underlies different aggressive behaviors, complex exogenous factors (i.e., social learning and the environment), which may alter the endogenous response, would still defy simple explanations. Focusing on one aspect of sexual aggression, that which involves repeated assault, narrows somewhat the frame of reference by excluding all those who have committed no acts of sexual aggression or only a single known act of sexual aggression. Even here, however, it is obvious that biological factors cannot be examined in a vacuum. The most compelling evidence to date underscores the powerful effect of social learning on the manner in which individuals learn to cope with and react to emotional experiences. Research on biological correlates of human sexual aggression must not only integrate theoretically meaningful social and developmental variables, but do so in models that permit the examination of complex interactions and temporal changes.

References

Abel, G.G., and E.B. Blanchard. 1974. The role of fantasy in the treatment of sexual deviation. *Archives of General Psychiatry* 30:467–475.

Bain, J., R. Langevin, R. Dickey, and M. Ben-Aron. 1987. Sex hormones in murderers and assaulters. *Behavioral Sciences and the Law* 5:95–101.

Brown, W.A. 1981. Testosterone and human behaviour. *International Journal of Mental Health* 9:45–66.

Burgess, A.W., C.R. Hartman, R.K. Ressler, J. Douglas, and A. McCormack. 1986. Sexual homicide: A motivational model. *Journal of Interpersonal Violence* 1:251–272.

Crepault, C., and M. Couture. 1980. Men's erotic fantasies. *Archives of Sexual Behaviour* 9: 565–581.

Dekker, J., and W. Everaerd. 1988. Attentional effects on sexual arousal. *Psychophysiology* 25:45–54.

Dorner, G. 1980. Neuroendocrine aspects in the etiology of sexual deviations, In R. Forleo and W. Pasini (eds.), *Medical Sexology* (pp. 190–98). The Third International Congress. Littleton, MA: PSG Publishing Company.

Douglas, R.J. 1967. The hippocampus and behavior. *Psychological Bulletin* 67:416–42.

Drummond, P., K. White, and R. Ashton. 1978. Imagery vividness affects habituation rate. *Psychophysiology* 15:193–95.

Ehrhardt, A.A. 1978. Behavioral effects of estrogen in the human female. *Pediatrics.* 62:1166–70.

Ehrhardt, A.A. 1977. Prenatal androgenization and human psychosexual behavior. In J. Money and H. Musaph (eds.), *Handbook of Sexology*, pp. 245–257. Amsterdam: Excerpta Medica.

Ehrhardt, A.A., and S.W. Baker. 1974. Fetal androgens, human CNS differentiation, and behavior sex differences. In R. C. Friedman, R.M. Richart, and R.L. Vande Wiele (eds.), *Sex Differences in Behavior*, pp. 53–76. New York: John Wiley and Sons, Inc.

Ehrhardt, A.A., J. Greenberg, and J. Money. 1970. Female gender identity and absence of fetal gonadal hormones: Turner's syndrome. *Johns Hopkins Medical Journal* 126:237–248.

Eicher, W., M. Spoljar, H. Cleve, H., J.-D.Murken, K. Richter, and S.Stangel–Rutkowski, 1979. H–Y Antigen in Transsexuality. *Lancet* 2:1137–38.

Farah, M.J., S.R. Steinhauer, M.S. Lewicki, J. Zubin, and F. Peronnet. 1988. Individual differences in vividness of mental imagery: An even-related potential. Paper presented at the Annual Meeting of the Society for Psychophysiological Research, San Francisco, October 19–23, 1988. *Abstract in Psychophysiology* 25:444–45.

Federman, D.D. 1981. The requirements for sexual reproduction. *Human Genetics* 58:3–5.

Flor–Henry, P. 1980. Cerebral aspects of the orgasmic response: normal and deviational. In R. Forbes and W. Pasini (eds.), *Medical Sexology*, pp. 256–262. The Third International Congress. Littleton, MA: PSG Publishing Co.

Gardner, H. 1985. *The Mind's New Science*. New York: Basic Books.

Gazzaniga, M.S. 1985. The social brain. *Discovering the Networks of the Mind*. New York: Basic Books.

Geschwind, N., and A.M. Galaburda. 1984. *Cerebral Dominance*. Cambridge, MA: Harvard University Press.

Goodman, R.E. 1983. Biology of sexuality. Inborn determinants of human sexual response. *British Journal of Psychiatry* 143:216–55.

Gosselin, C., and G. Wilson. 1984. Fetishism, sadomasochism and related behaviours. In K. Howells (ed.), *The Psychology of Sexual Diversity*, pp. 89–110. Oxford, England: Basil Blackwell

Hebb, D.O. 1968. Concerning imagery. *Psychological Review* 75, 466–77.

Isaacson, R.L. 1972. Neural systems of the limbic brain and behavioral inhibition. In R. A. Boakes and M. S. Halliday (eds.), *Inhibition and Learning*, pp. 497–528. New York: Academic Press.

Jarrard, L.E., and J.H. Korn. 1969. Effects of hippocampal lesions on heart rate during habituation and passive avoidance. *Communications in Behavioral Biology* 3:141–50.

Kaplan, H.S. 1979. *Disorders of Sexual Desire*. New York: Simon & Schuster.

Kardener, S.H. 1975. Rape fantasies. *Journal of Religion and Health* 14:50–57.

Kimble, D.P. 1968. The hippocampus and internal inhibition. *Psychological Bulletin* 70:285–295.

Kling, A., G. Borowitz, and R.D. Cartwright. 1972. Plasma levels of 17–hydroxycorticosteroids during sexual arousal in man. *Journal of Psychosomatic Research* 16:215–21.

Kafka, M.P. 1990. Successful antidepressant treatment of non-parahilic sexual addictions and paraphilias in males. Manuscript submitted for publication.

Konner, M. 1982. She and he. *Science* 82(September):54–61.

Kopera, H. 1983. Sex hormones and the brain. In D. Wheatley (ed.), *Psychopharmacology and Sexual Disorders*. Oxford: Oxford University Press. British Association for Psychopharmacology Monograph No. 4.

Kosslyn, S.M. 1988. Aspects of a cognitive neuroscience of mental imagery. *Science* 240:1621–6.

Kreuz, L.E., and R.M. Rose. 1972. Assessment of aggressive behavior and plasma testosterone in a young criminal population. *Psychosomatic Medicine* 34:321–32.

Lang, P.J. 1979. A bio–informational theory of emotional imagery. *Psychophysiology* 16:495–512.

Lang, P.J. 1985. The cognitive psychophysiology of emotion: Fear and anxiety. In A. H. Tuma and J. D. Maser (eds.), *Anxiety and the Anxiety Disorders* pp. 131–70. Hillsdale, NJ: Erlbaum.

Langevin, R. 1983. Sexual *strands: Understanding and Treating Sexual Anomalies in Men.* Hillsdale, NJ: Erlbaum.

Langevin, R. 1990. Sexual anomalies and the brain. In W.L. Marshall, D.R. Laws, and H.E. Barbaree (eds.), *Handbook of sexual assault: Issues, theories, and treatment of the offender,* pp. 103–13. New York: Plenum Press.

Langevin, R., M.H. Ben–Aron, P. Wright, V. Marchese, and L. Handy. 1988. The sex killer. *Annals of Sex Research* 1:263–301.

Leaton, R.N. 1965. Exploratory behavior in rats with hippocampal lesions. *Journal of Comparative and Physiological Psychology* 59:325–30.

Mabry, P.D., and B.A. Campbell. 1978. Cholinergic-monoaminergic interactions during ontogenesis. In L. L. Butcher (ed.), *Cholinergic-Monoaminergic Interactions in the Brain,* pp. 257–270. New York: Academic Press.

MacCulloch, M.J., P.R. Snowden, P.J.W. Wood, and H.E. Mills. 1983. Sadistic fantasy, sadistic behaviour and offending. *British Journal of Psychiatry* 143:20–29.

Marshall, W.L., G.G. Abel, and V.L. Quinsey. 1983. The assessment and treatment of sexual offenders. In S.N. Verdun-Jones and A.A. Keltner (eds.), *Sexual Aggression and the Law,* pp. 43–52. Vancouver, Canada: Criminology Research Centre, Simon Fraser University.

Meyer-Bahlburg, H.F.L. 1978. Behavioral effects of estrogen treatment in human males. *Pediatrics* 62:1171–77.

Meyer-Bahlburg, H.F.L., and A.A. Ehrhardt. 1982. Prenatal sex hormones and human aggression: A review, and new data on progestogen effects. *Aggressive Behavior,* 8:39–62.

Migeon, C.J., and M.G. Forest. 1983. Androgens in biological fluids. In B. Rothfield (ed.), *Nuclear Medicine in Vitro,* 2d ed. Philadelphia: Lippincott.

Miller, G.A., D.N. Levin, M.J. Kozak, E.W. Cook, A. McLean, and P.J. Lang. 1987. Individual differences in imagery and the psychophysiology of emotion. *Cognition and Emotion* 1:367–390.

Money, J. 1980. *Love and Love Sickness.* Baltimore, MD: Johns Hopkins University Press.

Money, J. 1986. *Lovemaps.* New York: Irvington Publishers, Inc.

Money, J., A.A. Ehrhardt, and D.N. Masica. 1968. Fetal feminization induced by androgen insensitivity in the testicular feminizing syndrome: Effect on marriage and maternalism. *Johns Hopkins Medical Journal* 123:105–114.

Prentky, R.A. 1985. The neurochemistry and neuroendocrinology of sexual aggression. In D.P. Farrington and J. Gunn (eds.), *Aggression and Dangerousness*, pp. 7–55. New York: John Wiley and Sons.

Prentky, R. A., A. Burgess, F. Rokous, A. Lee, C. Hartman, R. Ressler, and J. Douglas. 1989. The presumptive role of fantasy in serial sexual homicide. *American Journal of Psychiatry* 146:887–91.

Reinisch, J.M. 1981. Prenatal exposure to synthetic progestins increases potential for aggression in humans. *Science* 211:1171–73.

Reinisch, J.M., and S.A. Sanders. 1982. Early barbiturate exposure: The brain, sexually dimorphic behavior and learning. *Neuroscience and Biobehavioral Reviews* 6:311–19.

Ressler, R.K., and A.W. Burgess. 1985. Violent crime. *FBI Law Enforcement Bulletin* 54:18–25.

Ressler, R.K., A.W. Burgess, J.E. Douglas, C.R. Hartman, and R.B. D'Agostino. 1986. Sexual killers and their victims: Identifying patterns through crime scene analysis. *Journal of Interpersonal Violence* 1:288–308.

Ressler, R.K., A.W. Burgess, and J.E. Douglas. 1988. *Sexual Homicide: Patterns and motives*. Lexington, MA: Lexington Books.

Rose, R.M. 1978. Neuroendocrine correlates of sexual and aggressive behavior in humans In M.A. Lipton, A. DiMascio, and K.F. Killam (eds.), *Psychopharmacology: A generation of progress*, pp. 541–52. New York: Raven Press.

Rubin, R.T., A.J. Mandell, and P.H. Crandall. 1966. Corticosteroid responses to limbic stimulation in man: Localization of stimulus sites. *Science* 153:767–68.

Sano, K., H. Sekino, and Y. Mayanagi. 1972. Results of stimulation and destruction of the posterior hypothalamus in cases with violent aggressive, or restless behaviors. In E. Hitchcock, L. Laittinen, and K. Vaernet (eds.), *Psychosurgery*, pp. 57–75. Springfield, IL: Charles C. Thomas.

Schlesinger, L.B., and E. Revitch. 1983. *Sexual Dynamics of Antisocial Behavior*. Springfield, IL: Charles C. Thomas.

Simon, N.G. 1981. Hormones and human aggression: A comparative perspective. *International Journal of Mental Health* 10:60–74.

Singer, J.L. 1966. *Daydreaming*. New York: Random House.

Smith, D., and R. Over. 1987. Male sexual arousal as a function of the content and the vividness of erotic fantasy. *Psychophysiology* 24:334–39.

Stahl, F., F. Gotz, I. Poppe, P. Amendt, and G. Dorner. 1978. Pre- and early postnatal testosterone levels in rat and human. In G. Dorner and M. Kawakami (eds.), *Hormones and brain development*, pp. 99–109. Amsterdam: Elsevier–North Holland Publishing Company.

Valzelli, L. 1981. *Psychobiology of Aggression and Violence*. New York: Raven Press.

Venables, P.H. 1974. The recovery limb of skin conductants response in "high-risk" research. In S.A. Mednick, F. Schlusinger, J. Higgins and B. Bell (eds.), *Genetics, Environment and Psychopathy*. Amsterdam: North Holland.

Ward, I.L. 1984. The prenatal stress syndrome: Current status. *Psychoneuroendocrinology* 9:3–11.

Yalom, J.D., R. Green, and N. Fisk. 1973. Prenatal exposure to female hormones: Effect on psychosexual development in boys. *Archives of General Psychiatry*, 28:554–61.

Chapter 15

The Sex Killer

Ron Langevin
The Clarke Institute of Psychiatry
Toronto, Canada

■

Excerpts of this paper are taken from the author's forthcoming book Homicide: Clinical Assessment and Research Findings. *The material is reproduced by permission of Juniper Press, Oakville, Canada.*

■

Homicide involving sexual assault is one of the most socially despicable and frightening occurrences, especially for women, who are most often the victims of such crimes. Systematic information on the subject of sex killers would be of great value to police, correctional workers, probation and parole officers, and to mental health professionals attempting to understand and treat such individuals. However, there is a singular lack of systematic information on this topic, although to some extent this is true of homicide in general. The empirical data available at this time is incorporated into the following review, and the sex killer is compared to two pertinent populations: killers in general and nonhomicidal sexually aggressive men (rapists and sexual assaulters). These two populations share many features that may converge in the sex killer, namely substance abuse, history of violence, poor socialization, mental illness, and biological abnormalities. Pertinent to the sex killer and the nonhomicidal sexual aggressive is the presence of an unusual sexual preference, in particular, of sadism. First, definitions of terms and groups are undertaken.

Definitions

The terms serial killer, *mass killer*, and *sex killer* as well as *lust murder*, are often used interchangeably. Although some authors attempt to distinguish them, the empirical evidence to support distinctions is often lacking (e.g., Arboleda-Florez & Holley, 1985; and Dietz, 1986, for discussion). The serial killer, for example, is often a sex killer who has sexually assaulted and killed a number of individuals, usually one at a time; on the other hand, the serial killer will be labeled a sex killer if he has only one victim before being caught. The distinction between the two may reflect no more than the efficiency of law enforcement agencies.

Mass killers often manifest sexual anomalies, and there are case examples which number of females were held hostage and systematically destroyed. The sexual element in such crimes may be in doubt. Even in labeled "sex killing," the sexual motive is often inferred from the nature of the crime, rather than from any interview with the victim or from any assessment of his sexual behavior. The stab wounds and/or removal of the breasts and the uterus of the victim may be considered sufficient to label a crime sexual. In some cases, there is clear evidence of sexual assault and/or semen, whereas in others there is not. In one interesting case seen in our clinic, an individual showed a transition from one form of sexual assault to another. He started out hiring prostitutes whom he would beat and rape. Eventually, the beating of the victim became more exciting and totally satisfied him without ejaculation. This man, as well as others, described the physical assault as "sexually satisfying." He had a psychotic break shortly thereafter. If he had not revealed this earlier orgasmic behavior, the sexual nature of his presenting behavior (the beatings) may have been in doubt.

At present, so little systematic work has been done that it is not possible to sort out individuals who have a sexual anomaly based on phallometric testing, for example (noted later), from a criminal who may mutilate the sex organs of a body and possibly has no sexual motivation. It is interesting that, in criminal trials, the term, *sexual sadism*, is readily applied to the accused based only on the information gleaned from the scene of the crime. As noted later, we have much to learn about this topic.

A Comparison of Sex Killing with Homicide in General

Demographics Method and Motive

Sex killers are demographically similar to killers in general. That is, they tend to be young males, and their victims tend to be adult females, although homosexual and child sex killings have also been described in the literature. In terms of other demographic features, they may be indistinguishable in terms of education, occupation, marital status, socialization, criminal history, and so on. Two features do stand out, however. The victim of the sex killer is more often a stranger, whereas homicides in general tend to involve acquaintances. In a small sample of sex killers and non-sex killers (n = 13 per group) Langevin, Ben-Aron, Wright and Handy (1988) found that 69 percent of the sex killers had murdered a stranger, compared to only 8 percent of the non-sex killers. In the population of Canada in general, approximately 20 percent of homicides involve strangers as victims. Of course, as expected, many more victims were females (92 percent) for the sex killers compared to non-sex killers (38 percent) (cf. Langevin & Handy, 1987).

The second important distinguishing feature of the sex killer is the use of strangulation as a method of killing. Seventy-one percent of the sex killers strangled their victims, compared to 8 percent of non-sex killers. In addition, 38 percent used more than one means to kill, compared to only 8 percent of the non-sex killers. Contrary to popular belief, the use of excessive force and the mutilation of the body is common and occurred in approximately half of both groups. The use of strangulation as a method has been reported by others, such as Dietz (1986), and in the many case examples reviewed by Cameron and Frazer (1987). The use of strangulation as a means of prolonging the suffering of the victim and the pleasure of the killer, might be expected of a sadist. The most common method of killing, namely by gun or rifle (46 percent of non-sex killers versus 0 percent of sex killers), is too quick, and ends the pleasure of the killer in too short a period of time for his total gratification.

Strangulation provides a means of control as well, whereby the killer can stop and start and maintain control over his victim—an important feature in sadism.

The sex and non-sex killers differ also in terms of their motive for the crime. Sexual release occurs in no case of non-sex killers. Rather, anger was a motive for 77 percent of the cases (cf. Langevin, Ben-Aron, et al., 1988, for review). In contrast, 31 percent of sex killers appeared to be driven by pure sexual release, and an additional 69 percent appeared to fuse a sexual motive with anger in their crimes. It is not clear whether this anger is more general or specific to women or in fact is part of the scenario of sadism. As noted by a number of authors (see edited book by Weinberg & Kamel, 1983), the apparent anger of the sadist may be no more than role playing whereby he maintains control and power, critical elements for his sexual excitement. One suspects that a number of sex killers are not identified in the population of stranger homicides in Canada, in which one in five has an apparent sexual motive (cf. Langevin & Handy, 1987).

It has been stated that the sex killer seeks publicity and has an enormous ego (narcissism) that is satisfied by a police chase or the publicity that he commands through the daily newspapers and the fear of the masses. Of the thirteen sex killers in Langevin, Ben-Aron, and others' (1988) sample, only one was a publicity-seeker similar to the non-sex killers, in which one case was a narcissistic publicity seeker.

Substance Abuse

The role of substance abuse, and alcohol abuse in particular, in violent behavior has been debated over the last thirty years in the literature. Some authors maintain that it is unimportant, others that it is highly significant in homicide (see Langevin, 1990, in preparation). Criteria have been lacking for defining "alcoholism" or "heavy drinking" and, in some reports, it may be simply stated that the offender was drinking or was drunk. In the majority of reports, no information is provided about alcohol and drug use at the time of the crime. Information on substance abuse in the sex killer is almost nonexistent.

Alcohol influences behavior in a number of ways that are important in violence generally. First, it disinhibits, and can unleash angry feelings with considerably less provocation than might be necessary if the individual were sober. Moreover, many offenders are tolerant to alcohol and are functioning in a much different way from the typical drinking person who relaxes and becomes more sociable. Excessive consumption of alcohol, which may not be recorded reliably because the offender does not remember, may push him into the toxic range, if only temporarily. The tolerant drinker may walk a straight line for the policeman who stops his car, but his judgmental processes may be extremely confused, and he may act on impulse or act out of character.

Alcohol in some individuals also may lead to pathological intoxication. That is, a small amount of alcohol triggers extreme aggressiveness and/or psychotic behavior. One of the sex killers in our series apparently manifested this behavior. Although he acknowledged an interest in sadism prior to the crime under pressure from out-of-town visitors, he consumed one bottle of beer, whereas he did not drink at all prior to that time. He has no memory of leaving the bar until, after the homicide, he found himself covered in blood out in the countryside. A woman neighbor nearby had been sexually assaulted and brutally murdered.

Alcohol also has little impact on inhibiting libido. All the studies examining penile erection under the influence of alcohol found that even individuals at 100 mg % (legal limit in Canada, 80 mg %) have been able to maintain arousal to erotic materials, and their penile reactions were indistinguishable from controls who had no alcohol (e.g., Langevin, Ben-Aron, Coulhard, Day, et al., 1985, for review). Moreover, small amounts of alcohol (approximately 50 mg % blood levels) may stimulate libido. Whereas it is popular lore now that alcohol inhibits sexuality and causes impotence in the male, at the turn of our century alcohol was viewed to be an aphrodisiac. At the very least, alcohol appears to have little impact on erectile potency in young men, even at levels exceeding legal limits.

Sex killers, sexual aggressors, and non-sex killers were similar in the extent of their alcohol use and abuse in the Langevin, Ben-Aron, and others (1988) study. The criterion used for defining a heavy drinker was fourteen or more drinks per week, based on Statistics Canada guidelines (1981). Alcoholism was defined as MAST (Michigan Alcoholism Screening Test; Selzer, 1971) scores greater than 5. Over half of each group could be considered alcoholics based on this criterion, a tenfold increase over the percentages in Canada generally. Moreover, approximately half of each group had used one form of drug or another; the majority had tried marijuana, but similar numbers had tried hallucinogens and other drugs. The sex killers were closer to the sexual aggressors than to non-sex killers in their pattern of drug use, although the non-sex killers had not tried cocaine, whereas over one third of the sexually aggressive men had. At the time of the offence, over half of each group was drinking or on drugs. One-quarter of the sex killers were considered intoxicated, compared to half or more of the other two groups. This means that alcohol and drugs can play a significant role in sex crimes, as they do in other aggressive and homicidal crimes. This factor has been almost totally ignored in the professional literature, and substance abuse should be taken into consideration in any assessment that is carried out.

Mental Illness

It is uncertain whether sex killers in general are mentally ill. Two authors offer exact opposite points of view. Revitch (1965) based his claims on a study of newspaper reports and concluded that psychosis is a common feature of the sex killer. Dietz (1986), on the other hand, said that sexual sadism was much more prominent, and psychosis was not. It is perhaps the bizarre nature of the assault that is so repugnant to the average person and makes one believe that they must be "mad." In some historic cases, the presence of psychosis and psychiatric hospitalization have been noted (see, e.g., cases reported by Cameron and Fraser, 1987). However, the majority of reports remain only claims, and have no systematic data.

In our own small series of sex killers, non-sex killers, and nonhomicidal sexual aggressors, ICD-9 diagnoses were examined, and phallometric testing was available for a number of these individuals. Most in all three groups were labeled as personality disorders, typical of the criminal population seen at the Clarke Institute. However, only the sex killers were labeled as sadists, and 75 percent of them were so labeled, although multiple diagnoses were used in many cases. It is interesting that, in phallometric testing on nine sex killers, only 44 percent were aroused by sadistic stimuli, compared to 13 percent of sexual aggressors. There is an apparent discrepancy between the sexological criteria and psychiatric diagnoses for sadism.

Only 8 percent of the sex killers seen in our sample, as compared to 11 percent of sexual aggressors and 15 percent of non-sex killers were labeled as psychotic, a proportion that is not atypical of the population of clients seen in our forensic psychiatric facility. The majority of men seen had good reality testing and had no history of psychotic behavior. It is further noteworthy that none of the individuals we saw were hallucinating or delusional at the time of admission. The question remains whether the offenders were out of touch with reality at the time of their crimes and were hallucinating or delusional.

Fifty percent of the sex killers, compared to none of the sexual aggressors and 27 percent of the non-sex killers, were considered psychotic at the time of the offense. Some were considered psychotic at the time of the offense because of excessive drug use. One offender, for example, was high on amphetamines and had been so for many months when he killed a series of women. His motor skills and his sexual potency were unaffected—in fact, perhaps enhanced—by these drugs, but his judgment was extremely poor. The diagnosis of sex killers as psychotic or as sadistic requires much more research before adequate conclusions can be made.

Sexual Behavior

There is some dispute about the exact nature of sadism. According to DSM III-R, *sexual sadism* is defined as "a disorder in which recurrent, intense sexual urges and sexually arousing fantasies of at least six months' duration involving acts (real, not simulated) in which the psychological or physical pain (including humiliation) of the victim is sexually exciting. The person acts on these urges or is markedly distressed by them." These two criteria are at variance with other definitions of sadism over the past century. For example, the degree to which real pain is a factor in sadism has been disputed. In the edited book by Weinberg and Levi Kamel (1983), *S & M: Studies in Sadomasochism*, a variety of viewpoints were presented. Krafft-Ebing (1965) considered acts of cruelty and bodily punishment inflicted on others, and observing these being inflicted on others, to be the hallmark of sadism. He also noted that sexual feelings which resulted from being controlled or dominated by the will of another person, being treated by this person as a master, or being humiliated and abused, were also part of sadism. As Weinberg and Kamel noted, S & M is a form of social behavior, and they stress that is a scripted scenario of fantasy played out by two individuals in a relationship.

Albert Ellis (1926), on the other hand, made reference to pain, rather than cruelty, and considered erotically motivated pain the essence of sadomasochism. Ellis noted that sadists limit their love of pain to sexual situations, and in other respects may appear conventional. Weinberg and Kamel (1983) argue that very little pain is actually involved in sadomasochism, and in fact, many sadomasochists prefer verbal humiliation or abuse, cross-dressing, bondage, and mild spanking, in which there is no severe discomfort. They argue that the notion of being helpless and subject to the will of the other is what is most important. They further argue that at the very core of sadomasochism is not pain, but the idea of control, dominance, and submission.

It is also disputed whether sadists and masochists exchange roles and whether *sadomasochism* might not be a more appropriate term, because some argue, as Gebhard, Gagnon, Pomeroy, and Christenson (1965) have, that sadists and masochists are quite capable of switching roles, so that the sadist may become the masochist, and vice versa. Weinberg and Kamel state that the masochist is often the person in control of the S & M relationship and determines the tone of the actions between sadist and masochist. Gebhard and others (1965) hypothesize that the individual may have a set preference, but can switch roles because of the unavailability of partners. Weinberg and Kamel (1983) claimed that many sadists start their careers as masochists and that the best masters (sadists) are ones who know how to play the slave (masochist). Although Weinberg and Kamel considered S & M to be scripted, that no real pain is involved, and that neither S & M partner will go beyond certain limits, they also suggested that there are "dangerous" individuals. Potential S & M partners are very carefully "checked out," not only for the desired behaviors, but to rule out dangerous cases. Thus, it would appear that some individuals take S & M beyond the bounds of "script" and act out their own scenarios once in control. Possibly these dangerous cases include the sex killers.

A repeated theme in the psychological literature is that fantasies are particularly important to S & M and to the sex killer in particular. The enactment of an elaborate scenario that may involve dungeons and torture apparatus requires considerable cooperation in role playing. In many cases, the individuals who hope to act out their fantasies may request prostitutes to play the prescribed role for them. Cameron and Fraser (1987) and Prentky, Burgess, Rokous, Lee, Hartman, Ressler, and Douglas (1989) have examined the role of fantasy in serial sexual homicides. The latter researchers compared twenty-five serial sexual murders in which there were three or more victims with a sample of seventeen single sexual murders, with only one known victim. Prentky and others (1989) postulated that serial murders are driven by an internal mechanism, which takes the form of an intrusive fantasy life and is manifested as a higher prevalence of paraphilias, of organized crime scenes and of violent fantasies. They found support for their hypotheses in that 86 percent of the serial sex killers reported fantasies of rape, murder, or both, compared to 23 percent of single sex killers. Moreover, the serial killers were more likely to report fetishism (71 percent versus 33 percent single sex killers), and cross-dressing (25 percent versus 0 percent for single sex killers). Sixty-eight percent of the serial killers organized their crimes, compared to 24 percent of the single sex killers.

The nature of the sex fantasy life, as well as other details of the sex killer's crimes have often eluded examiners because homicide perpetrators in general tend to lie or to conceal the nature of their behavior (cf. Lang et al., 1987). In the Langevin, Ben-Aron and others study (1988), only 23 percent of killers provided unqualified disclosure, and 69 percent partial disclosure. Eight percent denied their behavior in spite of overwhelming evidence from the crime scene and in face of conviction.

Our own work supports Prentky and others' (1989) findings that sex killers tend to show multiple paraphilias, but this is not atypical of sexually aggressive individuals in general. There were no differences between sex killers and nonhomicidal sexual aggressors in the frequency of voyeurism, exhibitionism, toucheurism, and frottage, although over half of the cases in each group showed one or more of these anomalies.

There is an interesting and repeated finding that sex killers engage in transvestism. Langevin, Ben-Aron, and others (1988) found that 54 percent of sex killers (versus no non-sex killers) engaged in transvestism. Prentky and others (1989) found that 25 percent of serial sex killers did so. In another study on a non-homicidal sample, Langevin et al. (1985) found that approximately one in five sexually aggressive men engaged in transvestism. Although sample sizes are small, results suggest that more than double the number of sex killers engage in transvestism, compared to non-sex killers or nonhomicidal sexual aggressors.

It is also an interesting finding that 40 percent of the sex killers showed feminine gender identity as measured by the Freund Gender Identity Scale (Freund et al., 1977), compared to none of the other sexual aggressors. This is an uncharacteristic pattern of behavior, as expected by a number of theorists. Feminist theorists, for example (see Brownmiller et al., 1975 or Cameron and Fraser, 1987) hypothesize that it is the male domination and male aggressiveness that are operative factors in humiliating and embarrassing women, and it is manifested in extreme forms in sex killings. In contrast, Weinberg and Kamel note that the roles of male and female are frequently reversed in sadomasochism. A female partner may play a more aggressive role as a dominatrix, whereas the males are frequently passive and/or may be required to dress as women as part of the scenario. Thus, the males are the ones who would experience beatings and/or humiliation. Unfortunately, there is too little data on either of these topics to make firm conclusions. It is known, however, that most sex killers are labeled as sadists and tend to be male. The paradoxical presence of feminine gender identity and cross-dressing in these groups suggest that their behavior may fall within the realm of transvestism/ sadomasochism.

Wilson and Gosselin (1980) examined members of a transvestite's club and found a significant overlap of interest in sadomasochism and fetishism. It is possible for some men that being female is equated with being controlled, and that the female role is seen as inferior, as suggested by some feminists. It is also possible that the sex killer perceives the female as a controlling person. It is not unusual for men to consider women to "be in charge." They feel that men are at a disadvantage, having to ask women out, and that women control the direction and extent of sexual activity. It is clear that no one in the literature has made an attempt to examine the sex killer in terms of the features presumed to be important in sadomasochism, for example, reversing sex roles, the importance of role playing, the role of real pain versus control and domination, or the role of feminine gender identity and cross-dressing.

The Sex Killing

Four elements appear in sex killings which are considered aspects of sadism. These are:

1. Control or domination of the victim;
2. Fear, helplessness, pleading of the victim;
3. Injuries and/or rituals;
4. Death and/or necrophilia.

Not all of these elements are present in every case. Moreover, control may be the critical element in all of the sex killer's behavior. To have someone trapped in his power, tied up, and so on, is controlling, as in (1) preceding. However, if somebody is frightened, terrified, or pleading, it also suggests helplessness, and ipso facto, the control on the part of the offender, as in (2). Injuring someone also is power, and control over them—to use them or dispose of them as one wishes—as in (3). Finally, the dead body is utterly helpless and in the hands of the sex killer. He can do what he wants and frequently mutilates and/or sexually abuses it, removing organs and so on, which is the ultimate control over the individual's life.

Many sexually aggressive men who are not sex killers will report sexual excitement to the fear of their victims. It is possible that the four elements of sadism, in some modified form, are exciting to a wider range of sexual aggressors, and that only in some cases do they lead to the victim's death. It is possible, as Cameron and Fraser (1987) suggested in their book *The Lust to Kill*, that necrophilia is a different anomaly from sexual sadism. This remains unknown at present. However, having a "beautiful body" at one's disposal is also a form of ultimate control and can serve as a form of masochism—the degradation of having sex with a corpse.

Phallometric Test Results

The results of phallometric testing on sadists remain experimental at present. Gene Abel and his colleagues in 1977 examined penile circumference changes to descriptions of rape and consenting intercourse cues. He constructed a rape index, which was based on largest reactions to rape versus consenting intercourse cues. He found in his project that the more "sadistic" the crime, the higher the rape index. Other researchers have extended his findings using similar audio recorded materials. However, some have failed to replicate Abel and others' results (cf. Langevin, Bain et al., 1985, for review). In effect, sexually conventional men showed sizable reactions to rape cues for whatever reason, and with instructions (cf. Quinsey & Carrigan, 1978), can appear indistinguishable from the sex offender/rapist. These earlier conceptualizations of rape involved forced intercourse and/or violence with intercourse. Having seen a number of these stimuli, it is clear that the elements of control and domination that are so central to sadomasochism and perhaps to many rapists' behavior, were not consistently represented, or were not represented at all. This may explain the diversity of results in the various studies. In the experimental stimuli used in our own work (Langevin, Ben-Aron et al., 1988), four of the nine (44 percent) sex killers tested appeared to be sadists and responded more to such stimuli. It is possible that the degree of danger the offender presents may be detected in sexual arousal to various cues. For example, some individuals may be more aroused by the control and the entrapment game than by actual physical injury. This research remains a task for the future, and certainly phallometric testing will bring order to this topic where speculation has dominated.

Sexual Dysfunction

Sexual dysfunction and/or sexual inadequacy often have been attributed to the sexually aggressive male. Our earlier work (Langevin et al., 1985) suggested that there may be more sexual dysfunction in sadistic than in nonsadistic sexually aggressive men, but sample sizes were small. In the sample of Langevin, Ben-Aron, and others, (1988), there were no significant differences between the sex killers, sexual aggressors, and non-sex killers in the presence of impotence, premature ejaculation, or retarded ejaculation, but a total of 45 percent of the sex killers, versus 10 percent of other sexual aggressors and 33 percent of non-sex killers had some reported problem. Because this is a difficult area for males to accurately report, physical examinations would be valuable in further exploration of findings on actual sexual dysfunction.

Family Background and Childhood of the Sex Killer

It is frequently argued that the triad of enuresis, fire-setting, and cruelty to animals is an important one in identifying the violent individual. In our previous work (Langevin, Paitich, & Orchard, 1983 review), on a sample of non-sex killers, we found that less than 1 percent of the group showed this triad, and that there were no significant differences between killers and nonviolent controls. Case examples often quote excessive cruelty to animals in sadistic men, but no systematic data has been provided, so it is not known at present how predictive the triad is of adult sexual violence. In the small sample of cases by Langevin, Ben-Aron, and others (1988), 39 percent of the sex killers, 40 percent of the sexual aggressors and 10 percent of non-sex killers were cruel to animals at some time during their lives. Thirty-nine percent of the sex killers versus 33 percent of sexual aggressors, and 20 percent of non-sex killers had set fires. Sixty-two percent of the sex killers, 33 percent of sexual aggressors, and 33 percent of non-sex killers showed enuresis after age 5.

It appears there was considerably more disturbance in the homes of sex killers than in the homes of the other two groups, because 80 percent of the former group had run away from home as children, compared to only 11 percent of the non-sex killers. Moreover, 83 percent of the sex killers reported having temper tantrums as children, compared to 40 percent of the non-sex killers. When scores on the Clarke Parent Child-Relations Questionnaire (Paitich and Langevin, 1976) were examined for the three groups, the sex killers reported more aggression to their fathers and less affection from them than the other two groups reported. Overall, there was more family disturbance in the sex killers group, less in the sexual aggressors group, and least in the non-sex killers group. There was a trend for more of the sex offenders' fathers to be alcoholic than were the non-sex killers'; 60 percent of the sex killers reported that their fathers were alcoholic, versus 43 percent of sexual aggressors and 15 percent of non-sex killers.

Biological Factors

Sex killers are sometimes described as very intelligent, but it is rare that an IQ score is reported. In the sample of sex killers, non-sex killers, and non-homicidal sexual aggressors examined by Langevin, Ben-Aron, and others (1988), there were no significant differences in the three groups on WAIS-RIQ. There was a trend for the sexual aggressors to be less intelligent than the sex killers and the non-sex killers, but all cases still scored within average limits.

A brain scan was available on thirty cases, and 40 percent of the sex killers and 60 percent of the sexual aggressors versus no non-sex killers showed some abnormality. The majority of these abnormalities were in the right temporal horn area of the brain. Numbers, however, were too small for firm conclusions, although similar findings on sexual sadists have been reported in other studies (cf. Hucker et al., 1988, and Langevin, Bain et al., 1985). There were no group differences in the Halstead-Reitan or Luria Nebraska batteries.

Hormones were analyzed only for twenty cases (seven sex killers, six sexual aggressors, and seven non-sex killers), and there was a trend for significant elevation of testosterone of the sex killers as compared to the other two groups. These results should be replicated in further study.

Summary

Overall, there is considerable speculation about the nature of the sex killer but a shortage of empirical data and controlled research. What we do know suggests that some components of sadomasochism are operative in the behavior of the sex killer. He chooses a female victim and often strangles her, and/or may cut sex organs from the body.

Strangulation may be one method of controlling the very life of the victim, and of maintaining and prolonging sexual arousal, as well as torturing the victim, which is characteristic of sadism.

Too little data has been collected to argue whether the sex killer is insane, but it appears that psychosis is not the frequent diagnosis given. The ability of the offender to appreciate the nature of his act and a loss of touch with reality should be the ultimate criteria in deciding whether the sex killer is insane. It is perhaps the bizarre nature of the killing that leads the examining mental health workers to conclude that the offender is insane. It is not unusual in other sexual anomalies that a diagnosis, usually a personality disorder, is ascribed to an individual because of his sexual behavior, rather than independently based on other criteria. For example, a pedophile may be labeled as an inadequate personality because he interacts with children rather than adults. However, the decision for that criterion is not independent of his sexual behavior. Similarly, the nature of sex killing and of sexual sadism are not well understood. It is not known whether the individual is out of touch with reality at the time of his offense or during states of sexual arousal. Certainly, electroencephalographic information during sexual arousal could be used to examine some of these questions.

Substance abuse plays an important role in sex killing as it does in other homicides and in violent crimes generally. Its exact contribution to the crime, however, remains elusive and not well understood (see Langevin, Paitich, and Orchard, 1982). Sexual sadism is often ascribed as the underlying mental disorder/sexual deviation and/or motive for the crime in question. However, this conclusion should be treated with caution. In particular, it would be valuable to compare the general features of nonhomicidal sadists and sadomasochists with those of sex killers to determine if their patterns of behavior are similar. Phallometric testing could be used to evaluate the degree of sexual arousal to the components of sadism (control, fear, terror, injury, and death) as well as to masochism in order to determine whether the sex killer clearly fits into the S & M category.

The background of the sex killer is poorly understood. It is often assumed or reported in news articles (cf. Cameron & Fraser, 1987) that the offender had a disturbed childhood and/or a hatred for some woman in his life, but systematic information on this topic is nonexistent. It is possible that sex killers would not differ from other sexually aggressive men and/or criminals in general.

Finally, biological factors may play some role in the behavior of the sex killer. The study by Langevin, Ben-Aron, and others (1988) suggests that elevated testosterone may be a feature of the sex killers Other work on sexual sadists and non-sex killers has been mixed (see Bain, Langevin, Dickey, & Ben-Aron, 1987; Bain, Langevin, Dickey, Hucker & Wright, 1988, for more details). The possible role of neuro-cognitive distortion and impairment should not be overlooked at this time.

Feminine gender identity in the sex killer and the nonhomicidal sadist in our research remains paradoxical and interesting. Feminine gender identity is often associated with transvestism in noncriminal samples (cf. Buhrich, 1976; Steiner, Sanders, & Langevin, 1985) and transvestism is also associated with noncriminal sadomasochism and fetishism. It is possible that the sex killer represents no more than a transvestite sadomasochist who has poor socialization and is willing to carry his impulses to extremes in violating social norms. Gender has many possible explanations in the context of the sex-killer's makeup (cf. Langevin, 1985). It may reflect one facet of an antisocial or psychopathic personality. Because the sex killer has been poorly socialized in other respects and fails to incorporate many social mores and roles, it should not be surprising that he also fails to incorporate social sex roles but only plays along with them for his own convenience. Alternately, feminine gender identity may mean much more than a lack of socialization. It also is seen in autoerotic asphyxia (Hucker, 1985) and appears to play an integral role in sadomasochism. Playing the female role in their minds may mean being degraded socially and/or playing a role that is characteristically one controlled by the male. Much more work needs to be done to examine the role of sadomasochism and of gender disturbance in the sex-killer's makeup. Phallometry should prove a useful tool in exploring this area.

References

Abel, G.G., D.H. Barlow, E.E. Blanchard, and D. Guild. 1977. The components of rapists' sexual arousal. *Archives of General Psychiatry* 34:895–903.

Arboleda-Florez, J., and H. Holley. 1985. What is mass murder? *Psychiatry* 6:409–17.

Bain, J., R. Langevin, R. Dickey, and M. Ben-Aron. 1987. Sex hormones in murderers and assaultives. *Behavioral Science and the Law* 5:75–101.

Bain, J., R. Langevin, R. Dickey, S. Hucker, and P. Wright. 1988. Hormones in sexually aggressive men: I Baseline values for eight hormones: II the ATCH test. *Annals of Sex Research* 1:63–78.

Brittain, R.P. 1970. The sadistic murderer. *Medicine, Science and the Law* 10: 198–207.

Brownmiller, S. 1975. *Against Our Will: Men, Women and Rape*. New York: Simon & Schuster.

Buhrich, N. 1976. A heterosexual transvestite club: Psychiatric aspects. *Australian and New Zealand Journal of Psychiatry* 10:331–35.

Cameron, D., and E. Frazer. 1987. *The Lust to Kill: A Feminist Investigation of Sexual Murder*. New York: New York University Press.

Dietz, P.E. 1986. Mass, serial, and sensational homicides. *Bulletin of the New York Academy of Medicine* 62:477–91.

Ellis, A. 1926. Studies in the pathology of sex. In T. Weinberg and G. W. Levi-Kamel (eds.), *S and M Studies in Sadomasochism*. New York: Prometheus Books.

Freund, K., R. Langevin, J. Satterberg, and B. Steiner. 1977. Extension of the gender identity scale for males. *Archives of Sexual Behavior* 6:507–19.

Gebhard, P., J.H. Gagnon, W.B. Pomeroy, and C.V. Christenson. 1965. *Sex Offenders: An Analysis of Types*. London: Heineman Co.

Groth, A.N., A.W. Burgess, and L.L. Holstrom. 1977. Rape: Power, anger and sexuality. *American Journal of Psychiatry* 134:1239–43.

Hucker, S.J. 1985. Self-harmful sexual behavior. *Psychiatric Clinics of North America* 8:323–37.

Hucker, S.J., R. Langevin, R. Dickey, L. Handy, J. Chambers, and S. Wright. 1988. Cerebral damage and dysfunction in sexually aggressive men. *Annals of Sex Research* 1: 33–27.

Krafft-Ebing, R. von. 1965. *Psychopathia Sexuales*. Trans. F.S. Klaff, reproduced and edited in T. Weinberg, and G.W. Levi Kamel (eds.), *S and M Studies in Sadomasochism*. New York: Prometheus Books.

Lang, R.A., R. Langevin, R. Holden, N.A. Figia, and R. Wu. 1987. Personality and criminality in violent offenders. *Journal of Interpersonal Violence* 12:179–95.

Langevin, R. 1990, in preparation. *Homicide: Clinical Assessment and Research Findings*. Oakville, Ontario: Juniper Press.

———. 1985. The meanings of crossdressing. In B. Steiner (ed.), *Gender Dysphoria: Development, Research, Management*, pp. 207–26. New York: Plenum Press.

Langevin, R., J. Bain, M.H. Ben-Aron, R. Coulthard, D. Day, L. Handy, G. Heasman, S.J. Hucker, J.E. Purins, V. Roper, A.G. Russon, C.D, Webster, and G. Wortzman. 1985. Sexual aggression: Constructing a predictive equation. In R. Langevin (ed.), *Erotic Preference, Gender Identity, and Aggression in Men: New Research Studies*. Hillsdale, NJ: Erlbaum.

Langevin, R., M.H. Ben-Aron, R. Coulthard, D. Day, S.J. Hucker, J.E. Purins, V. Roper, A.E. Russon, and C.D. Webster. 1985. The effect of alcohol on penile erection. In R. Langevin (ed.), *Erotic Preference, Gender*

Identity and Aggression in Men: New Research Studies. Hillsdale, NJ: Erlbaum.

Langevin, R., M.H. Ben-Aron, P. Wright, M. Marchese, and L. Handy. 1988. The sex killer. *Annals of Sex Research* 1:263–301.

Langevin, R., and L. Handy. 1987. Stranger homocide in Canada: A national sample and a psychiatric sample. *Journal of Criminal Law and Criminology* 78:398–429.

Langevin, R., D. Paitich, and B. Orchard. 1983. Childhood and family background of killers seen for psychiatric assessment: A controlled study. *Bulletin for the American Academy of Psychiatry and Law II*: 331–41.

————. 1982. The role of alcohol, drugs, suicide attempts, and situational strains in homicide committed by offenders seen for psychiatric assessment. *Acta Psychiatrica Scandanavica* 66:229–42.

Paitich, E., and R. Langevin. 1976. The Clarke Parent-Child Relations Questionnaire: A clinically useful test for adults. *Journal of Clinical and Consulting Psychology*, 44:428–36.

Prentky, R., A.W. Burgess, F. Rokous, A. Lee, C. Hartman, R. Ressler, and J. Douglas. 1989. The presumptive role of fantasy in serial sexual homicide. *American Journal of Psychiatry* 146:887–91.

Quinsey, V.L., and W.F. Carrigan. 1978. Penile responses to visual stimuli. *Criminal Justice and Behavior* 5:333–42.

Revitch, E. 1965. Sex murder and the potential sex murder. *Diseases of the Nervous System* 26:640–48.

Selzer, M. 1971. The Michigan Alcoholism Screening Test: The quest for a new diagnostic instrument. *American Journal of Psychiatry* 127:1653–58.

Statistics Canada. 1981. *Special Report on Alcohol Statistics.* Ottawa: Health and Welfare Canada.

Steiner, B.W., R.M. Sanders, and R. Langevin. 1985. Cross-dressing, erotic preference, and aggression: A comparison of male transvestites and transsexuals. In R. Langevin (ed.) *Erotic Preference, Gender Identity, and Aggression in Men: New Research Studies.* Hillsdale, NJ: Erlbaum.

Weinberg, T., and G.W. Levi Kamel. 1983. *S and M: Studies in Sadomasochism.* New York: Prometheus Books.

Chapter 16

Serial Rape:
The Offender and His Rape Career

Janet I. Warren
University of Virginia

Robert R. Hazelwood
National Center for the Analysis of Violent Crime

Roland Reboussin
National Center for the Analysis of Violent Crime

■

This research was funded in part by grant #84-JN-AX-KO10 from the Office of Juvenile Justice and Delinquency Prevention to the University of Pennsylvania School of Nursing in conjunction with the FBI National Center for the Analysis of Violent Crime.

■

The most predatory of all rapists, the serial rapist, offers the researcher a unique opportunity for study. The multiplicity of his offenses, the extended nature of his rape career, and the general adeptness of his criminal activity allow for both theoretical and applied inquiry. Available from this type of inquiry is not only an assessment of those personality and behavioral factors that stay constant from one rape to the next but also those that change over successive rapes. Although the importance of these dynamics is viewed differently by theoreticians, clinicians, and law enforcement, an interest in studying the different aspects of rape as it develops incrementally for particular offenders is increasingly giving rise to interdisciplinary research and collaboration.

One such undertaking, initiated by the National Center for the Analysis of Violent Crime (NCAVC) of the FBI, was designed to study serial rapists who were responsible for at least ten rapes prior to their apprehension. The study, which developed in a form similar to that of an earlier study of serial murders (Ressler, Burgess, & Douglas, 1988), was undertaken in order to better inform the criminal investigatory analyses that were being conducted by the FBI. In 1978, the Behavioral Sciences Unit had formally begun to assist law enforcement across the country in the various departments' investigation of violent crime, and through a detailed analysis of crime scene data and information obtained from the victim, criminal investigatory analysts would outline, for the investigating agency, characteristics and traits of the offender that might help in streamlining or focusing the investigation. The process of "profiling" or "analyzing" these cases initially developed out of the investigatory experience of a small cadre of highly experienced Special Agents. Over the past decade, it has been complemented by quantitative research regarding serial murders, serial rapists, sexual sadists, arsonists, and child abductors.

The study of serial rapists, initiated in 1984 in conjunction with Dr. Ann Burgess of the University of Pennsylvania's School of Nursing, looked specifically at forty-one serial rapists who were responsible for 837 rapes and more than 400 attempted rapes. Data collection consisted of lengthy, in-depth interviews through which an attempt was made to "step into" the mind of the offender and, from that vantage point, fathom the motivation and behavior that characterized the development and execution of their rape behavior. Theoretically, the study evolved out of previous research by Groth, Burgess, and Holmstrom (1977); the law enforcement focus, however, highlighted the importance of crime scene information, the development of an offender's particular modes of operation, and his identifying behaviors both before and after his crimes. The results of this study are summarized subsequently under the following headings: (1) Methodology, (2) Case Vignettes, (3) Developmental History, (4) Sexual History; (5) Crime Scene Characteristics, and (6) Classification Analyses.

Methodology

Interviews were conducted with forty-one offenders who were incarcerated in prisons in twelve states. These offenders were identified initially by mental health professionals affiliated with sex offender treatment programs or state prisons, by law enforcement officers who had attended the FBI National Academy, and by FBI Special Agents. Of forty-three individuals who met the inclusion criteria, forty-one agreed to participate in the study. These men had exhausted all judicial appeals and therefore had no expectation that participating in the interview would either benefit or adversely affect their legal situation.

The data were collected in face-to-face interviews that lasted from four and one-half to twelve and one-half hours. Prior to the interviews all available documentation including police reports; victim statements; medical, psychiatric, and prison records; police investigatory reports; and presentence reports was reviewed. If any discrepancy was noted between the records and the respondent's reports, efforts were made to clarify the discrepancy during the interview. The interview itself covered all aspects of the respondent's developmental history and life situation prior to his incarceration as well as a detailed account of his first, middle, and last sexual assault.

Immediately following the interview, a seventy-page protocol was completed. The protocol had been developed as a collaborative effort between the FBI's NCAVC, the University of Pennsylvania School of Nursing, and Boston City Hospital. The protocol included sections on developmental history, education, employment, military history, psychiatric contact and treatment, sexual history, criminal history, sexual assault and crime scene characteristics, victim information, postoffense behavior, and motives for rape.

The Sample

The sample included thirty-five white males, five African-American males, and one Hispanic male. At the time of the interviews, their ages ranged from 23 to 55 years with a mean age of 35.2 years. The subjects' mean age at the time of the first, middle, and last rape was 21.8 years, 25.8 years, and 29 years, respectively.

Twenty-nine (71 percent) of the subjects had been married at least once; fourteen (34 percent) often had been married more than one time. The majority were living with parents, spouses and/or children, or a roommate during their rape career. Only twenty-one percent were living alone at the time of the last offense. At the time of their most recent arrest, the respondents had been employed at a job for an average of 2.4 years. Their reported annual income ranged from $5,000 to $52,000 with a mean of $16,446 a year. Of the rapists, twenty-one (51 percent) had served in the military: ten (50 percent) reported receiving an honorable discharge, two (10 percent) a medical discharge, three (15 percent) a general discharge, three (15 percent) an undesirable discharge, and two (10 percent) a dishonorable discharge.

The educational level of the men ranged from 5 to 17 years with a mean of 11.3 years. Twenty-two of the respondents (54 percent) had obtained a G.E.D., three (7 percent) had high school diplomas, and nine (22 percent) had procured either an associate's or a bachelor's degree. Formal intelligence testing, available for thirty-three subjects, indicated that only four subjects (12 percent) scored below average (below 90) and 12 scored within the average range (90–110) of intelligence. Overall, seventeen (51 percent) scored above average, obtaining scores within the bright normal (110–119) and very superior (130+) ranges.

Of the forty-one men, fifteen were participating in some form of sex offender treatment at the time of the interview. Collectively, they had accumulated 200 convictions. However, they admitted responsibility during this study for 837 rapes, more than 400 attempted rapes, and over 5,000 "nuisance" sexual offenses. The length of time over which they raped before the first rape arrest ranged from three months to twelve years.

Case Vignettes

Three case summaries are presented subsequently in order to illustrate the clinical richness encountered when interviewing the various respondents.

Case No. 1

J. was the youngest of four children; he had three sisters who were nine to sixteen years older than he. He recalled having been told that he was his parent's "last effort to have a son."

J. described his family as financially stable. His father was a store manager for a national retail store chain, and the family moved several times as a result of his father's transfers. Upon retirement from the company, the father purchased his own store, and the family remained in the same location for a number of years.

J. told the interviewers that his parents "had" to get married because his mother was pregnant, and he noted that his mother had conveyed to him that she experienced this as a deprivation of her "best years." According to J., his mother was also a very dominant person and would harass the father "continually." J. noted that she would tell people what to do, how to live, and how to dress, including any acquaintances he might bring home. J. attributed his lack of close friends to this, saying once he brought them home and they had a taste of his situation, they didn't want to stick around and experience it for any significant length of time. J. reported that his father would deal with conflict in the home by sulking and either going into his bedroom or back to work. He noted that he did not really know his father and that his father felt like an "abstract figure" to him.

J. recalled harboring a great deal of resentment toward his mother. He noted that he was not ill as a child, although his mother perpetuated the idea that he was frail and constantly gave him pills and vitamins. By his account, she would also discourage or forbid participation in sports or hunting with the father. J. emphasized that he felt "smothered" by his mother and felt that his mother's attitude led him to believe that women are "all-powerful" and were "objects of fear and dread." He also recalled that his mother had to have a hysterectomy following his birth, and many times while he was growing up, she would tell him that she had been damaged by his birth. J. noted that this was "a heavy load" of guilt for a young child to bear.

J. reported wetting the bed up through kindergarten and recounted how his mother dramatized the potential embarrassment of going to people's houses overnight until he was 12 or 13 years old. She would bring rubber sheets along and make an issue over having the bed prepared in case he had an accident. J. recalled that this prevented him from participating in Scouts, going camping, or spending the night at a friend's house.

J. explained that his family did not express affection openly. Embraces were ritualistic or expected, at arrivals and departures, and J. felt that they had no meaning, and he disliked the touching. He stated that he continued to avoid physical contact as he grew into adulthood.

J. was academically adept; he was in the top ten of his high school class and ranked third in his college graduating class. His graduation ceremony was a private one, however, as he had been arrested for assault and had spent a year in prison before actually graduating from college.

J. told the interviewers that he began window peeping in the ninth grade, explaining that the peeping itself did not sexually excite him although he derived a great deal of satisfaction from invading the privacy of his victims. He suggested that it was a way of cutting down on the power of the women, the dread with which he perceived them, and it gave him a sense of having done something to them and "gotten away with it."

J. reported that he began masturbating in his 20s. He had a couple of platonic relationships with women and had one consensual sexual experience when he was 24, which was a "one-night stand."

In detailing his criminal history, J. reported that he raped for approximately ten years before being arrested. He explained that he gradually developed his method for raping, which became increasingly complex over a large number of rapes. Prior to the rape, J. would go to a neighborhood where his appearance, dress and vehicle would "fit in" and go unnoticed, and through peeping, identify six potential victims. Returning on the night of the rape, J. would dress in his "going in clothes," which included surgical gloves and oversized sneakers. In this attire, he would cut the telephone and electric wires and enter the house, where he would locate the victim and his various means of escape. J. explained that his dress and behavior up until this point reflected that of a burglar rather than rapist, his assumption being that if he was observed or apprehended at this point, there would be nothing to connect him with his previous or anticipated sexual assaults.

After having familiarized himself with the residence, J. would open a window not far from where the victim was sleeping, and leaving the residence, return to his car. Once there, he would change into his "rape clothes"; these consisted of a pair of oversized coveralls and a second pair of sneakers that were of a different size from those he had worn previously. J. explained that he could remove the overalls easily prior to grabbing the woman and therefore would not be vulnerable while trying to disrobe once she was awake; the other size of sneakers were used to mislead the police into believing that there were two men involved in the assault.

Returning to the residence, J. would check to see if the woman had awakened and closed the window. If she had, he would move onto the next victim; if not, he would enter the residence a second time and complete the rape, generally using a knife to threaten his victim. He would subdue the woman, perhaps fondle her, vaginally assault her, and leave. J. explained that he was generally only with the woman five or ten minutes; he indicated he did not enjoy sex and that aspect of the assault was the least enjoyable. In fact, toward the end of his assaults, he would count to 10 to delay the rape as long as possible. As he explained, he would go ahead and rape the victim because "after all the trouble [of getting in], it would have been criminal not to."

Case No. 2

M. was conceived out of wedlock but eventually had a brother, sister, and a half-sister. He explained that his parents married because of the pregnancy, a fact that his mother allegedly blamed on him repeatedly throughout his developing years.

When M. was 5, he suffered severe injuries in an auto accident. He was subsequently diagnosed with an epileptic seizure disorder and was on medication for many years. Around the same time, M.'s father was discharged from the service for gambling, and not long afterward divorced M.'s mother when the subject was 7 years old. By his account, the subject blamed his mother more than his father for the divorce, even though his father physically abused him when drunk. He remembered his father occasionally taking him fishing and participating in other father/son activities, and M., therefore, considered himself to have been more severely abused by his mother because she did not interfere when his father began to be abusive toward him. M. reported that he has not seen his father since he was 7 years old.

M. explained that his mother was divorced for three years and brought home various boyfriends during that time. He remembered his mother walking around the house nude when she had a "friend" over. By his account, she would also give him alcoholic beverages after which she and her friends would laugh at his antics. M. reported that his mother remarried when he was 10 years old, adding that he was also beaten by his stepfather when he would get drunk.

Although M.'s IQ was scored at 139, he did not perform well in school. He failed second grade because he hit a teacher over the head with a chair. He also became "bored" with school in the fourth grade and had to repeat the sixth grade. The two-year age difference between him and his classmates apparently contributed to a feeling of nonacceptance and, at age 17, while in the ninth grade, M. was expelled from junior high for breaking into the school library and stealing the book fund. He never attended high school, but obtained his GED during his eighteen-day military career. He was discharged from the Army because of asthma. He attended one year of college when he was 17 and 18 years old and another year while in prison.

The theft of book-fund money was M.'s first major criminal offense. He was also involved in residential burglaries, for which he was arrested. The original charge of 114 counts of breaking and entering was reduced to 14 and then dropped when the judge found out that M. had arranged to enter military service.

M. recalled that his first sexual image was seeing his mother walk across the room nude when she had a "friend" over. By his account, he also watched his mother and stepfather having intercourse when he was 14 years old. He recalled being very excited, feeling jealous of his stepfather, and masturbating as he watched.

M. told the interviewers that he "blossomed" sexually when he was 14 years old. He explained that he began to think about raping, molesting, or sexually assaulting women and used photographs from *Playboy* for images in developing these fantasies. M. recalled, "At first I was OK and then I started humiliating them in my mind, degrading them, thinking things like 'fucking bitch' and stuff like that." By his account, he would think of forcing women into submissive positions and had fantasies of rape, although he would not focus on force, but rather on telling her what she was going to do and having her do it to him. He emphasized that in these fantasies, the woman was submissive to him and would always obediently follow his demands for various sexual activities.

M. explained that his first few incidents of sexual intercourse were rapes, adding that his rapes were either girlfriends or women/girls he knew. He stated that his sexual fantasies also became more aggressive after his first two rapes and that he became more demanding, telling the women to take their clothes off, "do this, bitch, or else," although he never fantasized what the "or else" was. According to M., he was also fantasizing about having intercourse with his mother, an act that was willing on both their parts. These fantasies started when he was 15 years old and continued until he was 17 years old. He explained that he also had returned home after his brief military service and attempted to rape his 11-year-old sister, but quit before he culminated the act as she became very frightened. M. noted that, soon after, his stepfather kicked him out of the house for stealing a relative's purse, and that, after his departure from the house, the fantasies about having intercourse with his mother subsided.

M. recalled that, after he was forced to leave his home, he went to live with a director of a runaway referral service. By his account, he started using drugs while living there and also raped a girl who came for help to the center. After that incident, he no longer felt welcome at the house, and soon after married a 26-year-old friend of friends (he was 17). He and his new wife used drugs heavily and separated after six weeks. M. recalled trying to commit suicide around that time by ingesting unrefined mescaline.

When M. was 20 years old, he attempted to rape his mother. When she resisted, he killed her. M. was tried and convicted of the offense and served a number of years in prison. He indicated that, by the time of his release, his fantasies had become increasingly more aggressive, involving knives or other weapons. In his last rape, he acted out most of his fantasies of threatening with a weapon and talking in a degrading manner, saying things like, "Suck it, bitch."

It is interesting to note that many of this subject's rapes were not reported. As he mentioned, all his rape victims were people who knew him. However, he was very manipulative in many instances, and the younger women he forced himself on were "from the wrong side of the tracks, with low self-esteem." He noted that he later found out one of his victims who had become very submissive to his demands had been molested by her father, and he assumed that she became submissive to him in the same manner as she did with her father.

M. diagnosed himself as being "antisocial." He clarified that he still does not care for people, although his therapist has told him that this does not mean that he cannot learn to live a responsible lifestyle and not hurt others. M. noted that he believes this and that he can recognize on an intellectual level the hurt he's caused other people although he cannot feel it emotionally.

Case No. 3

B. was the third of four children, and the only boy. One of his sisters died at an early age. The father was an alcoholic, a gambler, a womanizer, and a very violent and cruel man. He beat all the children, especially B. He also beat the mother. According to the subject, his beatings always involved his father telling him how "worthless [he] was."

B. explained that, from the age of 7, he believed that his mother did not love him. By his account, she would send him to his father when he wanted something, knowing that he was too frightened to ask him for anything, while always granting his sisters' wishes and showing strong favoritism towards them. B. noted that the combination of the mother's lack of affection and his father's mistreatment led him to believe there was something "wrong" with him.

B. recalled that his father's gambling was a constant problem for the family, causing them to run short of money on many occasions. The family also moved around several times, and his parents were finally divorced when he was 12 years old. B. explained that his mother took the girls but did not want him, and that he subsequently ran away and joined a carnival. According to B., this lasted a couple months, until his father found him and brought him home. He noted that he ran away another time, returned to his father at his mother's urging, and was then sent, by his father, to a reform school. At age 15, B. left home again and never returned.

In his reviewing of his sexual development, B. recalled being naked with his sister and an aunt. The girls were 9 and 11 and he was 5 years old. As he recalled, the girls took turns sitting on top of him. He noted that his parents caught them in these activities and that he was whipped, although the girls were not.

B. noted that the strongest image he has regarding sex from his early years is his father telling him that if a woman "don't give it to you, go ahead and take it because they want you to take it. They don't want to be looked at as easy and cheap." B. reported that he began masturbating at age 8, using his father's pornographic material as a stimulant. By 14 or 15 he was masturbating up to three or four times a day. According to B., when he was 9 years old, his father also began sexually abusing him. B. recalled craving his father's attention and love, and remembered going along with his sexual demands as a way of getting it. B. explained that for three years, from once a week to once a month, his father would anally assault him but stopped when he was 12, apparently because he became fearful that the subject would tell someone about the abuse.

When B. was 11 years old, his father started taking him out to bars. While there, his father would become friendly with a woman in a bar, buying her drinks, and late into the night, would suggest going to breakfast or some other place. According to B., he went along as a type of decoy, as the women always felt safer with a young boy accompanying his father. B. explained that when they left the bar, his father would then drive to a secluded location, and "force sex" upon the women. As time passed, he began to turn the women over to the subject. At first, B. was hesitant about participating, but his father insisted that the victims "service the boy," and he soon learned to be excited about the pursuits. B. reported that these "father-son" rapes continued until the subject was 16 years old, at which time, his father raped B.'s girlfriend. B. recalled enjoying the rapes from the time he was about 13 years old, but noted that when he was younger, he actually did not know that they were "rapes," as his father had convinced him that women like to be forced into having sex.

B. reported that his sexual fantasies involve a woman who "cares about him," and that the fantasy contains details of them "going together." He noted, however, that within the fantasy, "when it came to sex, it is always forced." He explained that, in his most forceful fantasy, he also uses a knife, and cuts the victim below the breasts during the rape. B. added that he often contacted his victims after the rape, feeling concerned about how they are doing, and after his first "solo" rape, returned and raped the same woman a second time.

When describing his feeling preceding a rape, B. explained that he would get a strong urge to rape; the desire would build up around his "relationship fantasy" and then become so strong that he would find a victim and rape her. B. noted that his fantasy would become more detailed over time, that he would become increasingly preoccupied with it, and that, at times, he would masturbate or try to otherwise occupy himself in order to get rid of the fantasies, although these alternatives never seemed to adequately satisfy his desire. B. added that some days he would have consensual sex and still go out and rape, emphasizing that between the two, the rape was always the more satisfying.

B. explained that when procuring his victim, he might impersonate police, pick a woman up at a bar, or follow a woman home. He would enter her residence to rape her as soon as he was convinced that she had gone to sleep. On the night of his arrest, B. recalled calling his wife from his place of business and telling her to get ready as he was coming home and was interested in having sex with her. Apparently, she responded in a receptive manner and, not long afterward, he left his business and began to drive home. B. explained that on the way, he stopped at a red light, looked over at a woman in the car next to him, and in a "split second" decided to rape her. Flashing his lights, he pulled her over, told her that he was a police detective, and indicated to her that he wanted to see her registration. Returning to his car, he acted as though he was checking her registration and then informed her that she would have to come with him as it had expired. Taking her to his car, he transported her to an isolated location and raped her vaginally. During the rape, the woman told him that her boyfriend would kill him if he ever found him. According to B., this statement enraged him, and turning her over, he raped her a second time anally. Following the rape, B. pushed the woman out of the car and drove away. Apparently, as he did so, she saw his license plate and later reported it to the police. In the interview, B. commented on the stupidity of this behavior, particularly in view of having a willing sexual partner at home.

B. told the interviewers that he had been convicted of six rapes but was, in fact, responsible for nineteen. He has been married twice and has three children.

Developmental History

Childhood Experiences

When describing their families of origin, over one-half of the respondents reported growing up in homes that were socioeconomically average (37 percent) or advantaged (17 percent). Fifty percent of the respondents viewed their mother as the dominant parental figure, and 40 percent their father as the dominant male figure. The relationship with these individuals was consistently described as being disappointing. Only a minority of the respondents viewed their relationship with their mother as being "warm, close," whereas 31 percent felt the relationship was "variable," 5 percent "cold, distant," 10 percent "uncaring, indifferent," and 18 percent "hostile, aggressive." Similarly, only a minority (18 percent) viewed their relationship with their father in a positive light. Thirty-one percent viewed the relationship as "variable," 31 percent as "cold, distant," 8 percent "uncaring and indifferent," and 18 percent as "hostile, aggressive."

Abusive behavior within these families was well documented. Thirty percent of the respondents reported being physically abused on a regular basis; 73 percent of the respondents reported being psychologically abused in terms of demeaning, degrading remarks; and 76 percent reported some type of inappropriate sexual exposure or contact. Interestingly, many of the respondents did not conceptualize themselves as having been sexually abused, and, only when asked about their first sexual experience, did they convey an experience that was clearly exploitive. For example:

> B., one of the rapists who initially denied being sexually abused, advised that when he was 7 years old, he went to a movie, and a man sat next to him and attempted to fondle him. He moved to another part of the theater and the man followed him and offered him two dollars to allow the activity. The boy agreed and continued to meet the man each weekend for a full year. The initial encounter bothered the boy enough to cause him to change seats, but as an adult, he rationalized it as a way of making money.
>
> Another rapist explained that at age 8, his parents hired a 17-year-old female to babysit him, and she "taught me how to go down on women." As an 8-year-old, the experience had to be frightening, but as an adult, he considered it a "score."

In a separate analysis of the forty-one rapist interviews, Burgess, Hazelwood, Rokous, Hartman, and Burgess (1988) found that thirty-one (76 percent) of the forty-one rapists reported some type of sexually abusive experience as children. Specifically, they found that eight (26 percent) of the thirty-one subjects reported being forced to witness disturbing sexual occurrences, seven (22 percent) reported being fondled or being involved in fondling another, and 16 (52 percent) in being forced to submit to penetration of their reported body. Burgess and others interpreted the etiological significance of these experiences according to Freud's repetition compulsion, wherein a victim attempts to gain mastery of a traumatic event by fantasizing and reenacting the trauma as the perpetrator rather than the victim. Katan (1973) suggests that these early sexual experiences lead to an overstimulation of the child's coping abilities and predispose him or her to interpret the acts as aggressive rather than sexual.

In an attempt to further assess the cumulative impact of these early descriptive experiences, the authors developed two indices: the Childhood Trauma Index and the Sexual Trauma Index. The Childhood Trauma Index comprises a number of variables that include: (1) the respondents' preadult institutional history; (2) the presence of a variety of chronic behavior patterns as a child or adolescent; (3) the general intactness of the respondent's family of origin; (4) the age at which either the respondent's father or mother departed from the family; (5) the socioeconomic level of the respondent's home as a child; (6) the overall stability and coherence of the home; (7) the quality of the relationships within the home; (8) the nature of the interactions within the home; (9) the presence of physical or psychological abuse; and (10) the evidence of harassment by peers during childhood and adolescence. The index had a value range of 0 to 62 with the respondents scores ranging from 6 to 45 with a mean of 22.5 (N=27).

Further analyses attempted to associate the Childhood Trauma Index with a number of offense-related variables including the type of approach used by the rapist, his method of control, the use of restraints, the amount of force used, the rapist's response to victim resistance, the perpetration of sadistic acts by the rapists, the amount of "pleasure" experienced by the rapist, the duration of the rape, the scene of the rape, the interval of time between rapes, and the total number of assaults. Only one relationship was significant: The Childhood Trauma Index was related to the rapist's method of victim control for the middle rape only. Because so many analyses were performed, however, and because no pattern of relationships with this variable emerged, it seems likely that this finding was due simply to chance.

The Sexual Trauma Index is also composed of a number of items. These include: (1) whether the respondent witnessed sexual violence or disturbing sexual activity on the part of parents or other family members; (2) whether the respondent experienced venereal disease or physical injury to sexual organs; (3) whether the respondent had experienced multiple sexual assaults; (4) whether the respondent had experienced a stressful sexual situation; (5) whether the respondent reported sexual problems among significant relations; (6) whether the respondent had experienced a history of childhood victimization. This index resulted in a scale with values of 0 to 12. On it the respondent's scores ranged from 0 to 8 with a mean of 2.6 (N=29).

This variable was also analyzed according to the same offense-related variables just mentioned. In this case, however, a pattern of significant relationships emerged. Specifically, an item measuring the display of a threatening physical presence by the rapists during the last rape ($t=2.3$, $p < .05$, $df=26$), the amount of "pleasure" experienced by the rapist during the middle rape ($r=.62$, $p < .001$, $n=27$), and the average length of time between assaults ($r=.50$, $p<.05$, $n=23$) were found to be significantly related to the Sexual Trauma Index. These findings indicate that those respondents who scored higher on the Sexual Trauma Index tended not to use a threatening physical presence as a method of control on the last rape, to experience a greater degree of "pleasure" on the middle rape, and to have more time between their various assaults. A further analysis demonstrated that the Sexual Trauma Index was positively correlated with three indices developed to reflect pathological behavior during childhood and adolescence. These results are discussed subsequently under Chronic Behavior Patterns.

Ressler and others (1988) report, in their study of serial murderers, that those offenders who had been sexually abused as children or adolescents were more likely to engage in sexual contact with animals, bondage sex, fetishism, obscene phone calls, indecent exposure, pornography, frotteurism, and cross-dressing. In the current study, no significant relationships were found between the Sexual Trauma Index and the occurrence of paraphilic behavior as an adult. Specifically, no relationship was found between the degree of sexual trauma experienced by the serial rapists as children or adolescents and their involvement with exhibitionism, voyeurism, fetishism, cross-dressing, obscene phone calls, coprophilia, urolagnia, and bondage.

In order to replicate more closely the results of Ressler and others (1988), a second analysis was run relating the occurrence of multiple sexual assaults in childhood or adolescence with various paraphilic behaviors in adulthood. A significant relationship between exhibitionism and multiple sexual assaults in childhood or adolescence was found (Fisher Exact test $p = .034$), although the relationship reported by Ressler and others with bondage sex, fetishism, obscene phone calls, or cross-dressing could not be replicated with the serial rape data. It is not clear why the similarities between these two samples should be limited to the relationship between sexual assault and exhibitionism while excluding the other paraphilias.

Chronic Behavior Patterns

The rapists were questioned about certain chronic behavior patterns that might have characterized their behavior either as children or adolescents. Stealing and shoplifting were reported by twenty-seven (71 percent) of thirty-eight respondents. Many rapists advised that a great deal of their thefts occurred through break-ins of homes within close proximity to their own residence, experiences that may account for their adeptness at entering the homes of rape victims years later. Temper tantrums/hyperactivity and alcohol abuse also had a high occurrence rate, with 63 percent of the sample reporting each behavior. Isolation/withdrawal occurred in twenty-four (62 percent) out of thirty-nine of the cases, and twenty-two (55 percent) out of forty of the respondents advised that they were assaultive to adults. Chronic lying was reported by twenty (54 percent) out of thirty-seven of the subjects.

Hellman and Blackman (1966) discuss the oft-cited hypothesis that enuresis, fire setting, and cruelty to animals are the triad of behavior patterns in childhood or adolescence that may be useful in predicting violent behavior in adulthood. In the current study, these behaviors were reported by 32 percent, 24 percent, and 19 percent of the respondents, respectively. Of respondents reporting these behaviors, two were reported by six (15 percent) respondents, and three by one (2 percent) respondent.

The data regarding chronic behavior patterns was also analyzed according to four cumulative indexes: Neurotic Behaviors, Neurological Deficits, Psychopathic Precursors, and Substance Abuse Disorders. The analysis demonstrated that most of the rapists had engaged in at least one of the behaviors on each of these scales. On the Neurotic Index, 71 percent (twenty-nine of the rapists) engaged in at least one of the seven behaviors, with a mean of 2.2 items; in the Neurological Index, 66 percent (twenty-seven of the rapists) engaged in at least one of the four behaviors, with a mean of 1.3; on the Psychopathic Precursors Index, 78 percent (thirty-two of the rapists) engaged in at least one of the nine behaviors, with a mean of 3.1; and finally, on the Substance Abuse Index, 66 percent (twenty-seven) had engaged in one of the three behaviors, with a mean of 1.3. These findings suggest that the rapists' developmental years were characterized by a number of behavioral problems, but that these did not clearly cluster according to any particular neurotic, neurological, psychopathic, or substance abuse substratum. As mentioned previously, the Neurological, Psychopathic, and Substance Abuse Indexes were found to correlate significantly with the Sexual Trauma Index ($r = .38$, $p = .056$; $r = .50$, $p = .011$, $r = .51$, $p = .005$, respectively), suggesting that sexually provocative or abusive experiences are associated with childhood and adolescent behavioral problems.

In terms of preadult institutionalization, 15 percent of the rapists reported residing in an orphanage, 41 percent in a detention center, 8 percent in a foster home, 26 percent in some sort of mental health facility, and 4 percent in a boarding or military school. These findings further suggest that a significant number of serial rapists were identified at an early age as being either delinquent or emotionally disturbed.

Sexual History

Fantasies of Rape

Ressler and others (1988) discuss at length the role of fantasy in the criminal behavior of serial murderers, asserting that "murder is compensatory in the fantasy world of the murderer" (p. 34). They observe from their sample of thirty-six serial murders that a "preference for fantasy" is clearly apparent in these men, and they note an early onset of aggressive and sadistic fantasy that is often realized in private and peer play. Later, these repetitive fantasies may be expressed in patterns of murder. As an illustration of their thesis, Ressler and others described one subject who, as a 3-year-old child, was found by his mother with a string tied around his penis; the other end of the string was shut in a bureau drawer. As an adolescent, the young man was found in the bathtub practicing autoerotic asphyxia with his penis and neck tied to the crossbar of the faucets; while, at age 14, he was taken to see a psychiatrist because of burns around his neck. By late adolescence, this same young man had begun to follow and bind young women and, after a period of incarceration, was responsible for the murder of three women by means of asphyxiation.

In their study of sadistic offenders, MacCulloch, Snowden, Wood and Mills (1983), similarly emphasized the role of fantasy as a precursor to violent criminal behavior. These authors note the presence of repetitive, sadistic masturbatory fantasies that "spill . . . over into overt behavior because the patient . . . [feels] compelled to seek and create increasingly dangerous in vivo 'try-outs' of their fantasies" (p. 20). They observed that the behavioral try-outs helped to maintain the effectiveness of the sadistic fantasy as a source of arousal, noting that in eleven out of thirteen cases the behavioral try-outs occurred within a year of the development of sadistic fantasies. They report that in seven of these instances, the subjects acted out parts of their fantasy with a frequency of once or twice a week, three reported infrequent behavioral try-outs, and one subject reported long periods without behavioral try-outs alternating with episodes "when he would try out parts of his fantasy several times each week" (p. 26).

In the current study of forty-one serial rapists, respondents were asked when they began to think or fantasize about raping, molesting, or sexually assaulting others. The youngest age reported by the respondents was 9, and the oldest was twenty-eight years of age. Of twenty-nine respondents, fifteen (52 percent) reported that they began to fantasize about rape between the ages of 9 and 15; eight (28 percent) between the ages of 16 and 22; and six (20 percent) between the ages of 23 and 28 years of age. These findings suggest that for one group of serial rapists the fantasy of raping and sexually assaulting a woman begins at an early age and apparently coincides with the advent of puberty, whereas for another group, this fantasy seems to build upon less aggressive fantasies as the rapist enters early adulthood. As suggested by MacCullough and others (1983), the time period between the appearance of the rape fantasy and its partial enactment in reality is also quite limited for the majority of the serial rapists. Specifically, of twenty-nine respondents, seventeen (59 percent) reported zero years between the "age of the fantasy" and the "age of action." Of those twelve respondents who reported a time interval, the range was from one to fourteen years with a mean of 5.2 years. There appeared to be no correlation between the age of the advent of the fantasy and the time interval until its enactment.

Paraphilic Behavior

Research by Abel, Becker, Cunningham-Ratner, Mittleman, and Rouleau (1980) suggests that paraphilic behavior tends to cluster in multiple form, with most paraphilics having had experience with a number of different types of deviant sexual behavior. Specifically, in a study of 561 nonincarcerated paraphilics, Abel and others found that only 10.4 percent of the paraphilics had one diagnosis; 19.9 percent had two diagnoses; 20.6 percent had three diagnoses; and 11.5 percent had four diagnoses. The remaining 37.6 percent were involved concomitantly or nonconcomitantly with five to ten different paraphilic behaviors.

These findings were supported by the self-reports of the serial rapists. Sixty-eight percent of the respondents reported that they became involved in voyeuristic activities as adolescents, a behavior that later often became associated with their selection of rape victims. Sixteen (41 percent) of the serial rapists reported fetishism, fifteen (38 percent) reported having made obscene phone calls, thirteen (33 percent) collected pornography, ten (26 percent) were involved in sexual bondage, nine (23 percent) had cross-dressed, six (15 percent) had been engaged in prostitution as either a prostitute or pimp, three (7 percent) reported being interested in coprophilia or urolognia, and two (5 percent), three (7 percent), and nine (22 percent) of the respondents described sexually sadistic behavior as a part of their first, middle, and last sexual assaults.

When the average number of paraphilic behaviors reported by each respondent was computed, it was found that six (16 percent) of respondents reported no paraphilic preferences other than their involvement in a series of rapes. Ten (27 percent) of the respondents, however, reported one paraphilic behavior, seven (19 percent) two paraphilic behaviors, six (16 percent) three paraphilic behaviors, five (14 percent) four paraphilic behaviors, one (3 percent) five paraphilic behaviors, and two (5 percent) six paraphilic behavior patterns. These findings support Abel and others, earlier observations concerning the multiple occurrence of paraphilic behavior and highlight the importance for informed inquiry by both mental health and law enforcement into the varied nature of the rapist's sexual activity.

Crime Scene Characteristics

The criminal investigative analyses conducted by the FBI organizes information regarding a rape according to seven main themes (Hazelwood and Burgess, 1987). These involve: (1) victim selection, (2) manner of approach, (3) means of controlling the victim, (4) the use of force, (5) sexual dynamics of rape, (6) verbal dynamics of rape, and (7) post offense behavior. The data regarding the serial rapists as it applies to this framework is summarized following.

Victim Selection and Characteristics

The serial rapists were asked a variety of questions about the 123 victims of their first, middle, and last sexual assaults. In 80 to 88 percent of the rape incidents, the victims were strangers to the offender. In only 10 (8 percent) instances did the rapist report raping an acquaintance, neighbor, friend, or date. This pattern of focusing on victims to whom they are unknown is believed to be instrumental in helping the rapist to avoid detection over a large number of successive offenses.

The average age of the victim for the first, middle, and last attack was 22.8, 26.1, and 24.4 years, respectively. The victims of the serial rapist were predominantly caucasian; of the 123 victims, 113 were Caucasian, 6 African-American, 1 Hispanic, 2 Asian, and 1 Native American. In this study, Caucasian rapists did not cross the racial line in their crimes against women, whereas the African-American offenders raped Caucasian and African-American women. The youngest victim in this study was 5 years old and the oldest was 65.

The majority of victims (79 percent) were alone at the time of the assault. Of the twenty-three victims who were not, four (13 percent) were with their children, two (2 percent) with a female friend, two (2 percent) with a parent, three (3 percent) with a spouse, and three (3 percent) with some other individual.

The scene of the sexual assault was relatively consistent. In fifty-nine assaults (50 percent), the rapists reported that the assault occurred in the victim's home. In seven assaults (6 percent), the offense occurred in a street or alleyway, and in seven (6 percent) instances, it occurred either in a parking lot or on a highway. Less often, the assaults occurred at the rapist's residence, public facilities, or at the victim's place of work.

As noted, the victim's residence was the scene of the assault in half of the rapes (50 percent). As mentioned earlier, 71 percent of the men had been involved in stealing as children and adolescents and many of them had done so by breaking into homes. Having this experience they no doubt felt more comfortable in gaining access to residences. Many of the rapists selected their victims through peeping activities or by following intended victims to their homes. Consequently, the offender learned the habits of the victim in her home (i.e., visitors, phone calls, sleeping hours, hours away from home). In several instances, the rapist entered the victim's home while she was absent and familiarized himself with the residence.

> One subject, a man who raped in excess of 50 women, would select potential victims through "peeping." He traveled great distances from his home town and would choose a residential area into which he easily blended socioeconomically. He made it a habit to target six women who lived alone and

through surveillance he established their routines. If, on the night of an attack, the victim was not at home, or she successfully resisted him, he had alternate targets readily available to him.

Methods of Approach

As delineated by Hazelwood and Burgess (1987b), three different styles of approach are frequently utilized by the rapists: the "con," the "blitz," and the "surprise." Each reflects a different means of selecting, approaching, and subduing a chosen victim, and as such, these categories are believed to provide information relevant to any indirect assessment of the personality and motivation of the offender.

The "con" approach involves subterfuge and is predicated on the rapist's ability to interact with women. With this technique, the rapist openly approaches the victim and requests or offers some type of assistance or direction.

> Mr. C., a man who raped more than 20 women, told the interviewers that he stopped one of his victims late at night and identified himself as a plainclothes police officer. He asked for her driver's license and registration, walked back to his car and sat there for a few moments. He then returned to the victim, advised her that her registration had expired, and asked her to accompany him to his car. She did so, and upon entering the car, he handcuffed her and drove to an isolated location where he raped and sodomized the victim.

The "con" approach was used in eight (24 percent) of the first rapes, twelve (35 percent) of the middle rapes, and fourteen (41 percent) of the last rapes. Various ploys used by the offenders included impersonating a police officer, providing transportation for a hitchhiking victim, and picking women up in singles bars.

Hazelwood and Burgess (1987b) note that in the "blitz" approach, the rapist uses a direct, injurious physical assault and in so doing makes use of his ability to physically overpower a woman. Interestingly, despite its simplicity, this approach was used in only 23 percent of the first rapes, 20 percent of the middle rapes, and 17 percent of the last rapes.

> Mr. T., a 28-year-old male, approached a woman loading groceries in her car, struck her in the face, threw her in the vehicle, and raped her. On another occasion, he entered a women's restroom in a hospital, struck his victim, and raped her in a stall. Exiting the restroom with the victim in his grasp, he threatened her as though they were involved in a lover's quarrel, and thus precluded interference from concerned onlookers who had gathered when she screamed.

The "surprise" approach, which involves the assailant lying in wait for the victim or approaching her after she is sleeping, presupposes that the rapist has targeted or preselected his victim through unobserved contact and knowledge of when the victim would be alone. Threats and/or the presence of a weapon are often associated with this type of approach; however, there is no actual injurious force applied.

> Mr. S., a 24-year-old male, would preselect his victims through "peeping" activities and would then watch the victim's residence to establish her patterns. After deciding to rape the woman, he would wait until she had gone to sleep, enter the home, and place his hand over her mouth. He would advise the victim that he did not intend to harm her if she cooperated with the assault. He raped more than 20 women before he was apprehended.

The "surprise" approach was used by the serial rapists in nineteen (54 percent) of the first rapes, sixteen (46 percent) of the middle rapes, and sixteen (44 percent) of the last rapes. This represents the most frequently used means of approach and according to criminal analysts is used most often by men who lack confidence in their ability to subdue the victim through physical threats or subterfuge.

Controlling the Victim

Hazelwood and Burgess (1987b) maintain that the manner in which a rapist maintains control over his victim depends on his motivation for the offense as well as the passivity of his victim. In categorizing this component of the rape, they outline four distinct methods that are frequently used in various combinations during a rape: (1) threatening physical presence, (2) verbal threats, (3) display of a weapon, and (4) the use of physical force.

The serial rapists across their first, middle and last rapes predominantly used a threatening physical presence (82 to 92 percent) and/or verbal threats (65 to 80 percent) to control their victims. Substantially less often they displayed a weapon (44 to 49 percent) or physically assaulted the victim (27 to 32 percent). When a weapon was displayed, it was most often a sharp instrument, such as a knife (27 to 42 percent). One rapist explained that he chose a knife because he perceived it to be the most intimidating weapon to use against women in view of their fear of disfigurement. Firearms were used less frequently (14 to 20 percent). Surprisingly, all but a few of the rapists who used bindings used bindings located at the scene of the rape. One exception was an individual who brought precut lengths of rope, adhesive tape, and handcuffs with him.

As indicated previously, the Childhood Trauma Index and the Sexual Trauma Index were both significantly related to methods of victim control. This was true as well for two of the behavioral clusters: the Neurological Cluster and the Psychiatric Precursor Cluster. Because each of these scales could be related to so few variables in this data set, it seems meaningful that four of them should significantly relate to the one item on victim control. Because the rapist's method of victim control reflects both the rapist's own psychic development and the dynamics of the rape at hand, further research of this topic would seem fruitful.

Use of Force

Attempts to differentiate the rapist's sexual arousal pattern from that of the nonrapist have focused on the role of force in either augmenting the arousal (Abel, Barlow, Blanchard, & Guild, 1977) of the rapist or in failing to exhibit it (Malamuth, Check, & Briere, 1986; Barbaree, Marshall, & Lanthier, 1979). Within the FBI context, the amount of force used during a rape is considered an important component of the criminal investigatory analysis for, as Hazelwood and Burgess (1987b) note, it "provides valuable insight into the motivational need [of the rapist]" (p. 157).

In the current study, the amount of force used by the forty-one serial rapists was examined in aggregate form across the first, middle, and last rape. Of interest, was the finding that the amount of force used was considered to be "minimal" (75 to 84 percent) across all three rapes. This has been defined by Hazelwood and Burgess (1987a) as involving no injurious force but rather mild "slapping" designed to intimidate rather than punish. Force resulting in bruises and lacerations or extensive physical trauma requiring hospitalization or resulting in death increased from 5 percent in the first rape to 8 percent in the middle rapes and to 10 percent in the last rapes. Two victims (5 percent) were murdered during the middle rapes and an additional two (5 percent) during the last rapes. Although these rapes clearly represented nonconsensual sexual contact, the amount of force used in most of them appeared to be designed to intimidate the victim rather than cause her physical harm per se.

In a subsequent analysis, the authors examined the change in force that occurred over the rapists' first, middle, and last offense. This analysis, which quantified force on a 6-point scale from 1 "no force" to 6 "fatal force," demonstrated that the amount of force used by the rapist did not change significantly across the first (1.9), middle (2.1), and last (2.3) offense, and, as indicated perviously, reflected a relatively mild form of physical coercion.

The analysis involving force, however, did indicate that even though there was no significant overall increase in the amount of force used by the serial rapists, ten of the rapists termed "increasers" did increase significantly in the amount of force used from their first to their last assaults. In an attempt to distinguish these "increasers" from the "nonincreasers," the two groups were compared on a number of variables including developmental characteristics, assault history, and behavior during the rape itself. As summarized in Table 16-1, it was found that the two groups did not differ on most variables including age at first and last assault, race, marital status, education, military record, the offender's acquaintance with the victim, mean pleasure at first and last assault, sexual abuse of the offender as a child, the general quality of the home environment, and the quality of the offender's relationship with his parents. As demonstrated in Table 16-1, the "increasers" did, however, assault more victims (a mean of 40 as contrasted to a mean of 22 reported for the nonincreasers), over a shorter period of time (a mean of every nineteen days as contrasted to every fifty-five days for the nonincreasers), inflicted more serious injuries during the last offense (nine out of ten inflicted "moderate" to "fatal" injuries), and were rated by the interviewers as having committed more sadistic acts during the last assault (Fisher Exact Test $p = .001$). The increasers were also reported to have performed anal sex on their victims at a rate almost three times that of the nonincreasers and ten times that of the rapists described in the Holmstrom and Burgess (1980) study, a finding, when assessed in light of the other differences, suggests that sexual sadism may be a motivating component of the "increasers" assaultive behavior (Dietz, Hazelwood, & Warren, 1990).

The different behavioral patterns of the two groups are described in the following two vignettes.

Nonincreaser

One nonincreaser, a 27-year-old white male, estimates that he had committed over 5,000 break-ins of homes to steal women's underwear. In 18 of those incidents he also raped the female resident, but never struck or physically injured his victims. Equating harm with physical force, he stated, "None of my victims were ever harmed and for a person to kill somebody after raping them, it just makes me mad."

Increaser

One increaser, a 32-year-old white male, vaginally raped his first victim using threats and intimidations, but did not strike

---

Table 16-1

COMPARISON BETWEEN THOSE SERIAL RAPISTS WHO INCREASED IN FORCE AND THOSE WHO DID NOT

Variable	Increasers (N=10)	NonIncreasers (N=29)	t	p
Amount of force used in first rape	1.8	2.0	.50	NS
Amount of force used in last rape	4.1	1.7	5.42	.0003
Victim injury during last rape	2.6	0.26	6.08	.001
Total assaults	40.7	22.4	2.3	.04
Mean days between assaults	19.7	55.2	2.3	.04
Age at first assault	20.1	22.1	1.0	NS
Age at last assault	30.0	28.4	0.8	NS
Mean pleasure at first assault	3.8	3.4	0.4	NS
Mean pleasure at last assault	4.2	3.7	0.5	NS
Childhood sexual trauma index	3.2	2.5	0.9	NS
Childhood general trauma index	9.8	24.0	0.8	NS

Note: The t-tests in Table 16-1 and all subsequent t-tests in this analysis take heterogeneity of variance between groups into account when appropriate.

or otherwise physically injure the woman. During a middle rape, he struck and otherwise punched the woman's breasts, leaving them bruised. In his last rape he so severely injured the victim's breasts that she required a double mastectomy as part of her recovery.

Victim Resistance

The amount of force used during a rape has been associated with the resistance strategies used by the victim. Prentky, Burgess, and Carter (1986) examined victim resistance and physical injury using subgroupings developed at the Massachusetts Treatment Center. They found that "compensatory," "displaced-anger," and "sadistic" rapists left combative victims either unconscious or with serious medical problems significantly more often than noncombative victims. In contrast, the degree of injury inflicted by exploitive rapists was unaffected by varying degrees of victim resistance. Honeyman (1981) studied the rapists' sexual arousal as it related to different victim resistance strategies and arrived at the tentative conclusion that anger and physical resistance were more arousing to an assaultive rapist than either calm or submissive resistance strategies. Hazelwood and Burgess (1987b) highlight the relevance, from a law enforcement perspective, of the rapist's response to resistance, again in understanding the perpetrator's motivation and general behavioral orientation.

In the current study, the rapists reported that their victims verbally resisted them in 53 percent of the first assaults, 54 percent of the middle attacks, and 43 percent of the last attacks. Physical resistance occurred in only 19 percent, 32 percent, and 28 percent of the first, middle, and last rapes, respectively. The relatively low incidence of passive resistance (i.e., 28 percent in the first rape, 17 percent of the middle rape, and 9 percent of the last rape) most likely reflects the rapists' inability to discern this type of resistance.

In this study, the offenders' most common reaction to resistance for the first, middle, and last rapes was to threaten the victim (41 to 50 percent) verbally. Compromise or negotiation took place in 11 to 12 percent across the three rapes, and physical force was used in 22 percent of the first rapes, 38 percent of the middle rapes, and 18 percent of the third rapes. The rapists also reported six incidents in which they left when the victim resisted; however, it is not clear at what point in the attack the resistance occurred.

Within the current study, victim resistance was also analyzed as it relates to the amount of force used by the perpetrator. Defined as the presence of verbal or physical resistance, the analysis demonstrated that there was no significant relationship between the presence or absence of victim resistance and the amount of force used by the rapists during any of the assaults. Victim resistance, however, was found to be correlated with the amount of pleasure experienced by the rapist. The pleasure variable was operationalized by asking the rapist to think back to his sexual pleasure during the rape (i.e., ". . . assuming 0 equals your worst sexual experience and 10 your absolutely best sexual experience, rate it according to the amount of pleasure you experienced"). The mean scores on this variable reflected a mean pleasure score of 3.7 for all three rapes, placing it at the lower end of the pleasure continuum. The rapist's pleasure was found to be significantly higher when the victim resisted during the first ($t = 4.15$, $p < .01$) and middle ($t = 2.48$ $p < .02$) assaults, although not in the last assault.

The analysis also demonstrated that when the victim resisted, either verbally or physically, the assault lasted significantly longer. For example, in the last assault, when the victim did not resist the assault lasted, on the average, 36 minutes, whereas when the victim did resist it lasted 94 minutes. (M-W $U = 2.24$, $p < .03$). Duration of the rape was also found to vary with the amount of pleasure experienced by the offender, suggesting that the rapist enjoyed a rape when it lasted longer, that he prolonged the rape when he found it particularly pleasurable, or that both variables are spuriously related to victim resistance.

Sexual Dynamics of the Rape

Holmstrom and Burgess (1980) studied 115 adult, adolescent, and child rape victims and, from their reports, delineated the sexual acts that occurred during the various rapes. They found that vaginal intercourse occurred most frequently (96 percent of the cases), with fellatio (22 percent), contact with the victim's breast (12 percent), cunnilingus (5 percent), anal intercourse (5 percent), manual touching of the genitals (5 percent), and urination on the victim or her clothes (4 percent) occurring in a decreasing order of frequency. They also found that victims who were aged 20 or older were more apt to have been anally raped than teenage victims.

In the current study, the sexual acts that the victims were forced to engage in remained relatively constant across all three rapes. The most common acts were vaginal intercourse (54 to 67 percent), oral sex (29 to 44 percent), kissing (8 to 13 percent) and fondling (10 to 18 percent). Anal intercourse (5 to 10 percent) and foreign object penetration (3 to 8 percent) were reported less often. As noted, the serial rapists' general interest in anal intercourse, a preference associated by Dietz, Hazelwood, and Warren [1990] with sexual sadism, is also greater than that detected among a more generic sample of rapes (Holmstrom and Burgess, 1980).

The occurrence of some type of sexual dysfunction is not an uncommon aspect of rape. In their study of 170 rapists, Groth and Burgess (1977) determined that 34 percent of the rapists experienced some type of sexual dysfunction during the rape. In terms of its relevance to law enforcement, Hazelwood and Burgess (1987b) note that "the occurrence of offender sexual dysfunction and an investigative understanding of the dysfunction may provide valuable information about the unidentified rapist" (p. 159). Particularly, this information may be of value in associating many offenses with one offender, as the nature of the dysfunction and the means the offender uses to overcome it are likely to remain constant over a successive number of rapes.

Among the serial rapists, the incidence of sexual dysfunction was surprisingly similar to that reported by Groth and Burgess (1977). During the first rape, 38 percent of the respondents reported experiencing a sexual dysfunction, 39 percent in the middle rape, and 35 percent during the last sexual assault.

Postoffense Behavior

The behavior of the rapist following the sexual assault is obviously of particular interest to law enforcement officials in their attempts to identify and apprehend the rapist. For the forty-one serial rapists, seventeen postoffense behaviors were examined, including, whether the perpetrator communicated with the police or news media, whether he interjected himself into the investigation, whether he confided the details of the crime, and so forth. For the serial rapists, the most frequent behaviors reported after their assaults included feeling remorseful and guilty (44 to 51 percent), following the case in the media (25 to 28 percent), and an increase in alcohol and drug consumption (20 to 27 percent).

Ressler and others (1988), in their study of serial murders found that although murderers' behavior after a crime was "tempered by the need for self-protection," a significant minority also returned to the crime scene, observed the discovery of the victim's body, kept souvenirs of the murder, and tried to interject themselves into the investigation, activities that the authors associate with the need to "sustain the excitement of murder." Among the serial rapists, 12 to 15 percent of the rapist reported revisiting the crime scene, 8 to 13 percent communicated with the victim after the crime, 7 to 10 percent took souvenirs, and only 2 percent attempted to involve themselves in the investigation.

Classification Analyses

Several schemes have been proposed for classifying different types of rapists (Guttmacher & Weihofen, 1952; Gebhard, Gagnon, Pomeroy, & Christenson, 1965; Seghorn & Cohen, 1980; Prentky, Knight, & Rosenberg, 1988). The classification scheme used most extensively by the FBI in its criminal investigatory analysis is that developed by Groth, Burgess, and Holmstrom (1977) and later modified by Hazelwood and Burgess (1987b). The scheme, which is based upon the assumption that power, anger and sexuality are fundamental components of all forcible rapes, posits that these factors combine in various ways to distinguish four discernible patterns of rape: the power-reassurance rapist who attempts in his rape behavior to restore "disturbing doubts about his sexual inadequacy and masculinity"; the power-assertive rapist who "regards rape as an expression of his virility and mastery and dominance"; the anger-retaliatory rapist who commits the rape as an expression of hostility and rage; and the "anger-excitation" rapist who experiences pleasure and excitement in response to his victim's suffering. These rape types serve as a basis for the criminal investigatory analysis conducted by the FBI's NCAVC and are used in organizing impressions derived from the crime scene in order help inform "the underlying purpose of the assault, thereby allowing the officer better insight into the type of person he is seeking" (p. 153).

For many years, the process of classifying offenders has been an intuitive process that would evolve out of years of investigatory experience. Recent attempts to train a second generation of criminal investigatory analysts at the NCAVC and to operationalize the classification process into systems of artificial intelligence, have underlined the importance of more objectively studying the process of classification. Using data from the original study of forty-one serial rapists as well as data from victims of a new sample of rapes submitted to NCAVC, research was subsequently initiated to address more clearly the dynamics of this classification process. Specifically, through the development of verbal, sexual and physical scales, an attempt was made to operationalize classification according to both rape type and increaser–nonincreaser status and to assess whether behaviors identified early on in an offender's rape career could be used to predict behavior during later offenses.

Method and Results

Both offender and victim data were used in conducting this study. The offender data consisted of transcribed accounts of the first, middle and last offenses of the forty-one sexual rapists reported in the original study (Hazelwood, Reboussin, & Warren, 1989). The victim data were derived from rape cases, including victim statements, that had been submitted for analysis by local law enforcement agencies to the NCAVC. Each rape, in both the offender and victim data sets, was coded according to 33 verbal, sexual, and physical scales as well as to overall rape type as delineated by Hazelwood and Burgess (1987b). Discriminant analyses was used to ascertain which scales, if any, could be used to classify each rape according to rape type and increaser status.

Offender Data

The offender discriminant analysis resulted in a discriminant function that accounted for 79 percent of the variance among rape types and resulted in 83 percent correct classification. Power-reassurance rapes were classified with 91 percent accuracy, power-assertive rapes with 83 percent accuracy, and the two anger categories together with 71 percent accuracy. The structure coefficients for the two discriminant functions (see Table 16-2) suggest that power-reassurance rapists tended to be less macho, more concerned about harming the victim, less angry, to use less force, and to be more apologetic than power-assertive and anger rapists. The second function, which separated the power assertive from the combined-power category, suggested that power-assertive rapists tended to act more macho and to use more explicit verbal sex and less force than the anger rapists. The other scales that appeared in the analyses but did not produce correlation with the discriminant function of .30 or greater included whether the rapist was complimentary or demeaning, the extent to which the rapist attempted to reassure the victim or not, whether the victim was transported, and whether a weapon was displayed or used during the offense (see Table 16-2).

Table 16-2

STRUCTURE COEFFICIENTS FOR DISCRIMINANT ANALYSIS BETWEEN RAPE TYPES ON BEHAVIOR SCALES FOR VICTIM AND OFFENDER DATA

Scale*	Scale Reliability		Offender Data		Victim Data	
	Pair A	Pair B	Funct. 1	Funct. 2	Funct. 1	Funct. 2
Sensitive/ Macho	.35	.66	.65	.34	.55**	-.22
Concern/ No concern	.57	.80	.57	−.08	.37**	.12
No anger/ Overwhelming anger	.57	.60	.41	-.13	.62**	.65
No force/ Brutal force	.51	.79	.37	−.37	.38**	.11
Apologetic/ Demanding	.64	.71	.37	.11	.51**	−.44
Complimentary/ Demeaning	.81	.49	.25	.00	—	—
Reassuring/ Not reassuring	.51	.46	.22	.17	.44**	−.02
No explicit sexual verbal content/extensive sexual verbal content	.46	.55	−.13	.36	.01	−.02
No effort to conceal ID/ Extensive effort to conceal ID	.58	.61	−.14	−.18	.04	−.08
No transportation/ Prolonged transportation	.88	.81	.15	.16	—	—
No weapon/ Weapon used	.93	.88	−.05	.08	−.02	.66

**r .05 = 29 (43df)

The discriminant analysis for "increaser status" was run stepwise using the same 16 scales used in the previous analysis. It resulted in a combined accuracy of 92 percent, correctly classifying 80 percent of the increaser and 96 percent of the nonincreaser. The analysis suggested that increasers tended to bind their victims and incapacitate them longer than the nonincreasers (see Table 16-3). The other scales that appeared in the analysis included whether the rapist transported the victim or not, whether the rapist negotiated or refused to negotiate with the victim, whether the rapist was complimentary or demeaning toward the victim, whether the rapist was perceived as being sensitive or macho, whether the rapist asked questions of the victim, whether the rapist spoke of himself, whether the rapist made efforts to reassure the victim, and whether there was a weapon displayed or used during the offense.

Victim Analysis

The victim data, as indicated, was derived from victim statements submitted to the NCAVC, and, as such, represented the victim's description of the offense, as contrasted to the offender's description of the offense used in the offender's analysis. These victim accounts represented different rapes and different rapists from those used in the offender analysis and were included in the sample only if the rapist was known to have perpetrated at least three rapes on different victims.

When the discriminant analysis for rape type was run with the victim data and the same scales found to be significant in the offender analysis, the classification potential of the discriminant function was found to improve. Specifically, the rape type analysis (see Table 16-2) accounted for 84 percent of the variance and resulted in an overall classification accuracy of 91 percent. Power-reassurance rapes were classified with 95 percent accuracy, power-assertive rapes with 93 percent accuracy, and the anger rapes with 80 percent accuracy. As in the offender analyses, the power-reassurance category tended to be less macho, more concerned about harm to the victim, less angry, to use less force, and to be more apologetic than the power-assertive and anger rapist. In the victim data, the power-reassurance rapists also tended to make repeated attempts to reassure their victims, whereas the other rapists did not.

The increaser discriminant analysis was also run using the same 10 scales found significant in the offender analysis. The analysis accounted for 57 percent of the variance between increaser group, correctly classifying 90 percent of the increaser rapes and 88 percent of the nonincreaser rapes, resulting in a combined accuracy of 89 percent. As summarized in Table 16-3, the scales with a correlation higher than .30 included the use of bindings, transportation of the victim, lack of negotiation between rapist and victim, and lack of attempts to reassure the victim. The remaining scales in the analysis included whether the rapist was complimentary or demeaning toward the victim, whether the subject asked the victim about herself, whether the rapist spoke about himself, and whether there was a weapon present or used during the offense.

Concluding Remarks

The information derived from these forty-one serial rapists illuminates the complex and intricate process by which these life histories have culminated in a long series of sexually aggressive acts against women. The stories of these lives as explored in the current study provides a rich context within which ideas of early development, sexual adaptation, and offense behavior can be pondered and perhaps more precisely understood. Familiarity with these men's behavior and their outlook on life is of immense importance for both law enforcement and clinical practice in the attempts of each to recognize and understand these particular offenders.

From a research perspective, the various analyses have also offered some interesting insights into the more general parameters of the offenders' rape careers. Perhaps one of the most important of these is the idea of sameness rather than change over time. The earlier analyses demonstrated that there was no significant change in the amount of force used, the pleasure experienced by the rapist, the extent of victim injuries incurred or the duration of the assault itself over the first, middle, and last offenses of forty-one serial rapists. These findings suggest that the modus operandi of the rapist, often subtly and incrementally developed, remains in many aspects unchanged over a surprisingly large number of offenses. This observation is consistent with the hypothesis that the behavior of the rapist during the sexual assault derives from the perpetrator more than the interaction that occurs between the perpetrator and his victim.

Second, although most rapists appear consistent in their rape behavior, there does seem to be a more dangerous minority that escalates in violence over successive offenses and who, by the end of their rape careers, are inflicting far more serious injuries and committing acts suggestive of a sadistic intent. It appears that this group of serial rapists is unusually prolific and dangerous and hence of particular importance for further study.

Third, victim resistance was found not to vary with the amount of force used by the perpetrator, although it was associated with the pleasure experienced by the rapist and the duration of the rape itself. These findings suggest that the resistance strategies used by a victim do not necessarily affect the aggression that is subsequently directed toward her, although they may prolong the duration of the assault. These are, however, only preliminary findings, and further research into the intricate relationship between victim resistance and victim injury is obviously required.

Finally, the classificatory analyses appear to be of theoretical interest in that they demonstrate that behavioral scales can be used to classify rapists both according to rape type and increaser status. These scales focus on the interaction occurring between the rapist and his victim and attempt to quantify behavior rather than the more complex systems of motivations lying behind it. As such, the scales hold potential for permitting reliable classification by those who have limited experience in recognizing a gestaltlike pattern within particular offenses. The fact that the offender analyses were replicated on victim statements describing serial rapists' first rapes also suggests that classification or prediction of rape type or increaser status can be implemented early in a series of offenses based solely on information supplied by the victim.

The classifications that can be derived from ratings of behavior—for example, rape type and increaser status—embody clinical information relevant to both mental health clinicians and law enforcement personnel. The clinician, in both treatment and evaluative settings, must try to understand the motivational underpinnings of an offender's behavior while also assessing his potential for future dangerousness. Investigators must alternatively prioritize investigations and decide which among a set of rapes should be attributable to a single offender. The behavioral scales offer a quantifiable means of informing these decisions. For example, it might benefit the clinician to know that the presence of excessive bindings, transportation of the victim to a

Table 16-3

SCALE RELIABILITY AND STRUCTURE COEFFICIENTS FOR DISCRIMINANT
ANALYSIS BETWEEN INCREASER AND NON-INCREASER STATUS ON
BEHAVIOR SCALES FOR VICTIM AND OFFENDER DATA

Scale**	Offender Data Scale Reliability Pair A	Pair B	Offender	Victim Data Victim*
No binding/Excessive binding	.93	.88	.45	.48*
Duration less than 30 minutes/ Duration greater than 3 hours	.90	.90	.35	.27
No transport/ Prolonged transport	.88	81	19	.34*
Extensive negotiation No negotiation	.71	.51	.15	.45*
Complimentary/Demeaning	.81	.49	−.14	.16
Sensitive/Macho	.35	.66	−.10	.55*
No questions/Many questions	.81	.51	−.09	−.04
No talk of self/ Much talk of self	.71	.78	-.07	−.09
Reassuring/Not reassuring	.51	.46	.03	.44*
No weapon/Weapon used	.99	.88	-.01	27

*r.05=.29 (43df)

different location, and sustained contact may be associated with an exacerbation in violence among a sample of serial rapists. Alternatively, the investigator can prioritize investigations based upon the same predictor variables while also using rape type to more fully understand, prior to his apprehension, the psychological processes motivating the offender. Along these lines, the victim-based classification scheme is currently being prototyped by the NCAVC in an expert system that questions the user about any given rape and provides a diagnosis of rape type and the probability that the rape was perpetrated by an increaser. This system, which can be run on a laptop computer, might well, increase the availability of this type of system to both law enforcement and mental health professionals.

References

Abel, G., D. Barlow, E. Blanchard, and D. Guild. 1977. The components of rapists' sexual arousal. *Archives of General Psychiatry* 34:895–903.

Abel, G., J. Becker, J. Cunningham-Ratner, M. Mittleman, and J. Rouleau. 1980. Multiple paraphilic diagnoses among sex offenders. *Bulletin of the American Academy of Psychiatry and the Law* 16:153–68.

Barbaree, H., W. Marshall, and R. Lanthier. 1979. Deviant sexual arousal in rapists. *Behavioral Research and Therapy* 17:215–22.

Burgess, A., R. Hazelwood, F. Rokous, and C. Hartman. 1988. Serial rapists and their victims: reenactment and repetition. In R. Prentky and V. Quinsey (eds.), *Human Sexual Aggression: Current Perspectives*. Academy of Sciences Annals 528:277–95.

Dietz, P., R. Hazelwood, and J. Warren. 1990. The sexually sadistic criminal and his offenses. *Bulletin of the American Academy of Psychiatry and the Law* 18:163–178.

Gebhard, P., J. Gagnon, W. Pomeroy, and C. Christenson. 1965. *Sex Offenders*. New York: Harper & Row.

Groth, A., and A. Burgess.. 1977. Sexual dysfunction during rape. *New England Journal of Medicine* 27:764–66.

Groth, N., A. Burgess, and L. Holmstrom. 1977. Rape, power, anger and sexuality. *American Journal of Psychiatry* 134:1239–43.

Guttmacher, M., and H. Weihofen. 1952. *Psychiatry and the Law*. New York: W.W. Norton.

R. Hazelwood. 1987. Analyzing the rape and profiling the offender. In R. Hazelwood and A. Burgess (eds.), *Practical Aspects of Rape Investigation: A Multidisciplinary Approach*, pp. 169–99. New York: Elsevier.

Hazelwood, R., and A. Burgess. 1987a. An introduction to the serial rapist: Research by the FBI. *FBI Law Enforcement Bulletin* (September): 16–24.

——— (eds.). 1987b. *Practical Aspects of Rape Investigation: A Multidisciplinary Approach*. New York: Elsevier.

Hazelwood, R., R. Reboussin, and J. Warren. 1989. Serial rape: Correlates of increased aggression and the relationship of offender pleasure to victim resistance. *Journal of Interpersonal Violence* 4:65–78.

Hazelwood, R., and J. Warren. 1989a. The serial rapist: His characteristics and victims Part I. *FBI Law Enforcement Bulletin* (January), 11–17.

———. 1989b. The serial rapist: His characteristics and victims Part II. *FBI Law Enforcement Bulletin* (February) 19–25.

Hellman, D. and N. Blackman. 1966. Enuresis, fire setting and cruelty to animals; A trial predictive of adult crime. *American Journal of Psychiatry* 122:1431–35.

Holmstrom, L., and A. Burgess. 1980. Sexual Behavior of assailants during reported rapes. *Archives of Sexual Behavior* 9:427–39.

Honeyman, B. 1981. Rapists' sexual arousal in response to audio-taped victim resistance styles. Doctoral dissertation, University of Oregon, 1981. *Dissertation Abstracts International* 42:02-A.

Katan, A. 1973. Children who were raped. In R.S. Eisler et al. (eds.) *The Psychoanalytic Study of the Child*, pp. 208-24. New Haven: Yale University Press.

MacCullough, M., P. Snowden, J. Wood, H. Mills. 1983. Sadistic fantasy, sadistic behavior and offending. *British Journal of Psychiatry* 143:20–29.

Malamuth, N., J. Check, and J. Briere. 1986. Sexual arousal in response to aggression: Ideological, aggressive, and sexual correlates. *Journal of Personality and Social Psychology* 50:330–40.

Prentky, R., A. Burgess, and D. Carter. 1986. Victim responses by rapist type: An empirical and clinical analysis. *Journal of Interpersonal Violence* 1:73–98.

Prentky, R., R. Knight, and R. Rosenberg. 1988. Validation analyses on a taxonomic system for rapists: disconfirmation and reconceptualization. In R. Prentky & V. Quinsey (eds), *Human Sexual Aggression: Current Perspectives*, pp. 21–40. New York: New York Academy of Sciences, Annals.

Rada, R. 1978. *Clinical Aspects of the Rapist.* New York: Grune and Stratton.

Ressler, R., A. Burgess, J. Douglas, J. 1988. *Sexual Homicide: Patterns and Motives.* Lexington, MA/Toronto, Canada: Lexington Books/D.C. Heath and Company.

Seghorn, T., and M. Cohen. 1980. The psychology of the rape assailant. In W. Cerran, A.L. McGarry, & C. Petty (eds.), *Modern Legal Medicine, Psychiatry and Forensic Science*, pp. 533–51. Philadelphia: F. A. Davis.

Warren, J., R. Reboussin, R. Hazelwood, and J. In press. Wright prediction of rape type and violence from verbal, physical and sexual scales. *Journal of Interpersonal Violence* (March 1991).

Index

∎